FORGOTTEN REALMS

NEVERWINTER NIGHTS

SHADOWS OF UNDRENTIDE™

Official Strategy Guide

By Michael Lummis

Neverwinter Nights™
Shadows of Undrentide™
Official Strategy Guide

Table of Contents

BradyGAMES would like to extend very special thanks to everyone at Atari, especially Rachel Hoagland and Dorian Richard. Without your help, this guide would not have been possible!

Author Acknowledgments: I am very happy to thank my killer gaming team of Edwin Kern, Christopher Burton, and Kurt Ricketts! These three got the job done and came up with enough strange character ideas that we'll still be trying new combinations when the next expansion pack comes out. Also, great thanks to Tim Fitzpatrick for a ton of editing and advice, and to Kathleen Pleet for her ongoing cleaning of my laughable draft material.

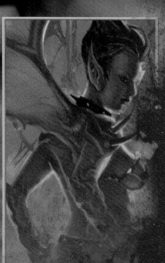

A Call to Arms

Far from the gates of Neverwinter is the village of Hilltop, a place of quiet and solitude that knows little of suffering or world politics. Yet, a dwarven wizard has chosen such a place for his studies, training, and intrigue. While taking on students, this mage has continued to work for a secret organization. As with many choices, however, there are consequences that this wizard must face even in retirement.

When Drogan Droganson is attacked and loses several items of great importance, the tremendous task of returning the artifacts falls to a younger generation. A new hero will have to save Hilltop, but that is only the beginning. Where do the Harpers fit into all of this mystery, and what of the rumors that there is a dragon pulling the strings behind this horrible attack? Indeed, what else could be lurking in the shadows, just waiting for a chance to make away with the artifacts?

The answer will take our hero into distant lands, where desert ruins and ancient magic bear the weight of a terrible legacy. Pride and folly once laid waste to an empire of legendary beauty; now the stage is set for an abandoned city and its deceased to alter the world's course again. Can this be prevented before the spirits of the arcane stir?

In Neverwinter Nights: Shadows of Undrentide, players will find a campaign that uses the Neverwinter Nights engine to its fullest. There are many alignment-based quests and decisions to be made, and the style of dungeons brings some of the system's best features to the forefront. Secret doors, more interesting traps, and many complex events should give players and module creators many hours of excitement and a host of new ideas. This guide will serve as a reference for this process. Beyond a thorough walkthrough, you'll find developed character sections, battle strategies, enhanced descriptions for old and new skills and feats, and plenty of tricks for getting the most out of campaigns. Whether someone is looking for the most obscure piece of treasure or the strangest ways to solve every quest, this is the place to look.

How to Use this Guide: Understanding the Tomes

Understanding this book is the key to power, glory, and honor (or whatever else you seek). This brief chapter explains how to navigate the library of gaming knowledge that is stored within these pages.

Lists of Attributes for Races and Classes

Learning to create a character for *Shadows of Undrentide* necessitates the study of many races and classes. The Character Development chapter covers both the general purpose of these categories and the details of their use. Information in these areas will be displayed in the following form:

HUMAN

- ✠ Favored Class (Any): When determining whether a multi-class human suffers an XP penalty, his highest-level class does not count.

- ✠ Quick to Master: 1 extra feat at 1st level

- ✠ Skilled: 4 extra skill points at 1st level, plus 1 additional skill point at each level up

This is followed by a description of humans (their strengths, weaknesses, etc.).

Tables for Skills, Feats, and Equipment

The mathematic nature of certain abilities within Third Edition *Dungeons and Dragons* makes it useful to display some sections as tables. The following example comes from the skill for using magical devices.

Skill Requirements for Magical Devices

Skill Value	Class Restricted Item	Race Restricted Item	Alignment Restricted Item
1	1,000 gp or fewer	Impossible	Impossible
5	4,800 gp or fewer	1,000 gp or fewer	Impossible
10	20,000 gp or fewer	4,800 gp or fewer	1,000 gp or fewer
15	100,000 gp or fewer	20,000 gp or fewer	4,800 gp or fewer
20	100,000 gp or fewer	100,000 gp or fewer	20,000 gp or fewer
25	100,000 gp or fewer	100,000 gp or fewer	100,000 gp or fewer

Walkthrough Maps

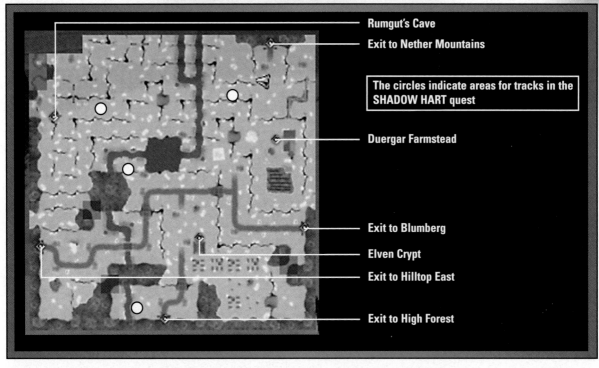

Rumgut's Cave

Exit to Nether Mountains

The circles indicate areas for tracks in the SHADOW HART quest

Duergar Farmstead

Exit to Blumberg

Elven Crypt

Exit to Hilltop East

Exit to High Forest

The in-game maps make it possible to quickly understand where characters have been and where they still need to explore. These maps are used throughout the walkthrough so that players will always have a reference for their movements that relates to the text.

Quest Tips

Quests and other side actions within the game are explained through tips. These can be general, covering a wide range of possibilities.

Quest Tip

WHAT TO DO WITH THE PEOPLE OF BLUMBERG
Good characters will be excited by this opportunity to really make a difference. Tell the prisoners that Hilltop is safe and give them 100 gold pieces to help rebuild their lives (total alignment shift of four points toward good).

Demanding payment from the villagers doesn't really do much because the sorry lot has nothing to offer. This can be done multiple times with no effect other than to shift your character's alignment one point toward evil with each occurrence.

Lying to say that Hilltop is in ruins will also push your character one point toward evil.

Killing the prisoners may be an effective way to end their suffering, but it sure isn't a kind or productive way to accomplish this end. This is an extremely evil act and will push your character far toward the side of evil.

Or, these tips can be alignment-specific.

This second tip type quickly gives players an idea of an action's consequences. Devoted good- or evil-aligned characters will be able to follow their alignment closely through intelligent use of the game's many branching points.

Loot Notes

Areas with especially useful, expensive, or obscure treasure are pointed out with an extra note.

Inside the chest are 50 gold pieces, a Focus Crystal, a magic ring, a journal, and a small magical item that is intended to reflect something about your character.

The ring, Mystra's Hand, does not have to be worn to be useful; it only has to be in your inventory. If your character is in trouble and has a Focus Crystal, the ring's unique power can be used to teleport the character back to Drogan's manor. This item can be dragged down onto the quickbar for faster and more efficient use.

The magical item is determined by your character's class, and it will serve to boost a skill once per day for most of the items. A fighter can get a Discipline buff, for example.

The journal will give players a fairly quick rundown on the other members of the manor. Other students have been training under Drogan, and it sounds like they cover a wide range of professions and philosophies.

Warnings

Warnings are given in areas with especially dangerous traps or ambushes. Spotting one of these in the text ahead will prepare you for a nasty trap, or at least give you time to save your game.

There are more traps along the passage to the north. These are more dangerous because they are accompanied by kobolds that will take advantage of your party's failures.

The first trap is connected to a large crossbow at the other end of the hallway—it's more of a small ballistae! It isn't easy to skirt this trap, so a rogue will have to disarm the trigger unless you are willing to run the risk of taking a hit. If you're willing to spend some time, you can destroy the automated crossbow from a distance, before crossing the trigger's threshold, by using missile weapons, such as a Longbow.

Around the next bend are some barrels that will explode when the archers at the other end of the hall make their missile attacks. Hurry past these to avoid the effects of darkness and fire that ensue. Even less militant characters will have better luck moving with haste through this part of the hall.

A final word of caution involves the crates through the dungeon. Starting at the next hall, there are crates you can search through for treasure. There isn't much of value to uncover, and there are kobold slashers inside a few of these containers.

Mini-Bestiaries

Each area has its own monsters and enemies. Instead of leaving hundreds of creature variants in the greater bestiary, each section is given a more pertinent selection of upcoming challenges. This makes it easier for players to known what is on the horizon. The statistics covered in these mini-bestiaries include Alignment (for spell purposes), Creature Type (racial hatred), Saving Throws (to figure out whether to use will magic or evocation), Armor Class, and Hit Points.

ORC

Alignment:	Chaotic Evil
Creature Type:	Humanoid
Fortitude Save:	2
Reflex Save:	0
Will Save:	0
Base AC:	10
Base HP:	4

ORC CHIEFTAIN

Alignment:	Chaotic Evil
Creature Type:	Humanoid, Ranger
Fortitude Save:	6
Reflex Save:	1
Will Save:	1
Base AC:	11
Base HP:	18

What Gleams in the Silver Marches

Regions

This section of the guide discusses the locations and characters of the game without giving away any of the critical plot events that will soon dirty the waters beneath Hilltop.

THE SILVER MARCHES

The Silver Marches covers a huge collection of wilderness that is home to a host of races. For generations, humans, elves, dwarves, and monsters have roamed this savage frontier and occasionally tried to settle within its borders. Even in the areas where trade and natural routes of travel have given rise to cities, there is always a sense of danger and freedom in the Silver Marches. Though war and fate push people away at times, the mystique and beauty of the land have always given settlers cause to return.

HILLTOP

Hilltop is one of the 'Free Towns' in the Silver Marches. Recently founded by ex-soldiers from the armies of Zhent, the towns are looked upon with suspicion by neighbors familiar with Zhent's expansionist history. The folks of the Free Towns maintain that they are happy to be rid of the yoke of Zhentarim control and wish to make a new life for themselves. In addition to former Zhent soldiers, the Free Towns tend to attract folk who are drawn to the local attitude of 'live and let live' and the lack of questions about a stranger's past.

The town is composed mostly of human settlers, though members of other races occasionally come to Hilltop, many to study under the town's most powerful resident, a mage named Drogan Droganson. Because of Drogan's good reputation, these assorted students are treated with an air of importance and comfort by most of the town's residents.

ANAUROCH

Known as the Great Waste, this tremendous desert was created through foul magics carried out by the nation of Netheril's enemies who dwelt above then-grassy plains in floating cities raised by magic. Now, few make it their home, except for the nomadic Bedine and the Zhentarim, who seek to forge a permanent trade route through the desert that they call the Black Road.

Individuals with great courage seek fame and glory in the desert, searching perhaps for the resting sites of the Lost Kingdoms and the Cities of Gold. Rumors of treasure and magics are only dwarfed by the tone of fear and danger that pervade this wasted land. Very few can brave to tread where the winds wail.

BLACKSANDS

Named after a mishap created by the original settlers (worshippers of the fire god Kossuth), Blacksands is a small settlement on the edge of the Anauroch desert. It has fallen into disrepair over the years, with many inhabitants moving west toward more temperate climes. The recent Zhentarim attempts to make their trade route permanent have brought back some life to the town.

THE FLOATING CITIES OF NETHERIL

The mages of the ancient Netherese Empire worked spells far beyond the reach of the mages of these latter days. Perhaps chief among their creations was the *mythallar*, the wondrous magical device that enabled the Netherese to raise their fabled floating cities. High above the earth, the floating cities were mighty citadels safe from virtually all enemies.

And indeed, the cities were eventually brought low not by any outside force, but by the pride and folly of the Netherese archmage Karsus, who attempted to seize the power of the goddess of magic. He instead managed to shatter the *mythallars*, sending all the cities of Netheril plummeting to earth.

The sands of the Anauroch desert swallowed the ruins, and Netheril passed into history, and then into legend. Now only the bravest explorers and adventurers dare to seek the lost cities, for the magical treasures hidden within are easily matched by the dangers of long-lost magic traps and the twisted creatures that lurk in the buried chambers.

The Cast of Characters

The central hero of the story has been training with Master Drogan for some time at his estate in Hilltop. From the outset, the player learns that the hero has done quite well in training. Though untested in true conflict, either arcane or physical, it seems that everyone has high hopes for the future career of this character. Yet, few people can go into the darkness alone, and there are many allies who will come and go throughout the adventure. The following spread of non-player characters will be available at different points in the game.

DORNA TRAPSPRINGER

When she heard Drogan had established a school for adventurers and was taking on apprentices in Hilltop, Dorna was one of the first to arrive and apply. She traveled nearly 200 miles alone across the wilds of the Silver Marches from her clan home in the mountains, which many would consider proof enough that she needed no instruction in survival. Still, she seems convinced that she is destined to face even greater danger; it's unlikely that she's wrong.

DROGAN DROGANSON

After a long career as an adventurer and explorer, Drogan has retired and set up shop in the village of Hilltop as an instructor. He teaches lessons learned from years of close calls and narrow escapes to a small class of youths who are anxious to start their own lives of adventure. Aside from his stories and lessons of adventure, Drogan speaks little of his past, though he exhibits all the hardened pragmatism typical of the northern Shield Dwarves.

XANOS MESSARMOS

Born to the upper middleclass of Chessenta, Xanos found his razor-sharp wit a strong counter to the barbs of his schoolmates in his youth. While now older, Xanos still has an acerbic nature, but it now masks his desire to fulfill the role of a true adventurer and gain renown throughout the realms.

MISCHA WAYMEET

The daughter of two mages, Mischa was something of a changeling in her family, with no gift for magic and a fascination with swordplay. Her talents brought her to Drogan's school in Hilltop for the training she could not find at home. Now a paladin of Mystra, she continually works to improve her skills and to protect the helpless from rogue spellcasters.

DEEKIN SCALESINGER

Deekin is a rather remarkable member of the Dripping Fang clan of kobolds. Unlike other kobolds, Deekin aspires to something 'bigger' than mining, marauding, and looting. He aspires to be a skald, a noble northern bard of legend. His goal is to write a heroic saga that will rival any of the classics… His chief problem is that his fellow kobolds are anything but heroic. Deekin has recently decided that he'll have to look a little further if he is going to find a hero befitting his saga.

KATRIANA DOROVNIA

One of the few non-Zhents allowed to traverse the Zhentarim's Black Road freely, Katriana is a halfling who has carved out her place in the world. She's garnered a reputation as a hard-nosed but fair bargainer who can be counted on for an even deal. She's always looking for people who can further her trading company, either by dealing with it or by keeping it from harm as it travels through dangerous climes.

Character Development

Character Development: The Path to Glory

Before a single step is taken on the journey toward greatness, players should sit back and envision the characters that will accompany them on the quests ahead. This is the most exciting aspect of a good role-playing game; each person has the power to choose a unique character from many thousands of options. Though these choices are a matter of personal preference, this section of the guide will provide players with a valuable list of advantages and challenges that are associated with each fork in the road.

As you read through this chapter, you'll encounter the "Shadows of Undrentide Exclusive" icon (see below). These mark elements or features that are new to the game (i.e., not part of the original Neverwinter Nights game).

EXCLUSIVE
Shadows of Undrentide

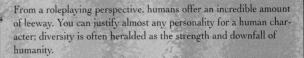

There are many powerful races that walk the Forgotten Realms. Many of these are too strange or fantastic to play, but a substantial number of options remain. These races add a lot to every character because they provide a chance to customize your character's statistics and background. Though many of the races have a few classes that they are geared toward, there are very few rules that are set in stone. If you want to play a gnome fighter from the very beginning, don't worry about whether that is a standard role. When played well, almost any choice of race will fit with the class that one desires. As with many of the choices in roleplaying games, power and opportunity are available from many angles. Of course, a half-orc sorcerer may draw more than a few stares, but maybe that is what you are looking for!

HUMAN

- ✛ Favored Class (Any): When determining whether a multi-class human suffers an XP penalty, his highest-level class does not count

- ✛ Quick to Master: 1 extra feat at 1st level

- ✛ Skilled: 4 extra skill points at 1st level, plus 1 additional skill point at each level up

Humans are the living currency of the world; these diverse people cover almost all regions and have many cultural and racial backgrounds. Though very short-lived, compared to a number of races, humans have been able to carve quite a niche for themselves; the penchant for technology and fast breeding have probably played a heavy part in this. Humans can have a number of skin tones from black to extremely pale white, and their hair covers the same range of dark, light, and moderate colors. Some men will grow facial hair that can be sparse or thick, though other human males may keep themselves cleanly shaven. Dress styles vary by region, as do religious callings, language, and other aspects of human life.

From a roleplaying perspective, humans offer an incredible amount of leeway. You can justify almost any personality for a human character; diversity is often heralded as the strength and downfall of humanity.

Humans are geared to take advantage of their diversity. All of the racial advantages that are offered to humans are generic, and these will serve well on any path. Because humans don't have a specific favored class, players will be very happy when it comes time to make a multi-class character with one. Players who plan on triple classing will certainly want to consider humans if they want to avoid experience penalties and the like.

Having an extra feat is nice for some classes and a godsend for others. Sure, fighters won't mind getting yet another tool for their early levels, but clerics and mages (who often feel starved for feats, even at high levels) will be very happy for this boon.

Again, the extra skill points are there to supplement any chosen class. Rogues may not need too many spare skill points to throw around, but barbarians and other classes with low natural skills and a tendency toward a mediocre intelligence will benefit from the steadfast nature of human learning.

DWARF

- Dwarven Ability Adjustments: +2 Constitution, -2 Charisma
- Favored Class (Fighter): A multiclass dwarf's fighter class does not count when determining whether he suffers an XP penalty for multiclassing

Many dwarves are as hard as the mountain stone. These are a people of crafts, be it smithing, mining or warfare. Whatever profession drives a dwarf will become a dominant factor in that character's life. Many people see the quiet and cold nature of dwarves and think that these are a people without emotions or joy. The truth is that dwarves often see great beauty in the things they create, and their love of such things has tremendous depth. Many dwarves are better at obscuring the truth than actual deception, and these people are renowned for their steadfast qualities when their word has been given.

Though dwarves only stand between four and four-and-a-half feet when they are fully-grown, a strong male would end up being almost as wide as he is tall! Dwarves are perfectly built for the diminutive tunnels and crags of the underworld. Most dwarves have slightly darker skin, ranging from a deep tan to light brown. These people have thick hair that is black, gray, brown, or auburn. Beards are a sign of age and power, so dwarven men grow these to substantial length.

Special Abilities

- Stonecunning grants all dwarves a +2 bonus on skill checks that involve unusual stonework: sliding walls, stonework traps, etc. This sixth sense about stonework is so strong that dwarves have a chance to notice unusual stonework even if they are not searching for it.
- Darkvision is a form of sight that requires no light at all. Creatures with darkvision can only see in black and white when there is no source of light, but it otherwise functions as normal vision.

- Hardiness vs. Poisons gives a +2 racial bonus on saving throws versus poisons.
- Hardiness vs. Spells gives a +2 racial bonus on saving throws versus spells and spell-like effects.
- Offensive Training vs. Orcs provides a +1 racial bonus to attack rolls against orcs.
- Offensive Training vs. Goblinoids provides a +1 racial bonus to attack rolls against goblinoids.
- Defensive Training vs. Giants allows characters to add a +4 dodge bonus when giants strike at them.
- Skill Affinity (Lore) adds a +2 racial bonus on lore checks.

For roleplaying, there are a number of nifty options that come out of dwarven society. Many may enjoy the common sight of a taciturn dwarf, evoking memories of many famous characters out of adventure novels, but dwarves can take other avenues as well. These mountain folk are extremely driven, whether it comes to crafts, war, or kinship. Religious fervor is not out of question when it comes to a dwarf, and that could lead to some very interesting roleplaying depending on the character's deity.

Dwarves are a very wise choice for a person who is interested in getting out of tough situations without too much of a thrashing. It isn't that dwarves are any stronger than humans or many of the other races; they simply won't fall unless they take an absurd amount of punishment. This seems like a perfect trait for a variety of warriors, and it is, but that doesn't preclude dwarves from becoming various types of mages and rogues, or men of faith. The constitution bonus that goes to each dwarf is welcome for any class that will be doing work on the front lines (whether by choice or lack thereof). Thuggish rogues are a very good example of a class that direly needs extra hit points.

The ability to multiclass as fighters without penalty is useful for people who want to grab skills or abilities from other classes. Dwarven fighter/clerics work extremely well because of their high hit points—it's almost like playing a full fighter who also has healing.

ELF

- Elven Ability Adjustments: +2 Dexterity, -2 Constitution

- Favored Class (Wizard): A multi-class elf's wizard class does not count when determining whether he suffers an XP penalty for multiclassing

Elven culture is known throughout the lands as being a haven of song, poetry, arcane study, and beauty. This does not preclude the elves from more mundane or even martial activities though. Elves often seek a balance between the pursuit of art and the necessity to protect the things that they care about. Because elves can live to be over 700 years old, everything takes a lot more time in their society. People often take a long time to judge others, and they are just as slow to indulge their emotions when something new is encountered.

Many elves are thin of build and stand over a foot beneath a human counterpart. On the whole, elves are pale-skinned and have green eyes and dark hair. Neither men nor women grow any facial hair. Elves apply their sense of beauty and grace to their clothing and buildings, so there is almost a sense of poise to the things that are associated with elves. This causes many races to have a natural attraction toward elves and elven things.

Special Abilities

- Immunity to Sleep from all magical sources.

- Hardiness vs. Enchantments reflects a +2 racial bonus toward enchantment spells and effects.

- Bonus Proficiencies (Longsword, Rapier, Shortbow, Longbow) are given to all elven characters.

- Skill Affinity (Listen) adds a +2 racial bonus on listen checks.

- Skill Affinity (Search) adds a +2 racial bonus on search checks.

- Skill Affinity (Spot) adds a +2 racial bonus on spot checks.

- Keen Senses make it possible for elves to spot secret doors even if they aren't looking for them; elves are given a spot hidden roll even on a casual pass.

- Low-light vision gives creatures twice the normal range of sight under minimal light conditions, while retaining their sense of color and detail.

Role players have a limitless trove of wealth when it comes to portraying an elf. On the happy side, a person can play a free spirit who adventures for a number of fair and gentle reasons: to see the world, to find strange magic, or just for the excitement. On the other hand, people who want to enjoy a darker side of elves can play a character that is driven by the urge to defend natural things or the elven way of life. When threatened, the elves are fierce and brutal, and this side of the fey folk is often disconcerting to others.

The statistics that elves gain are no less interesting or useful. Elves may be more than a little frail, but they gain so much in exchange. There are a number of spells that just aren't useful in the least against elven characters. This is especially a boon at lower levels, when basic enchantments and sleep spells are slung about. It is also nice, especially for classes without heavy battle training, to gain free proficiencies with common elven weapons. This gives even a mild character the option to bring a blade or bow into a fight, and neither of those are weak choices. It is really nice to have an elf in the party with a fair bit of dedication toward finding secret doors.

Many classes work wonderfully as an elf. The chaotic nature of barbarians is a bit much for the fey, but almost anything else can be worked into a good character. Rogues are a choice that many people lean toward quickly, because of the bonus to dexterity and the ability to detect secret doors so easily. Rangers and druids are also intuitive, especially from a roleplaying perspective (the guardian of nature aspect of elven society and all that).

If an elf is selected for a militant class, such as a ranger or fighter, there are a number of things to consider. First, elves don't have many hit points compared to humans or dwarves. For this reason, it is important to figure out how to defend on the frontlines. It isn't wise to let armor do all of the talking when one lucky shot can really put a hero out of action. For a better combination of defenses, use lighter armor and a high dexterity. Leather armor on a very quick character can outdo even a heavy fighter in full plate in terms of defensive capabilities. If damage isn't a major issue, take a shield as well, especially if you are a fighter; rangers are geared toward dual wielding, and their combat abilities fall behind a fighter unless you make incredible use of this.

To supplement an elf's offensive power, use finesse to let speed control melee bonuses instead of strength; this feat is wisely purchased for elves because there is usually at least a four-point difference between strength and dexterity, and this only grows with levels. People who want to play brute force warriors should already be looking elsewhere.

GNOME

- Gnome Ability Adjustments: +2 Constitution, -2 Strength

- Favored Class (Wizard): A multi-class gnome's wizard class does not count when determining whether he suffers an XP penalty for multiclassing

Gnomes are hailed as the great tinkers of the land. These tiny folk are fascinated with alchemy, industry, and the more technical side of things arcane. Not often seen adventuring in the overlands, gnomes are a reclusive and eccentric people. Still, visitors will find these people to be friendly and interested in trade, jokes and gossip. Gnomish culture places a great deal of importance on learning through trial and experience, which sometimes gets these people into trouble. "Just because it failed for him doesn't mean it won't work for me, eh?" Singed eyebrows are not uncommon on gnomish inventors.

In build, the gnomes are quite like the dwarves, though they aren't quite as thick. Adult gnomes are often a bit of three feet in height and have darkly tanned or even woody-colored skin. These people have fair hair and light eyes; this is offset by their love of brown tones in their buildings and clothing. Males carefully trim their beards. The lifespan for these affable creatures varies between 350 and 500 years.

Special Abilities

- Small Stature means that these characters gain a +1 size bonus to their armor class and attack rolls. They also have +4 due to size on their hide checks. As a penalty, these characters must use weapons one size smaller than their larger counterparts. They also have only a 75% carrying capacity.

- Hardiness vs. Illusions gives gnomes a +2 racial bonus against all kinds of illusions.

- Offensive Training vs. Reptiloids provides a +1 racial bonus to attack rolls against reptiloids.

- Offensive Training vs. Goblinoids provides a +1 racial bonus to attack rolls against goblinoids.

- Defensive Training vs. Giants allows characters to add a +4 dodge bonus when giants strike at them.

- Skill Affinity (Listen) adds a +2 racial bonus on listen checks.

- Skill Affinity (Concentration) adds a +2 racial bonus on concentration checks.

- Spell Focus (Illusion) adds a +2 racial bonus on lore checks.

- Low-light vision gives creatures twice the normal range of sight under minimal light conditions, while retaining their sense of color and detail.

While a person could always try to play a nasty or lazy gnome, this would be a very far stretch for such a specific race. Gnomes really do stick to their mold most of the time, and roleplayers will be interested in gnomes more for the application of a character type rather than the creation of one. Gnomes usually adventure for knowledge or to obtain new materials for their experiments. Less intellectual gnomes can certainly be in the employ of other forces, which could lead to some interesting situations.

By the stats, gnomes are an odd combination. Though many gnomish skills are a boon for mages (specifically wizards), there are a few things that are very useful to warriors in this mix. A higher constitution is always desirable, whether a person stands on the frontlines or hides in the back. Having a small stature is also nifty when it comes to situations with large, stomping beasts that are quick to squish even the toughest characters. This dichotomous mix of perks makes it possible to do many interesting things with gnomes.

The most obvious choice is to make a gnomish wizard. Gnomes make incredibly useful spellcasters, and they certainly tend toward a wide mix of spells, unlike sorcerers and evocation specialists. With higher hit points, gnomes can stay a bit closer to the front without being in mortal terror for more than half of the time. This opens to door for using more buff spells to enhance party members, and for more direct magic during battle. Evokers tend to stay back and play like archers, throwing brutal spells into the mix. Gnomes can come forward and disrupt enemies, especially considering the gnomish tendency toward illusion magic.

Warriors are often happier with a dwarf, particularly if one is interested in gaining many of the same perks that gnomes are given, but someone with a real flair for the odd could choose a gnome for this. The roleplaying aspects of this idea are boundless, and it would certainly be a fun way to get involved with online play. Push around a few half-orcs and threaten them with the back of your hand if they get too cheeky. Make sure to use finesse weapons, having items with range to soften enemies, and consider multi-classing with another class to gain some tricks (i.e., get some rogue levels for sneak attack damage).

HALF-ELF

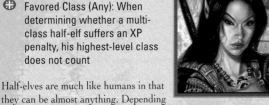

- ✛ Favored Class (Any): When determining whether a multi-class half-elf suffers an XP penalty, his highest-level class does not count

Half-elves are much like humans in that they can be almost anything. Depending on where the person was raised, a half-elf could have the adoration of nature and art that typifies elves, or the individual could be a raging lunatic who burns tree stumps for a living. Some societies accept half-elves without judgment; this is often in regions where humans and elves get along well, of course. In other lands, half-elves live without the support or kinship of either race.

Physically, half-elves can bear any mixture of human or elfish features. The tendency is for these people to have fair skin, but even this isn't dependable. Though these people enjoy longer lives than pure humans, it is rare for a half-elf to live much past 180 years.

Special Abilities

- ✛ Immunity to Sleep from all magical sources.

- ✛ Hardiness vs. Enchantments reflects a +2 racial bonus toward enchantment spells and effects.

- ✛ Skill Affinity (Listen) adds a +1 racial bonus on listen checks.

- ✛ Skill Affinity (Search) adds a +1 racial bonus on search checks.

- ✛ Skill Affinity (Spot) adds a +1 racial bonus on spot checks.

- ✛ Low-light vision gives creatures twice the normal range of sight under minimal light conditions, while retaining their sense of color and detail.

A role player can do anything with a half-elf. Some people tend toward being a misfit who hasn't found a place in the world, while others come from a loving background and have known the strengths and joys of two worlds. Whatever class and style a person desires, there is certainly a history to justify why a half-elf could fall into that role.

It is almost a crime not to use multiple classes as a half-elf. In a crude view of statistics, it is a waste of half-elven versatility (one of their greatest assets) to stay as a single class. An elf has extra dexterity and several useful abilities that a half-elf lacks, and a human gets extra skill points and an entire feat. As such, the most powerful use of a half-elf is to take the elven advantages that are gained and apply them to a mix of classes that can use such powers.

Half-elves make very effective rogue/fighters because of their versatile stats and bonuses to roguish skills. A person who plans on making a very lethal sneak attack rogue will also enjoy the resistance to enchantments and the low-light vision of these creatures.

HALF-ORC

- ✛ Orc Ability Adjustments:
  +2 Strength, -2 Intelligence,
  -2 Charisma

- ✛ Favored Class (Barbarian): A multiclass half-orc's barbarian class does not count when determining whether he suffers an XP penalty for multiclassing

Half-orcs are rarely seen as a quiet and peaceful folk. Indeed, it is rare to find a half-orc who doesn't have a hard story to tell. Human societies are not often gentle enough to nurture a person with a bit of orc heritage, and it is quite unlikely that a half-orc would be raised in orcish tribes without having a lot of grief while proving himself. These hard knocks make it common for half-orcs to be fierce, short-tempered, and still oddly reflective. Caught between two worlds, these people have no peaceful home or culture, so they are driven to action and decisions on their own inspiration. This individualism can lead half-orcs into trouble with the law in many lands and also aids the notion that they are a chaotic group.

Though partially human in appearance, half-orcs are often very well muscled and have darker skin. These creatures have the same life span as humans, save for their troublesome lifestyles, and will reach 70 or more years if they are fortunate.

Special Abilities

- ✛ Darkvision is a form of sight that requires no light at all. Creatures with darkvision can only see in black and white when there is no source of light, but it otherwise functions as normal vision.

Though the statistics of a half-orcs are very limiting, the roleplaying opportunities for these pariahs are not. Half-orcs can be brutal savages, artists, lonely travelers with a bond to the world itself, or poets who carry axes in their hands and songs in their hearts. Players of half-orcs are entirely free to choose whether they speak in monosyllables or iambic pentameter.

As stated though, the stats for these creatures can be difficult to bear. Half-orcs are the only playable race that has a deficit in their starting attribute points. Losing two from intelligence and charisma almost forces a player to choose from a limited class list. Still, there are so many interesting aspects to playing as a half-orc that the fun balances this race even if they look a bit weak on paper.

Any barbarian player has a strong option in the form of a half-orc. It won't hurt anyone much to lose intelligence or charisma as a barbarian, and the added strength goes wonderfully with a greataxe and the heavy application of barbaric rage. This is a very safe way to grab a character that does truly devastating damage from the very beginning of his or her career. Because half-orcs can take a second class without penalties, a single level of fighter can kick a barbarian off on the right foot (free feat and full armor options can pave the way nicely).

HALFLING

- Halfling Ability Adjustments: +2 Dexterity, -2 Strength

- Favored Class (Rogue): A multi-class halfling's rogue class does not count when determining whether he suffers an XP penalty for multiclassing

Halflings are a short and clever bunch that always finds its way into the strangest sort of places. In many ways, halflings are brave and tough, even though they aren't physically impressive; this comes from a stiff resolve that few anticipate until they have dealt with the little folk. Though halflings enjoy money and possessions, they prefer to use these resources and revel rather than hoard and prepare for distant times. This tendency gets halflings into trouble sometimes when bill collectors come knocking on their door.

Halflings have ruddy skin, dark and often straight hair, and brown or black eyes. The men don't let their hair grow too long, though they let their sideburns grow out. Other facial hair is often avoided and kept to a minimum. Halfling clothes are comfortable, practical, and allow freedom of movement. A good halfling never knows when he'll need to make a run for it, after all. These short people are only about three feet tall. Many halflings live to an age around 150 years.

Special Abilities

- Small Stature means that these characters gain a +1 size bonus to their armor class and attack rolls. They also have +4 due to size on their hide checks. As a penalty, these characters must use weapons one size smaller than their larger counterparts. They also have only a 75% carrying capacity.

- Skill Affinity (Move Silently) adds a +2 racial bonus on move silently checks.

- Skill Affinity (Listen) adds a +2 racial bonus on listen checks.

- Lucky is a wonderful trait that gives halflings a +1 racial bonus on all saving throws.

- Fearless gives halflings a +2 bonus on saving throws against fear (stacks with innate luck bonus).

- Good Aim grants a +1 racial bonus with thrown weapons.

Though halflings aren't easy to spot next to some of the larger races, they more than make up for it with the size of their personalities. Halflings are chatty, and they work themselves into everyone's affairs whenever possible. This makes some halflings into dear friends, but others find opulent living as charlatans and rogues. It's hard to trust these short people, yet many of the races have to fight against a natural tendency to believe and care for halflings (perhaps because they have a childish aspect to their physical and mental perception). Roleplayers can use this to their full advantage!

It's almost hard to try anything beyond a rogue when playing as a halfling. Though there are many races that play well as rogues, but halflings excel beyond all of the others. Having a high dexterity is a plus, and losing strength is no major price to pay for it (the elves lose constitution instead, which is a nasty trade). Beyond that, halflings enjoy a smaller profile, some bonuses to survival from their special abilities, and the ability to become a multiclass rogue without any penalties. It doesn't get much better than that. The Thuggish style of rogues isn't really meant for halflings, but almost all of the other choices are perfect.

Yet, there are other options if a halfling player doesn't want to walk down the same thiefly road that has been tread by so many before. Looking at a halfling's stats, a player will notice that there are a ton of defensive goodies in that little package. A defensive fighter or paladin will have a lot to gain from trying a halfling. Natural defense from being small combines nicely with expertise to make a character that won't be hit by normal attacks. Combine this with high saving throws (especially as a halfling paladin) and the final product is the ultimate survivor. It is true that the damage potential of this combination is laughable, but holding up enemies while an archer or mage does the dirty work is certainly possible.

Classes

A character's class or classes will determine almost all of the statistics that grow and develop as the character progresses through the levels of the game. Indeed, a great deal of roleplaying is based around class selection and assertion as well. This means that class selection is more important than almost any other choice for a character's identity.

This part of the guide not only lists the strengths and weaknesses of each class; it also gives a template for a possible character for each class. Rather than listing a fairly generic model for each character type, a number of interesting and uncommon character mixes have been tested and reproduced here. These are primarily meant to get people thinking about the thousands of possible character ideas that lie off the beaten path.

BARBARIAN

- ✚ Alignment Restrictions: Any nonlawful
- ✚ Hit Die: d12
- ✚ Proficiencies: All simple and martial weapons, light armor, medium armor, and shields
- ✚ Skill Points (Int Modifier *4 at 1st level): 4 + Int Modifier
- ✚ Barbarians are unable to progress in levels if their alignment ever becomes lawful

Barbarians do not live by the civilized laws of mankind. These warriors have a feral calling that keeps them from falling into the ruts that others so often do. Barbarians gather strength from their emotions, and the rage that comes over them in battle allows these savages to survive some of the most punishing engagements. People who want to be strong and tough will be very happy as barbarians; they have even more hit points than normal fighter classes, better attacks through their abilities, and still have an incredible bonus to attack.

Barbarian rage, which increases over the levels, can be used several times a day. Initially, this ability grants a +4 bonus to strength and constitution for a short time. At fifteenth level, this bonus extends to +6 for both stats. Though a modest armor class penalty is applied during a rage, the loss of 2 armor class points is a trivial matter compared to change in overall damage potential.

Through the levels, barbarians gain additional abilities that are also useful for getting them out of tough situations. Because barbarians often wear light or medium armor, the focus of these abilities is toward mobile, defensive fighting. Barbarians can't be caught flat-footed (2nd level) or flanked (5th level), and their natural bonus of movement is nice for protecting a party from multiple attackers. Later on, barbarians also acquire a natural damage reduction (which increases at levels 11, 14, 17, and 20).

Barbarians are a very good class to take all the way up to 20 because of these abilities, though they work well as multiclass characters with fighters (for extra feats and grabbing weapon specialization) and rogues (for sneak attack).

Good henchmen or companions for a barbarian include clerics (for buffs and healing), mages, and archers. The barbarian can tear through and tie up almost anything that comes down the corridor, so a nice support character will be happy and unmolested in the background.

Barbarian Fighter (Berserker)
HALF-ORC BARBARIAN/FIGHTER (16/4)

Strength	20 (+4)	Dexterity	15 (+1)
Intelligence	6	Constitution	14
Wisdom	8	Charisma	6

Primary Attribute	Strength
Weapon Choices	Dual Kukri
Armor Preference	Breastplate
Primary Skills	Discipline, Listen
Starting Feats	Exotic Weapon Proficiency, Ambidexterity
Additional Feats	Two-Weapon Fighting, Weapon Specialization, Weapon Focus, Power Attack, Improved Critical, Improved Two-Weapon Fighting, Cleave, Improved Power Attack, Greater Cleave

This hybrid class is quite evil on the field of battle. At first appearance, the sight of a gigantic half-orc with a couple of kukri will draw a snicker from various enemies; this will soon change. As the levels progress, the many penalties of two-weapon fighting will drift away as the proper feats are taken. By the end of the process, this half-orc will still have a substantial bonus to strike even while using power attack (or even improved power attack if the enemies are slow enough). This allows the barbarian to take at least six kukri attacks per round (ignoring spell buffs, full cleave potential, and attacks of opportunity). With all of the bonuses from a high strength, power attacks, and weapon specialization, those kukris won't seem so trivial. If this character is lucky enough to grab keen kukri one day, having a 12+ threat range will make things even worse for anyone who tries to play games with a berserker!

This is not a class combination for complete beginners. It takes a lot more time to get this barbarian off the ground compared to a more generic model, but the end result is fast, exciting, and vicious. Many players see rangers as the master of dual wielding, but this template has a ton of benefits: higher hit points, barbarian rage, faster movement, and better armor. Considering that this character only loses one feat to the ranger (the fighter levels add two feats but it takes three to gain the dual wielding abilities), the barbarian should be a strong contender for the crown of twin weaponry.

As a side note, it is best to take the fighter levels early on. Try grabbing them at levels 2, 3, 4, and 6. This will ensure that the character can take weapon specialization (a fighter-only feat) and get a lot of the dual wielding feats out of the way before wasting too much time whiffing in the early levels.

An optional version of this character could focus on a greataxe instead of the kukri. Ditch the three feats for dual weapons and grab point blank shot, rapid shot, and weapon focus (longbow). This model is a bit less creative, but he still carries a lot of weight in battle. The enhanced missile capabilities of this barbarian can help early in a fight too.

Characters who wish to go through the game and find all of the options and solutions for each problem will want to steer clear of this character (and most barbarians in general). Berserkers lack finesse, intelligence, and persuasion, and that makes the whole world look a bit like a nail. Berserkers can still play as either good or evil characters, but they won't have a lot of extra conversation options or quests to take care of during their journeys.

BARD

- ⊕ Alignment Restrictions: Any nonlawful
- ⊕ Hit Die: d6
- ⊕ Proficiencies: Simple weapons, light armor, medium armor, and shields
- ⊕ Skills Points (*4 at 1st level): 4 + Int Modifier
- ⊕ Spellcasting: Arcane (Charisma-based, no spell preparation, spell failure from armor is a factor)

⊕ Bards begin the game knowing all cantrips

⊕ Bards cannot gain levels of experience while they are of any lawful alignment

Bards are a difficult class to understand until a person has played a few of them. The inherent problem of a bard is that she is a warrior, poet, negotiator, scout, rogue, mage-of-sorts, and a bit of everything else. To truly master a bard, a person has to have a bit of experience with all of these roles. Critics of this complex class decry that bards are outdone at every path; fighters beat them in melee and at range, mages outcast them, clerics can buff just as well, and rogues sneak and assassinate with more grace. All of these are true! However, bards fight better than mages, cast well enough to outdo a rogue, buff well, and sneak well enough when they need to. There are advantages to being a jack-of-all-trades. This is often the case in large parties where a bard can always fill in for a person who is having problems of some sort. When playing alone, it is a lot harder to get everything out of a bard.

For special abilities, a bard can draw upon bardic magic, music, and lore. Bardic magic is arcane in nature (and is disrupted by armor), so bards are often forced to switch in and out of their armor depending on the situation. Otherwise, bardic spells are a mix of enchantments. Buff spells, moderate healing capabilities, and a fair bit of illusion potential make the bardic school a fairly exciting one. As with other bard elements, this magic won't overpower a dedicated caster of similar level. Instead, the school offers a mix of everything for each section. Bards have a number of nice buffs for combat work (haste and invisibility derivatives).

Bardic Archer (Skald)
ELF BARD/FIGHTER (16/4)

Strength	10	Dexterity	16 (+4)
Intelligence	12	Constitution	14
Wisdom	10	Charisma	15 (+1)

Primary Attribute	Dexterity
Weapon Choices	Longbow or a Composite Longbow
Armor Preference	Chainmail or Breastplate
Primary Skills	Perform, Hide, Move Silently
Starting Feats	Point Blank Shot
Additional Feats	Rapid Shot, Weapon Focus, Weapon Specialization, Improved Critical, Dodge, Mobility, Spring Attack, Skill Focus (Perform or Discipline), Toughness

Bards don't bring too much power into a standard melee, but people who give them a chance with a missile weapon will find that they are one of the premier classes to send arrows into a fray. The reason for this rests on the fast and plentiful bardic buffs that are ideal for increasing archer damage whether in or out of armor. Adding a few levels of fighter to the mixture will increase the attack rating of final characters to the point where they gain a fourth attack and can take weapon specialization (always a perk).

Though bard players always need to be fast on their feet, having a modest hit point spread is not damning. Rather, it encourages people to play this template the way that a tried and true archer should be played— using hit-and-run tactics all the way. Bards are ideal for this aspect of archery too, because they have invisibility spells, haste magic, and a spread of additional spells to make things more difficult for pursuers.

Bardic music is a great way to enhance a party. Through the use of several songs, a bard can give the party bonuses toward combat attacks, damage, hit points, and saving throws.

Bards are a somewhat poor class for taking up to 20. After level 14, bards don't get anything that will make their music too much more effective for a party. Beyond that, they lose out on a fourth attack and a chance for more hit points. Thus, there are a number of interesting multiclass options for a bard's later levels. As a fighter or paladin, bards can increase their bonus to hit and make a successful bid for that final attack. Fighters also get extra feats, but a paladin benefits from the bard's natural charisma. With rogue as a side class, the bard gains a modest sneak attack that polishes off the notion that this class can do a bit of anything. Monks and spell-wielding classes are not as effective because six levels won't get the character very far.

As a side note, it is very difficult to pull off a paladin/bard combination because it takes such a specific turn of events to create one. A person would have to be created as a lawful good paladin and turn to a neutral alignment when she wants to become a bard. The concept is extremely cool, and roleplaying opportunities abound, but the feasibility of this character is quite troublesome. Players who are driven to make this work can use the aurora toolset to create a scenario to play out this change of heart; alternatively, there are modules on the major sites that accomplish the same thing.

Bards thrive on the strength of their companions. This class is almost driven to find a full party for adventuring, so playing with only a henchman is a bit stifling. If that is the only option, play against the bard's weaknesses. A combative bard should take a good caster to stay in the back and buff or attack. Gun-shy bards should seek a more militant companion who can control the front lines and exposure enemies to sneak attacks, missiles, or whatever else the bard has up her sleeves.

It is nice to take this character template through the game because almost every quest option will be possible. Bards have trouble staying on the lawful end of things for too long, but that doesn't prevent these characters from doing honorable things when they are in the mood. Beyond that, they can be nasty, friendly, or whatever else the player enjoys. Having a full spread of skill and well-rounded attributes can be a bonus for this too.

Skalds are incredible fun to play, especially for people who have a bit more experience with the game. Though battles take longer, especially if the skald only has a henchman around to help out, the style of combat is quite active. This template comes highly recommended, especially for people who haven't yet found a bard character to fall in love with.

CLERIC

- ⊕ Hit Die: d8
- ⊕ Proficiencies: All simple weapons, all armor, and shields
- ⊕ Skill Points (*4 at 1st level): 2 + Int Modifier
- ⊕ Spellcasting: Divine (Wisdom based, armor-related chance of spell failure is ignored)

Many clerics who seek adventure are warriors of faith. Though the various gods differ greatly, both malicious and benevolent deities allow their clerics to don incredibly heavy armor and wield all manner of capable spells. Clerics can be kind, gently, wary, cruel, spiteful, idiotic, or anything else that exists in the nature of man and beast, and so roleplayers are given a dramatic number of choices for personalities.

One of the sacred abilities of clerics comes in their struggle over the living dead. Undead can be turned, controlled, and destroyed by the power of the divine. Because this touches upon a cleric's ability to supplicate and call down the essence of the divine, this can only be done several times per day. The higher a cleric's charisma bonus, the more chances the character is given to turn or rebuke undead. Clerics normally can turn undead three times per day plus their charisma modifier.

This power over death gives clerics a sense of awe, and these people of faith can even return people from the clutches of the afterlife.

Air

| Spell Level Three: Call Lightning |
| Spell Level Six: Chain Lightning |

The cleric can turn elementals as if they were undead of equivalent level. This ability by itself can be useful, especially in certain dungeons. The two spells for this domain add a substantial amount of direct damage potential for the cleric to draw upon.

Animal

| Spell Level Two: Cat's Grace |
| Spell Level Three: True Seeing |
| Spell Level Five: Polymorph Self |

Animal domain clerics summon monsters that are enhanced beyond that normal level of the cleric's summoning spells. This is a mediocre ability for most clerics, but characters that solo a great deal and rely on their creatures to tank for them may find it useful. The spells of this domain are not terribly powerful, but they add a slight druidic flavor to a cleric, if that is desired.

CLERIC

For direct conflict, clerics are only given the use of simple weapons and must rely on their superior armor to carry them through. Fortunately, the divine magic of these characters will work no matter what armor they are wearing, so encumbrance is not a major concern during a fight. Wisdom allows clerics to cast higher levels of divine spells, so this is often the central attribute of a player character.

Finally, each cleric can choose to focus on two domains from which to draw power. These godly realms provide certain spells that are not available normally to the clerics, so it is a very important choice. For proper roleplaying purposes, a person should simply decide which spirits grant the cleric his power. However, players with a very specific urge toward certain spells or powers will appreciate the accompanying sidebars. If roleplaying is not an issue, take the two domains that provide the best abilities for the cleric that is being created.

Death

Spell Level Four: Phantasmal Killer

Spell Level Five: Enervation

Death clerics can summon an avatar from the negative elemental plane. This has a certain malicious appeal to it, but this creature will not be as effective for clerics who travel with henchmen and groups. As for spell selection, the domain of death is limited. Phantasmal killer is an autokill spell that comes a bit earlier than its peers, but it rarely turns the tide of a larger battle. Enervation is certainly good for its intimidation value against living creatures, but it has no worth against many of the more vicious opponents out in the world. Death has a lot more importance as a domain if the planned cleric will be playing against other player characters.

Destruction

Spell Level Three: Stinking Cloud

Spell Level Six: Acid Fog

Destructive clerics can use their ability to turn undead to harm constructs. Considering the significant danger posed by such creatures, this is a nifty power for people to have. The nice spells that are granted from this domain are a boon as well, for both bring a sorcerous element to the priestly caster. Clerics on the backline of the party will be served well by this domain.

Earth

Spell Level Four: Stoneskin

Spell Level Five: Energy Buffer

Earth clerics turn elementals as if they were undead of equivalent level. Being able to cast stoneskin is a fine bit of luck for melee clerics, considering that such a spell is quite powerful for medium-level characters. Energy buffer, coming just a spell level later, is also a splendid buff for preventing damage. Dwarven Fighter/Clerics are heavily drawn to this domain, for practical and spiritual reasons.

Evil

Spell Level One: Negative Energy Ray

Spell Level Three: Negative Energy Burst

Spell Level Five: Enervation

Evil clerics can turn outsiders as if they were undead of equivalent level. This grim domain's primary ability does not come in handy very often because many outsiders are hard to find and then hard to turn even when they do show up. The spells from this domain are mediocre for doing direct damage to one's enemies, but it is hardly worth the taint that follows from accepting the realm of evil. Now, if the domain granted horrid wilting as an ability…

Fire

Spell Level Four: Wall of Fire

Spell Level Five: Energy Buffer

Fire priests can turn elementals as if they were undead of equivalent level. Though the domain of earth offers a better spread of magic, the ability to summon a wall of fire will often surprise enemies who are used to seeing clerics shy away from such strong elemental magics.

Good

Spell Level Four: Stoneskin

Spell Level Five: Lesser Planar Binding

Clerics of goodness can turn outsiders as if they were undead of equivalent level. As always, stoneskin is an ability that everyone wants to have. Having a spell to summon or control some outsiders is nifty too.

Healing

Spell Level Two: Cure Serious

Spell Level Five: Heal

Healers are able to cast all healing spells as if they were used with the feat of empowerment. This is perhaps one of the finest abilities granted by any of the domains, and clerics who serve a party or even a dedicated melee henchman will feel blessed in making such a choice for their gods. Being able to master cure serious wounds and heal ahead of time is also a major gift in the grand scheme of things.

CLERIC

Knowledge

Spell Level One: Identify

Spell Level Two: Ultravision

Spell Level Three: Clairaudience/Clairvoyance

Spell Level Four: True Seeing

Spell Level Six: Legend Lore

Though clerics of knowledge don't have any special abilities to draw upon, their extensive library of special spells is nice for players who want to round out their party. Identify and Legend Lore are useful when there aren't mages and bards around to identify items, while ultravision, true seeing, and clairaudience make it possible to detect sneaky types even if a fellow rogue isn't around to do the work.

Magic

Spell Level One: Mage Armor

Spell Level Two: Melf's Acid Arrow

Spell Level Three: Negative Energy Burst

Spell Level Four: Stoneskin

Spell Level Five: Ice Storm

The study of magic is not preclusive to the worship of gods. Indeed, clerics who study magic gain no special abilities from their gods, but they master many rare spells that other clerics are forbidden or unable to cast. Melf's acid arrow and ice storm bring a fair bit of direct damage into the cleric's repertoire. Stoneskin gives protection to make the package a bit sweeter. Backline clerics do very well with this domain.

Plant

Spell Level Two: Barkskin

Spell Level Seven: Creeping Doom

Plant domain clerics can turn various vermin as if they were undead creatures of equivalent level. This is not one of the better domains for most clerics because so few vermin pose a dire threat to a party (compared with undead, constructs, elementals, and such). Barkskin is a good addition at low levels, and creeping doom adds a whole level of style to a fight, but there are more powerful domains to choose from.

Protection

Spell Level Four: Minor Globe

Spell Level Five: Energy Buffer

Clerics who believe in the powers of protection have the ability to create a field of divine protection once per day. This is a form of sanctuary that has a [DC of 10 + Caster's Charisma Modifier + Number of Cleric Levels]. The duration is (1 round per caster level + Caster's Charisma Modifier). The spell selection for this domain is adequate, though energy buffer can be found elsewhere with better combinations. Anyone who is really interested in the domain of protection should do it for the chance to have sanctuary at his disposal.

Strength

Spell Level Three: Divine Power

Spell Level Five: Stoneskin

Clerics of strength can enhance their own physical powers once per day. This increases the strength of the cleric for (5 rounds + Caster's Charisma Modifier). The bonus strength equals [2 + (1 for every 3 Cleric levels)]. Divine power and stoneskin are both powerful buffs, making this a domain that is wonderful for militant clerics who want to supplement their skill up on the lines of battle.

Sun

Spell Level Two: Searing Light

Spell Level Seven: Sunbeam

Those clerics who worship the sun are even more ferocious enemies of creatures who tread the line between the living and the deceased. As a special ability, sun clerics have a greater ability to turn undead! Sun clerics add 1d6 to the maximum hit dice of undead that are turned, and 1d4 additional undead per turning are affected by the divine power. Even the bonus spells for this domain are entirely centered around maintaining the proper balance of life; clerics who want to savage the undead have no better option in all the planes of existence.

Travel

Spell Level One: Entangle

Spell Level Two: Web

Spell Level Three: Freedom of Movement

Spell Level Four: Slow

Spell Level Five: Haste

The domain of travel does not have any direct powers to give a cleric, but the numerous spells from this selection are quite good. Entangle and web are brilliant for disrupting enemies, especially at the lower levels. Freedom and movement is nice for getting out of trouble before better dispel powers are at the cleric's disposal, but having slow and haste are the real treats. Haste is the crown jewel of this domain, and it tops off a buff clerics repertoire perfectly!

Trickery

Spell Level Two: Invisibility

Spell Level Three: Invisibility Sphere

Spell Level Four: Improved Invisibility

Clerics who worship tricksters have a touch of roguishness in them, and that comes through in the powers that they gain. Once a day, these clerics can increase the following skills by [1 for every 2 Cleric Levels]: Hide, Persuade, Search, Disable Trap, Move Silently, Open Locks, Pick Pockets. This effect lasts for (5 turns + Caster's Charisma Modifier). Having invisibility is a hefty bonus as well, for both buff clerics, sneak characters, and for militant casters.

CLERIC

War

Spell Level Two: Cat's Grace

Spell Level Seven: Aura of Vitality

War clerics are able to drive themselves into a brutal frenzy once per day. This malevolent ability grants the cleric [1 + (1 for every 5 Levels)] to Dexterity, Constitution, Attack Rolls, Damage, and an equal level of Damage Reduction from incoming attacks. This power lasts for (5 rounds + Caster's Charisma Modifier). In addition to this potent buff, war clerics can cast cat's grace and aura of vitality; this complete package makes war one of the best domains for almost any cleric. Militant clerics and buffers should both be quite happy to draw from this domain (so long as the touch of Ares doesn't taint the purpose of the cleric's actions).

Water

Spell Level Three: Poison

Spell Level Five: Ice Storm

Water clerics can turn elemental creatures as if they were undead of equivalent level. The spells from their domain are fairly weak compared to many of the others, but poison and ice storm provide a bit of direct damage potential for a cleric who stays at the back of the party.

Many classes are made to be paired with one or two types of henchmen for an ideal couple. With clerics, the options are quite numerous because these characters are good at fighting, buffing others and themselves, healing, and casting some offensive spells too. Like bards, clerics are made to join and supplement any party. Thus, a cleric should look for a companion who has specific needs that can be attended. Heal those barbarians, protect the rogues, buff the fighters, and chase off any undead who poke their heads out of the dirt.

Warrior Cleric (Crusader)
DWARF CLERIC/FIGHTER (16/4)

Strength	14	Dexterity	10
Intelligence	10	Constitution	16
Wisdom	15 (+5)	Charisma	12

Domains	War and Strength
Primary Attributes	Strength, Wisdom
Weapon Choices	Longsword
Armor Preference	Full Plate and a Tower Shield
Primary Skills	Discipline, Concentration
Starting Feats	Luck of Heroes
Additional Feats	Dirty Fighting, Weapon Focus, Weapon Specialization, Improved Critical, Toughness, Empower Spell, Lightning Reflexes, Dirty Fighting, Power Attack

Dwarves are a bit surly for a run-of-the-mill cleric, but they are ideal for a crusader. Because of the high constitution that comes so easily to this template, the character will easily have as many hit points as a normal warrior; that by itself is pretty nifty. With a longsword, full plate, and a tower shield, most people are not going to assume that there is actually a man of faith under all of that steel and bravado.

These clerics are meant to go up on the front lines. Attribute buffs and other long-lasting spells for the party can be cast during the quiet times, then the crusader can take his place along any of the best tanks in the game. By choosing war and strength as domains, this cleric gets some absurdly wonderful spells (stoneskin and aura of vitality are simply evil in a warrior-cleric's hands). The ability to draw on divine strength and battle mastery is incredible too, though the dwarf's meager charisma limits the duration on these—everyone has to have a weakness somewhere!

These tanks won't deal as much damage as a heavy fighter or barbarian, but they can absorb attacks (both mystical and mundane) without being phased in the least. Using stoneskin and the various spells for attribute buffs and saving throw bonuses, this cleric can become an unstoppable beast!

On the offensive end of things, this template has sacrificed level-nine spells for a fourth melee attack. For many spellcasters, this would be folly, but the decision is reasonably justified here. Warrior clerics won't often need the same level of creature summoning to stay alive that soft casters do (thus the gate and the highest summoning spell are dispensable). There are no additional healing spells at level nine, nor are there are major buffs; the new enchantment against undead is nice, but it is very specific in what it can do for a party. Thus, the fourth melee attack wins the day. However, players who are interested in the spells at the price of a melee attack should simply follow a 17/3 model of the same template.

Players who want to have a more charismatic crusader should switch to playing as a human; lower the constitution, raise the charisma, then take paladin levels if immunity to fear is worth losing weapon specialization. Either way, the character type will bring a lot of love into the world (one way or another).

DRUID

- ⊕ Alignment Restrictions: Must be neutral good, lawful neutral, true neutral, chaotic neutral, or neutral evil

- ⊕ Hit Die: d8

- ⊕ Proficiencies: Proficient with the club, dagger, dart, sickle, scimitar, spear, sling, and quarterstaff, as well as shields and light and medium armor

- ⊕ Skill Points (*4 at 1st level): 4 + Int Modifier

- ⊕ Spellcasting: Divine (Wisdom based, armor-related chance of spell failure is ignored)

- ⊕ A druid that is no longer neutral cannot gain levels

Druids are a power that does not exist inside the struggles of man, elf, nor monster. Druids bow to a higher calling, but a more terrestrial one than their cleric brothers. Nature itself is the source of strength and worship for these mystic people, and they will heed the call of no other for long.

In disposition, many druids are quiet and contemplative. This does not prevent them from being kind to others or violent against those who try to taint the land. Though many people tend strongly to lean toward good or evil in their passage through life, the druid tries to look at the balance of nature instead (though only a few druids are perfect at doing this).

Undead and other artificial things are some of the greatest enemies of this order. Druids cannot abide the creation or existence of such things, and they will risk themselves and others to cleanse the area of these monstrosities. To accomplish this, druids are given divine magic that can harm enemies, heal allies, and enhance creatures. In addition to these normal clerical spells, druids have a wide range of summoning magics and shapechanging abilities.

Druids are very limited in their choices for weapons and armor. The articulate plate suits of a cleric and heavy weapons of a warrior came from the land, but they have been twisted by the needs of society. Instead of taking these into battle, druids prefer the comfort of basic wooden and metal implements, like sickles, scythes, and leather or hide armor.

As with most divine magic, druids rely on their wisdom to learn and cast spells of higher levels. Because druidic magic has nine full levels of spells, it is best to take a high level druid up to an extremely high wisdom for accessing these powers of nature.

Druids are unable to level the field in both melee and with direct magical damage (at least, at low levels). For this, it is best if they seek companions who are good at putting direct damage into the equation. A druid can do many things to slow down enemies (negative enchantments, animal summoning, and even tanking), so arcane casters are good allies. Because druids can heal fairly well, full tanks aren't bad to have around either. The most important thing to remember is that druids just aren't meant to be alone; as long as a druid finds someone nifty to travel with, they will do perfectly well.

Armored Druid (Force of Nature)
HUMAN DRUID/FIGHTER (19/1)

Strength	14 (+1)	Dexterity	10
Intelligence	14	Constitution	14
Wisdom	16 (+4)	Charisma	8

Primary Attribute	Wisdom
Weapon Choices	Scythe
Armor Preference	Full Plate
Primary Skills	Animal Empathy
Concentration, Spellcraft, Persuade	
Starting Feats	Exotic Weapons,
Knockdown, Power Attack	
Additional Feats	Cleave, Weapon Focus,
Improved Knockdown, Improved Critical,	
Empower Spell, Combat Casting	

Start a druid's career out as a neutral fighter of some sort. Take exotic weapons to have a run with a scythe (just to pay tribute to the forest). This isn't the most efficient choice because of the template's moderate strength, so some players may opt for a katana and shield combination instead. Either way, this sets a path for a druid with a lot more combat survivability than the normal model.

With the following 19 levels all devoted to the life of a druid, this character will have access to all nine spell levels of druidic magic. Unlike clerics, it is almost insane not to take a druid up to his final spell level; mass healing, some needed summoning magic, and one of the best damage over time spells in the game are hidden up there. With a finishing wisdom of 20, the druid won't have any problems casting these, and this makes for a very efficient druid whether a party calls for healing, buffing, a tank, or even a bit of a damage caster.

People who are somewhat tentative about the combat worthiness of a druid will especially like this template. Adding melee feats over the levels won't limit the druid's spell too much, and it will drastically improve the way this druid can land blows on the front line. With improved knockdown in the mix, the druid is set for joining with either melee henchmen or mages with equal capability.

In smaller fights, this druid's best tricks are to go in buffed, use the closing period to cast enchantment spells that will harm the enemies during the fight (entanglement, spike growth, hold spells, quillfire, etc.). This way, the weaker melee skills of the druid are offset by the strength of the buffs and the crippling effect of the harmful enchantments on the enemies. Though these techniques are more complex and challenging than those of a pure melee type or a heavy arcane caster, the potential for victory is just as high. Indeed, a skilled druid can level a playing field under all manner of conditions!

A nifty point for those who enjoy the shapeshifting spells: at the highest levels, a druid can take on the form of a dragon. Though the breath weapon of these sacred beasts is not gained through this magic, there are some evil perks. When in dragon form, a druid can still use the knockdown feat against various enemies. Even giants can be put down on their rumps with this! Cast premonition, then storm of vengeance, and finally transform into a form of a wyrm. Enemies will take damage over time from the cruel storm, the dragon will be hard as steel and quite difficult to damage, and enemies will spend most of the battle looking up at the sky. They won't call anyone a treehugger after that.

FIGHTER

- ⊕ Hit Die: d10

- ⊕ Proficiencies: All simple and martial weapons, all armor, and shields

- ⊕ Skill Points (*4 at 1st level): 2 + Int Modifier

Almost anyone can become a fighter: trained mercenaries, knights of a secular leader, barmaids who get a little too much experience breaking fingers, etc.

Unlike many classes, fighters don't have anything that is common to all of them, save a certain level of skill in combat. Even in that respect that class has a lot of variety; fighters can focus on missile combat, melee, dual wielding of weapons, heavy weapons, defensive styles of combat, or just about anything else.

It is true that fighters feel a bit generic because of this. That is just about the only downside of a good warrior; they are a dime a dozen in most nations. Unlike rangers, clerics, druids, and paladins, fighters have to find their own calling. For glory, money, or just for the love of adventure, a fighter has to have a reason to take the field each day.

As for things that a fighter can do, there are few limitations. Fighters start with access to all forms of armor and training in every non-exotic weapon! Add to this a free feat at first level and the result is a master of everything related to combat.

Over the levels, the gap between fighters and the other classes widens. Because these warriors focus on combat with such intensity, a bonus feat is granted every even level that a fighter gains. Characters who want to use very complex mixes of weapons and styles will benefit immensely from training this way.

Fighters add damage and defense to a party at the same time. They are the perfect guardians for archers, rogues, and casters. If a fighter needs healing instead, a cleric with buffs and a focus on the domain of healing will supplement the warrior greatly.

Pure Fighter (Armsman)
HUMAN FIGHTER (20)

Strength	16 (+4)	Dexterity	12
Intelligence	13	Constitution	15 (+1)
Wisdom	10	Charisma	9

Primary Attribute	Strength
Weapon Choices	Greatsword, Longbow
Armor Preference	Full Plate
Primary Skills	Discipline, Heal, Lore
Starting Feats	Power Attack, Cleave, Weapon Focus
Additional Feats	Toughness, Knockdown, Weapon Specialization, Expertise, Improved Power Attack, Improved Critical, Improved Knockdown, Lightning Reflexes, Called Shot, Greater Cleave, Weapon Focus (Longbow), Weapon Specialization (Longbow)

This is a generic fighter template that will serve many players well, especially if a person is somewhat new to third edition gaming and wants to try something simple while learning the ropes. As a human fighter, a person has an almost unlimited amount of feat potential, so this character will get to try out many of the combat feats that are available. High hit points, heavy armor, and various special bonuses to saving throws (from extra feats) make this a durable class with modest potential at long range and fair damage in melee. Alone, this fighter will survive and excel, and in a party a good fighter is always needed.

Optionally, a person could sacrifice the saving throw feats (iron will, lightning reflexes, and such) and put those feats into weapon focus and specialization for a one-handed weapon to go with the rest of the set. This way, the fighter could switch to a sword and shield style if there was a need for high armorclass fighting during an adventure. Fighters have so many feats that it isn't a bad idea to have points put into an offensive and a defensive configuration. It often takes a bit of time to assemble the equipment for all of this, but the added flexibility is worth the trouble.

Using improved knockdown makes a fighter very dangerous against creatures that aren't gigantic. As long as there aren't more than two beasties whacking on a warrior at the same time, the fighter will be able to use tandem knockdowns to force the monsters into a defensive role. This lets the damage add up over time, and it truly rips most enemies to shreds. If there is a rogue in the party to take advantage of this, the knockdown style becomes even more fun to watch.

MONK

- ⊕ Alignment Restrictions: Any lawful

- ⊕ Hit Die: d8

- ⊕ Proficiencies: Proficient with club, dagger, handaxe, light crossbow, heavy crossbow, kama, quarterstaff, shuriken, and sling

- ⊕ Skill Points (*4 at 1st level): 4 + Int Modifier

Though similar to clerics and druids in their level of devotion, monks are not bound to the gods or the land. Instead, monks look for wisdom and strength inside themselves. Though there is tremendous arrogance in this form of self-pursuit, many monks tread a path of humility and kindness, perhaps realizing that the power they have is secondary to how it should be used. The few monks who assert themselves and their will over others have come to different conclusions: that those of "weaker" wills should be forced onto their proper paths.

Few people are afraid of monks until they have seen one applying his art. Instead of using weapons and armor to keep themselves alive in the heat of conflict, monks seek enlightenment to carry them through. Who would imagine that this would succeed, but it does! As a monk grows in power, he finds a path to victory that others could hardly imagine. Deflecting arrows with a bare hand, absorbing damage without harm, and ignoring pain and injury to the body with only a simple thought; this is the legacy of a monk's training.

When fully unencumbered, monks gain substantial bonuses to their armor class. Having a higher wisdom pushes this bonus even higher, thus giving monks a fair amount of defensive power over the course of their training. Wearing any form of armor, no matter how light, will negate these bonuses.

Offensively, monks quickly become better in hand-to-hand combat than they could ever be with any type of weapon. Each monk increases his base damage by gaining levels. Toward the highest levels of mastery, monks can do more damage with their hands than many warriors can with even two-handed weapons!

Monks can deal a ton of damage, but they lose hit points quickly if they run into a monster that can break through an enlightened defense. Because of this, monks are much better off if they can travel with a cleric or druid. Having a healer nearby means that the monk will have a lot of staying power that would normally be hard to maintain. Of course, high-level monks are nearly deities in their own right, but it's a long road to 20 for someone who wants to go it alone.

Aggressive Monk (Student of the Dragon)
HALF-ORC MONK (20)

Strength	18 (+4)	Dexterity	15 (+1)
Intelligence	6	Constitution	14
Wisdom	14	Charisma	6

Primary Attribute	Strength
Weapon Choices	Fists, Feet, Head, Kidneys, etc.
Armor Preference	Training
Primary Skills	Tumbling
Starting Feats	Power Attack
Additional Feats	Improved Power Attack, Circle Kick, Improved Initiative, Weapon Focus, Improve Critical, Toughness

Some of the templates in this section are fairly well balanced. This is obviously not one of those, but there are some honestly good times to be found while trying out this style of monk. Even at low levels, when monks in general struggle to keep up with other classes, this template has enough power to get through the sticky spots. A very high strength improves the damage potential for the monk, and adding a nice bonus to the character's armorclass and hit points is worthy of note. Losing skill points and persuasion potential is sad, but it isn't the end of the world for the template that is destined to become a walking deity.

As the higher levels approach, this monk will start to inflict truly lewd amounts of damage. Monks have about as many attacks as a dual wielder (and even worse penalties to hit in some ways), but the half-orc's bonus to attack should make up for these. Using circle kick will help to add even more attacks and damage, but the monk's natural cleave is just over the top when it comes to unfair advantages. Having toughness toward the end and a high constitution should make up for the generally low hit points that are seen in most monks; for someone who isn't wearing any armor, even a d8 per level just doesn't seem to last.

This template doesn't stray from pure monk levels because of the final abilities that are available to monks. These various protections from damage are so tempting that there are only a few alternatives that may lure people away from the devoted path of a monk. One of these is a monk/rogue (12/8) combination. This is a poor choice for solo work, but a monk with several dice of sneak attack damage can be frightening in a party! Ditch power attack, cleave, and toughness for this template and head toward dodge, mobility, and spring attack. This monk won't be the destroyer of worlds, but it is extremely rewarding to play a hit-and-run monk with sneak attack.

PALADIN

- ✠ Alignment Restrictions: Lawful good only
- ✠ Hit Die: d10
- ✠ Proficiencies: All simple and martial weapons, all armor, and shields
- ✠ Skill Points (*4 at 1st level): 2 + Int Modifier
- ✠ Spellcasting: Paladin Spells. Divine (Wisdom based, armor-related chance of spell failure is ignored)
- ✠ A paladin that is no longer lawful good cannot gain levels until their alignment is lawful good again

Paladins are the shining light of civilization. These warriors of faith see goodness and importance in almost every aspect of existence, and it is for the heart of all honest creatures that they fight. Paladins are trained in combat and worship and charge into every challenge with a zeal that most find either encouraging or horrific.

This fire that burns inside each paladin protects the warrior from harm. In game terms, paladins gain a bonus to all saving throw types based on their charisma modifier. Beyond that, the early levels grant immunity to diseases and fear because of a paladin's devotion to life.

Though paladins can never heal others with the same miracles as a cleric, it is possible to use light healing magic through persistent training. For spells along these lines, paladins should have a wisdom of at least 13 or 14.

In battle, paladins fight well, but their greatest strength is directed against creatures of true evil. Paladins can turn undead and smite evil. There are even specific weapons and pieces of armor that meant to be carried by a paladin. These are often quite powerful, having been made to face the darkest creatures of evil.

To remain a paladin, each warrior must remain lawful good. If a person's faith ever fails, it will be impossible to continue training in this class. The road of a paladin is ever rigid.

Paladins are wonderful allies for mages because these warriors can tank and heal. Having high saving throws also means that a paladin won't quickly be turned aside by charm magic or other ailments (this prevents the lighter members of the party from being exposed). Paladins work well with other backline characters, too: archers, rogues, etc. The only major limitation is that paladins really shouldn't travel with any characters that aren't fairly close in alignment; this isn't a specific limitation of the game system, but it is a strong aspect of roleplaying one of these defenders of faith.

Defensive Paladin (Vigilant)
HUMAN PALADIN/FIGHTER (12/8)

Strength	14 (+1)	Dexterity	12
Intelligence	10	Constitution	14
Wisdom	14	Charisma	14 (+4)

Primary Attribute	Charisma
Weapon Choices	Bastard Sword
Armor Preference	Full Plate and a Tower Shield
Primary Skills	Discipline
Starting Feats	Exotic Weapon Spec, Power Attack
Additional Feats	Cleave, Great Cleave, Weapon Focus, Divine Might, Divine Shield, Improved Critical, Toughness, Weapon Specialization, Weapon Focus (Longbow), Weapon Specialization (Longbow)

Pure paladins are pretty darn cool; they have several levels of spells to draw upon, and they essentially have the same attack and damage potential as fighters (minus a few bonus feats). The Vigilant template bridges this gap by stealing a number of free feats and giving up only level-four paladin spells in the process. Because most of the really juicy spells are gained in the third rank, this is not a huge blow to the paladin's ultimate power.

This character is perhaps the most well rounded good guy that people will come across. As a lawful good character, this paladin won't have every option in the game when it comes to solving puzzles and defeating enemies, but it is nice to shake off the murky grey of the real world now and then to don the view of a pious warrior.

The Vigilant template has a high armorclass during the entire rise through the levels, and the damage output from this class is very nice for a sword and shield user. All of the extra feats are responsible for this! Having a high charisma will lead to a pleasant saving throw bonus and the chance to really kick things into high gear when using the divine feats.

For an even more defensive character, drop the Constitution down to 11, raise Intelligence to 13, and take expertise and improved expertise instead of the longbow feats. Put one point into Constitution later and that will make up for half of the difference.

RANGER

- ✥ Hit Die: d10
- ✥ Proficiencies: All simple and martial weapons, light armor, medium armor, and shields
- ✥ Skill Points (*4 at 1st level): 4 + Int Modifier
- ✥ Spellcasting: Divine (Wisdom based, armor-related chance of spell failure is ignored)

People assume a lot of things about rangers. Enemies of nature often cross paths with druids, and many assume that rangers are just a more militant branch of this sect. That isn't true in many cases. Rangers are warriors who have trained themselves to fight in the wilderness, without heavy armor, without support from legions of allies, and without a warm home to return to. Not all rangers love or ever care about nature. Fighters train themselves to deal with combat; rangers train to deal with tracking, stealth, and survival.

Rangers aren't given the freedom to come into their own in most settings. Because of the way most dungeons and modules are arranged, the greatest glory of this class is rendered moot. Adventurers are often met head-on by their enemies, so the hit-and-run tactics of the ranger are reduced in power. For this reason, rangers are one of the hardest classes to play in many games outside of paper and pencil roleplaying.

That said, there are still many tricks that rangers have in their set. People focus quite heavily on the fact that rangers are given dual-wielding abilities without cost. Ambidexterity, two-weapon fighting, and improved two-weapon fighting are all class benefits for a ranger. This does not mean that every ranger should dual wield. In fact, fighters are still better at dual wielding than rangers in most circumstances (fighters gain 10 extra feats, which more than makes up for having to purchase the dual-wielding feats on their own). The only huge ranger advantage in this regard is the removal of the dexterity 15 requirement for ambidexterity and improved two-weapon fighting.

Rangers should dual wield when the player feels comfortable getting the most out of the two-weapon system. A ranger with the wrong weapon combination ends up being a very weak character indeed; this forces ranger players to decide on many things before even rolling up to the PC.

Rangers have a limited amount of druidic magic that they learn after a few levels. This requires a fair amount of wisdom (a 14 to gain all of the spell levels). An odd mix of healing, summoning, and enchantments are thrown together for this school of magic. These fit the role of a ranger well, but it takes a lot of practice to master the time and place for each spell.

Because rangers have specific training in their intended targets, they gain a natural hatred toward the targets of their attacks. Over the levels, rangers get to choose several targets for their animosity. It is best the take the most powerful target (or the most common target) at level one, because the hatred bonus rises the most for the original choice.

Rangers also have animal companions that will help to distract enemies from the real threat of an engagement.

As for additional allies, rangers can serve as tanks for casters and do fairly well. Rogues and bards are good to have around too, because they have a similar style of fighting. This makes for an organized party that is fast, flexible, and fun to play.

Heavy Ranger (Survivalist)
HALF-ORC RANGER/FIGHTER (16/4)

Strength	20 (+4)	Dexterity	10
Intelligence	6	Constitution	14 (+1)
Wisdom	14	Charisma	6

Primary Attribute	Strength
Weapon Choices	Doubleaxe, Doublesword, Diremace
Armor Preference	Light Armor
Primary Skills	Discipline (somewhat)
Starting Feats	Exotic Weapon
Additional Feats	Power Attack, Cleave, Weapon Focus, Weapon Specialization, Improved Power Attack, Blind Fighting, Improved Critical, Toughness, Greater Cleave

This character gets away from the stereotype of a fast and free ranger without wasting a lot of time. Instead of going for high dexterity weapons and skills, this ranger template takes advantage of the paired weapons feats that don't require a minimum dexterity (one of the few true perks of the ranger's "free" feats). The concept behind this half-orc is to get a melee guy up on the lines that has upwards of six attacks per round, plus any opportunity or cleave strikes, and can deal a solid amount of damage with each attack. With weapon specialization and a decent list of hated foes, this template can go head-to-head against various fighter and barbarian models that scoff at the light tank that is a ranger.

The feat selection is meant to maximize extra attacks per round while expanding on the options that this ranger has against different foes. With improved power attack, poorly defended enemies are just savaged; six attacks with +10 damage per hit is a nightmare for everything on the receiving end. Of course, it is pretty rare to pull that out of the hat because most powerful enemies aren't easy to hit. Everything is about having options with this template; the trick is to know when to use everything (as with druids and some of the other challenging classes).

Having entangle and grease around is nifty for the lower levels. These spells open the door for a bit of damage at range by slowing the approach of melee enemies. Rangers are always pressured to switch between weapons quickly, from missile to melee, which is another reason why a double weapon is nice to keep around instead of two individual items.

This ranger template has almost as many hit points as a barbarian, and that will help quite a bit in the somewhat longer fights that come about. Of course, this is lessened by the need for light armor; without either good protection or a high dexterity, this poor soul is a sitting duck if too many enemies engage him at the same time. For this reason, a heavier tank or a cleric should be considered more than usual for a henchman.

RANGER

This character lacks intelligence, persuasion, and skills. In fact, for a well-rounded trip through the game, this ranger is terrible. However, the purpose of this template is to show that it is possible to create a battle ranger that is fairly potent. For a much more relaxed character, switch to a human and tone down the strength (a lot). With a 14 strength, the ranger can afford to put intelligence and charisma up by four each; this still leaves two more points for dexterity as well. Though the character won't deal nearly as much damage, the change in skills and role-playing is tremendous.

Rangers can be very well balanced, and that makes them ideal for getting a variety of quests and side elements of the main game and extra modules.

ROGUE

⊕ Hit Die: d6

⊕ Proficiencies: Proficient with club, dagger, dart, light crossbow, heavy crossbow, mace, morningstar, rapier, shortbow, short sword, and quarter-staff. They are proficient with light armor, but not with shields.

⊕ Skill Points (*4 at 1st level): 8 + Int Modifier

Society has its own set of rules, and they are meant to be flexible! Rogues don't have the same view of what is important or necessary as most people. Of course, not all rogues are scoundrels and thieves. Certainly, some people train in stealth, picking locks, and other forms of spying and such for only the best of reasons. True, but this is not common.

On the whole, rogues are quick with the tongues and fast on their feet. These slippery sorts can present themselves as warriors, mages, or almost any other type of person; it is rare for them to be honest about who they are and what they are doing. To aid this, rogues have elements of the other classes that they train with. Rogues can fight, use all manner of magical items, and use a modest mix of weapons and armor. Combine this with a good wit and some fair acting, and a rogue can replace anyone in a party.

Like bards, these characters can train in a huge variety of skills. This combines nicely with the massive number of skill points that rogues get per level (especially at level one, where a character who chooses rogue will be able to score dozens and extra points). Though many players will lean toward spot, move silently, search, and hide, these are not skills for every rogue. Battle rogues (thug types) will often prefer use magic item, spot, and search, but may not care at all for move silently and hide. Likewise, a high charisma rogue will enjoy a bit of persuasion, but it isn't worth the points for most half-orcs to be diplomatic.

The most vicious aspect of the rogue class is the ability to make sneak attacks. When an opponent is unable to defend himself, the rogue can add an additional 1d6 damage to a strike for every couple of levels that he has in the class (starting at level one). This turns into some vicious numbers after a rogue has trained for a while!

Because rogues can fake it enough to use other class' magical items, it is very nice to have a stash of wands and potions. Healing items and evocation wands are some of the best things to keep around; this way, a rogue always has something that he can do for a party, even if he is injured and out of the melee.

To survive, rogues have a few feats that they gain later in their class levels; these aren't available to anyone else, and all of them are fairly nifty.

Crippling Strike

Use: Automatic

Bonuses: Any successful sneak attack deals two points of Strength ability damage to the target.

Opportunist

Use: Automatic

Bonuses: The rogue gains a +4 competence bonus to attack rolls when making an attack of opportunity.

Skill Mastery

Use: Automatic

Bonuses: The rogue can take 20 whenever using the Disable Trap, Open Lock, or Set Traps skills, even if in combat.

ROGUE

Slippery Mind

Use: Automatic

Bonuses: If the rogue fails his save against a mind-affecting spell, he makes an automatic reroll.

Improved Evasion

Use: Automatic

Bonuses: In situations where a successful Reflex saving throw would allow others to take only half damage, the character escapes unscathed on a successful roll and takes only half damage even if the saving throw fails.

Defensive Roll

Use: Automatic, once per day

Bonuses: If a potentially lethal blow strikes you (i.e., you suffer weapon damage that would normally drop you below 1 hit point), you make a Reflex saving throw (DC = damage dealt). If successful, you take only half damage from the blow (which may still be enough to kill you). If you are caught flat-footed, you may not make a defensive roll.

A rogue can join up with almost any other henchman or party. Often, tanks make some of the best buddies for a skilled rogue. If another character can hold the attention of the rogue's enemies, sneak attacks will be easy to pull off and quite devastating to watch. The worst pair that would likely come up would be a rogue and an arcane caster. Rogues can inflict as much damage as a fighter (given the right circumstances), but they cannot tank worth a darn. Measly hit points, weak armor, and a mix of attributes mean that rogues last about two seconds when the big monsters decide to have at one of them.

Militant Rogue (Thug)
DWARF ROGUE/FIGHTER (13/7)

Strength	16 (+4)	Dexterity	14
Intelligence	12	Constitution	15 (+1)
Wisdom	10	Charisma	10

Primary Attribute	Strength
Weapon Choices	Greatsword
Armor Preference	One light suit, One heavy suit
Primary Skills	Discipline, Hide, Move Silently, Pick Pockets, Persuade, Spot, Search, Use Magic Device
Starting Feats	Dodge
Rogue Feats	Slippery Mind, Improved Evasion
Additional Feats	Mobility, Weapon Focus, Weapon Specialization, Spring Attack, Improved Critical, Power Attack, Cleave, Knockdown, Toughness, Great Cleave

Sure, rogues can be sneaky and such, but they can also slip into the middle of a brawl and deal wicked damage to a few unsuspecting chaps. This template makes that easier by raising the rogue's paltry hit points through fighter levels and a higher constitution.

So much rogue damage is frontloaded that spring attack is an absolute essential. Being caught in a drawn-out melee just means wasting time and hit points that could be spent elsewhere, perhaps by looting treasure before anyone else can get their hands on it. Either way, the feat selection for this template ensures that the player can pull the rogue back as soon as the desired target has gone on to join the choir invisible.

By taking the fighter levels here and there, it is quite possible to keep discipline perked all the way up to its maximum without having to endure the cost of raising it as a rogue. Taking a fighter level every few times this character gains should help to keep the progression of the thug quite sound.

Slippery mind is a wonderful tool to compensate for the low will of this character. Any way to keep from having enchantments land should be looked into. For thwarting warriors, a spare suit of armor should be kept around. A heavy suit of plate will get in the way of a good rogue's talent, but having the ability to use it during an unsuspected fight is pleasant. To take this even farther, a thug could carry a tower shield and a lighter weapon too! This adds a lot of defensive potential when it would be needed the most. Remember that spring attack and many other subtle activities are not possible or tenable when wearing heavy armor, so don't forget to take the heavy stuff off when the maelstrom has calmed.

It is sad to lose a few d6 of sneak attack damage by multiclassing as a fighter here and there. Still, the extra hit points, feats, weapon specialization, and a defensive set of gear should compensate for the loss.

This is a good character to play through most adventures, including the main story of *Shadows of Undrentide*. With a fair intelligence, acceptable charisma (for a dwarven rogue, at least), and nice stats all around, a player should enjoy a thug under most circumstances. Most alignment paths are open to this template as well, though lawful good just isn't going to happen.

SORCERER

➕ Hit Die: d4

➕ Proficiencies: All simple weapons. No armor or shields

➕ Skill Points (*4 at 1st level): 2 + Intelligence Modifier

➕ Spellcasting: Arcane (Charisma-based, no need for preparation, armor-related chance of spell failure is a factor); sorcerers begin the game knowing all cantrips.

Sorcerers wield the power of arcane magic without study or rote mastery. Instead, these are mages who use their emotion and will to force the land into action. Many sorcerers are found in odd locations, seeking power from objects and people that others fail to understand.

There is a great deal of potential in the sorcerer class. These spell-wielders can cast more times per day than any of the other mages or divine classes. It also helps that sorcerers can use any of their memorized spells at any time. Being able to react to a variety of situations without stopping to rest and re-memorize spells is a huge asset. The downside of this is the lack of spells that each sorcerer will master; only a precious few are chosen from each level.

Luckily, these mages are given a chance to change their mind during the leveling process, so a poor choice early on will not force a sorcerer to live the rest of her life in regret.

Because of the intuitive way that sorcerers use their magic, it is impossible to devote one of these characters to a specific school of magic. Wizards are able to do that through intensive programs of study, but it simply isn't possible for a sorcerer to understand magic in the same way.

It takes a very high charisma to master the full range of arcane magics, so every sorcerer will want to reach at least a 19 with that ability.

Though sorcerers have more time and training with basic weaponry, it is still quite dangerous to take them into any battle directly. These mages have few hit points and weak attack bonuses, so the back or middle of the party is the best place for them in times of trouble.

Sorcerers gain a magical companion for their journeys. These beings can be summoned once per day and increase in power as the sorcerer rises in level.

Sorcerers work well in almost any party, but their best combinations are with very fast and flexible henchmen or player characters. Because many arcane casters do blast damage with their best spells, a full group of tanks will run into problems when a sorcerer can't learn to control her fire. An easier combination would be a sorcerer and a cleric, defensive warrior, or an archer of some sort.

Paladin Sorcerer (Theologian)
HUMAN SORCERER/PALADIN (18/2)

Strength	8	Dexterity	12
Intelligence	10	Constitution	14
Wisdom	10	Charisma	18 (+5)

Primary Attribute	Charisma
Weapon Choices	Anything with nice bonuses
Armor Preference	Heavy suit of armor, shield, one set of magical robes
Primary Skills	Concentration, Lore, Spellcraft
Starting Feats	Combat Casting, Toughness
Additional Feats	Still Spell, Empower Spell, Maximize Spell, Quicken Spell, Spell Penetration, Greater Spell Penetration

After taking two levels of paladin, this character devotes herself fully to the mastery of arcane lore and spells. At first glance, this is a deeply awkward mix of potential, but there is method within the madness. For one, the paladin's immunity to fear and intense saving throw bonuses are a huge asset for a budding sorceress. Combine that with an early dose of hit points and the ability to wear heavy armor and a shield during times of trouble, and the final product is an evil lady indeed!

At the sorceress' final level, only two castings per day of level-nine spells are wasted; everything else still reaches its highest rank, and it is well worth the sacrifice to gain a possible +7 or more on all saving throws. This character can survive fortitude problems almost as well as a warrior and will saves are an absolute dream.

For greatest area of effect damage, fill every spell level from three up to nine with fireballs. The order should progress like this: Fireball, Stilled Fireball, Empowered Fireball, Maximized Fireball, Delayed Blast Fireball, Stilled Delayed Blast Fireball, and finally an Empowered Fireball. Magic Missile and Melf's Acid Arrow are decent choices for the early levels, though Burning Hands will polish off the image of a true fire mage.

Using still spell, the sorceress can keep a number of powerful spells memorized for use while wearing heavy armor. This way, the caster can keep a high defense despite the paper doll that is quivering within. In safer dungeons, the mage can take her armor off and blow through enemies will full arcane power.

There are a few downsides to this type of sorcerer. First off, creatures with a substantial amount of fire resistance are a real threat. Keep a quickbar with backup spells ready to take on such targets (ice storm, cone of cold, and other non-fire choices are great here). Obviously, melee is an even greater threat, but having a suit of armor around will help if things go sour.

The other major problem with this template is that this sorceress is dripping with powergaming goodness. Roleplayers will still appreciate any player who brings a good attitude and a lot of style into an adventure, but playing this character can feel a bit ridiculous at times. To lessen some of the evil, try to add a few non-fireballs to the mix, and don't blast everything down all the time. A bit of moderation rarely hurts.

WIZARD

- ⊕ Hit Die: d4

- ⊕ Proficiencies: Proficient with club, dagger, light crossbow, heavy crossbow and quarterstaff. No armor or shields.

- ⊕ Skill Points (*4 at 1st level): 2 + Int Modifier

- ⊕ Spellcasting: Arcane (Intelligence-based, requires preparation, armor-related chance of spell failure is a factor); wizards begin the game knowing all cantrips and four 1st-level spells.

Wizards are the intellectual students of arcane magic. Instead of using raw emotion and spirit to summon the powers of the mystic world, wizards practice and hone the scientific techniques that bring about change. In ancient libraries, high towers, and sheltered studies, these mages pour over scrolls that will expand their base of knowledge. Though sorcerers learn spells quickly and master few, wizards are able to master every single spell that they come across; this makes every wizard adept with a versatile mix of enchantments and attacks.

It takes a very high intelligence to use the most devastating spells from the school of the arcane. Wizards should try to have at least a 19 intelligence as they proceed toward the conclusion of their craft. Because of interference with movement, it is also wise to avoid donning armor unless the caster is using the feat of still spell to prevent this problem.

One downside of wizardry is that spells must be prepared ahead of time. This makes the use of a wizard quite strategic; knowing what a person will need the next day as they lie down to sleep is half science and half art. The simple part is to memorize combat magic and enchantments during adventures, then to use secondary spells when there is time and safety to rest and figure everything out.

Wizards are often ravenous for new scrolls. These can be transcribed into the caster's own spellbook, thus permanently giving them access to a new ability.

As with other devoted mages, the society of wizards is not one for direct conflict. Wizards are physically dismissible, and their paltry hit points make it almost suicidal to engage in melee combat.

Like rangers, wizards are often associated with a companion. In this case, the caster summons a familiar who can help out with scouting, drawing away enemies, and drinking foul smelling liquids to see what color it turns them.

Wizards are so versatile that they are great for playing with almost any companion. Because of a wizard's wide spell range, a player has more options in a fight than a sorcerer would. It is easier for a wizard to start off fights with a nasty area of effect spell (before the other creatures and allies have joined) then switch over to more cautious battle spells (magic missile, hasting allies, etc.). If forced to choose a single henchman, a strong tank is a wise investment.

Pure Wizard (Illusionist)
GNOME WIZARD (20)

Strength	8	Dexterity	10
Intelligence	18 (+5)	Constitution	16
Wisdom	10	Charisma	10

Primary Attribute	Intelligence
Weapon Choices	Wands
Armor Preference	Something that won't chafe
Primary Skills	Concentration, Spellcraft, Lore, Heal
Secondary Skills	Spot, Persuade
Starting Feats	Spell Penetration
Additional Feats	Toughness, Combat Casting, Greater Spell Penetration, Greater Spell Focus, Silent Spell, Empower Spell, Maximize Spell, Quicken Spell, Expertise, Improved Expertise

Let the sorcerers have their beloved evocation spells. They can throw fireballs all day long, but can they identify? What about a broad range of buffs? Well, this template makes for a guy or gal with a ton of skill and class in everything (well, everything except conjuration). Gnomes are slick with illusions, and being able to learn almost everything else under the sun isn't a detriment.

Indeed, the best way to play a gnome illusionist is to keep a bit of everything around. Have potions, scrolls, wand, and a wide mix of spells at the ready. Accept that there are better arcane damage dealers; fire evocation sorcerers are the winners for that ticket every day. Instead, cover everything else that a party might ever need. Elemental resistance buffs? Sure. Invisibility, haste, ultravision for the henchmen and allies while casting an area of darkness on enemies? Absolutely. Not only are these combinations great for avoiding friendly fire casualties from wanton fireballs, but the creativity involved in playing a well-learned wizard is also vastly rewarding.

The gnomes aren't just useful for their good looks! Though small, each gnome is a package of sturdy earthenware construction. Though wizards are fragile on their best days, a 16 constitution will put these wizards at least on par with the average bard who is strumming away on his lute. Adding toughness at an early level tops this off nicely, and the ability to survive a stiff breeze makes it a lot safer in the dank pits of evil where knowledge and glory are so often found.

It's nice to have improved expertise, especially at high levels. Because mages aren't knocked out of this feat when they cast spells, it's possible to get a huge boost to a character's armor class without losing anything substantial. If a person doesn't need or want to do this, try taking extended spell and a second spell focus instead. Also, this trick may be seen as an exploit, so it may not be around forever.

Prestige Classes

Prestige classes are only available to characters that have met certain criteria, usually involving multiple levels of other classes and skills. Many of these special classes grant a mix of interesting and powerful skills, making the pursuit of these careers all the more exciting.

ARCANE ARCHER

- ✛ Hit Dice: d8
- ✛ Proficiencies: All simple and martial weapons, light and medium armor, and shields
- ✛ Skill Points: 4 + Int. Modifier
- ✛ Required Race: Must be a Half-Elf or Elf.
- ✛ Required Base Attack Bonus: Must be +6 or Higher.
- ✛ Required Feats: Must have Point Blank Shot and Weapon Focus Longbow or Shortbow.
- ✛ Required Spellcasting: Must have the ability to cast level-one arcane spells.

Sometimes even the supreme archery of the elves isn't enough to defend their homelands from outside threats. When war calls, the arcane archer must respond in kind. These elven warriors focus on using evocation to enhance the power of their arrows. This takes a great deal of training to master, but it ultimately leads to an apex of ranged potential. Almost nothing commands the same respect at range as an arcane archer.

As a prestige class, it is always a bit of a trial to create an arcane archer who won't have a few downsides. For one, the best templates for this class invariably run into experience penalties for at least a few character levels. Beyond that, it takes quite a bit of planning and patience to grow into a person's full potential down this route.

Arcane archers can fill multiple roles within a party at the same time. As an archer, these characters are wonderful for keeping enemy mages, missile attackers, and light melee troops at arm's length. The natural enchantment that arcane archers bestow on their arrows makes it even easier to wound special creatures that some bowmen would barely be able to touch. Add area of effect and even some of the less evocative mages start to get jealous.

Only fighter-based archers end up having more hit points than this class. Arcane archers will appreciate the full d8 that comes with the extra abilities!

Special Abilities

- ✛ Enchant Arrow: Arcane Archers are able to fire arrows with both increased precision and destructive power. All arrows fired by these archers are automatically treated as magical, and the power of this ability increases over the levels. At level one, Arcane Archers fire arrows that are +1 to hit and damage enemies, this becomes +2 at the third level, +3 at the fifth, +4 at the seventh, and +5 at the ninth level.

- ✛ Imbue Arrow: At second level as an Arcane Archer, the character can shoot three fireball arrows every day. These have a mage's blast radius, and the result can wound many enemies very quickly.

Arcane Archer/Bard (Arrow Singer)
HALF-ELF FIGHTER/BARD/ARCANE ARCHER (2/8/10)

Strength	10	Dexterity	16 (+4)
Intelligence	10	Constitution	12 (+1)
Wisdom	10	Charisma	16

Primary Attribute	Dexterity
Weapon Choices	Longbow
Armor Preference	The best armor to maximize AC by dexterity
Primary Skills	Discipline, Perform, Lore
Starting Feats	Point Blank Shot, Rapid Shot
Additional Feats	Weapon Focus, Toughness, Lingering Song, Extend Spell, Improved Critical, Skill Focus (Perform), Skill Focus (Discipline)

This character functions in much the same way as the Skald. The only major changes are in the class' progression and in the use of arcane archer abilities.

For a slow but immensely powerful route into the prestige class, take two levels as a fighter, followed by all eight bardic levels. This gives the character a solid set of skills and feats for missile attack and buffs. When the final ten levels of arcane archer are used, this person will simply be stacking the mystic power on top of his existing abilities. Many other templates for this class have to switch roles while they progress, from mage to archer or tank to mage to archer.

Imbued arrows are the key to happiness. Against creatures without elemental resistance, this special ability gives the archer a nice trick for frontloading his damage; slam one of these into a group before battle begins to soften everyone. This makes the hit and run tactics of all archers a lot easier to pull off! Add bardic mage (for Expeditious Retreat/Haste) to top this off.

- ✛ Seeker Arrow: At fourth level, Arcane Archers can fire an arrow once per day that cannot miss. At sixth level, they learn to do this twice per day.

- ✛ Hail of Arrows: At eighth level, Arcane Archers can use an attack to shoot an arrow toward every target in range.

- ✛ Arrow of Death: At tenth level, these archers can summon the power of ancient magics once per day to loose an arrow that will automatically slay its target (provided that the creature cannot resist the arcane power of this attack).

ASSASSIN

- Hit Dice: d6

- Proficiencies: Light Armor

- Skill Points: 4 + Int. Modifier

- Required Alignment: Any Evil

- Required Skills: Hide in Shadows (8 ranks), Move Silently (8 ranks)

Assassins are very similar to the rogue class in fighting capabilities, hit points, and such, but these nasty characters are bent toward mastering the most vicious techniques for taking enemies down. Though assassins gain fewer skill points, there are some nice perks that a combat-oriented rogue can gain by going in this direction.

The assassin Death Attack stacks with a rogue's normal Sneak Attack damage, so there isn't a downside to having both of these in the same template. The entire point of the assassin special attack is to cripple enemies even if they are not slain outright. Often, this sounds like a good idea for thug-styled rogues, but that is not always the case.

In fact, assassins are even more fragile than rogues in some ways. Because this is a prestige class, rogues who train to become assassins will lose out on taking a heartier side class (i.e., a barbarian or fighter). That leaves these sneaky PCs with low hit points, trivial armor, and a lot of combat exposure despite their weakness.

To compensate for these problems, a third class should often be taken to round out the template. Perhaps even a couple levels as a barbarian (for a nice dose of hit points, the rage buff, and a slight speed increase). Or, as the class template below, try to learn some of the Shadow Dancer skills so that the assassin will be able to hide under even the most adverse conditions.

Special Abilities

- Death Attacks are a special form of Sneak Attack that have a chance of paralyzing opponents. Death Attack damage increases with experience: +1d6 at 1st level; +2d6 at 3rd level; +3d6 at 5th level; +4d6 at 7th level; and +5d6 at 9th level.

- Uncanny Dodge: The assassin is able to avoid and deflect incoming attacks. At 2nd level, the assassin retains his or her Dexterity bonus to armor class, even if flat-footed. At 5th level, the assassin gains a +1 to Reflex saving throws. At 10th level, the assassin gains a +2 to Reflex saving throws.

- Spells: At 2nd level, the assassin gains the ability to cast Ghostly Visage once per day. At 5th level, the assassin gains the ability to cast Darkness once per day. At 6th level, the assassin gains the ability to cast Invisibility once per day. At 9th level, the assassin gains the ability to cast Improved Invisibility once per day.

- The assassin's expertise with deadly toxins gives the assassin an unnatural resistance to poisons of all types. This ability improves with experience: +1 Fortitude save vs. poison at 2nd level; +2 at 4th level; +3 at 6th level; +4 at 8th level; and +5 at 10th level.

Sneak Attack Assassin (Deathshadow)
HUMAN ROGUE/SHADOW DANCER/ASSASSIN (8/2/10)

Strength	14 (+2)	Dexterity	14 (+2)
Intelligence	14	Constitution	14 (+1)
Wisdom	10	Charisma	12

Primary Attributes	Strength/Dexterity
Weapon Choices	Greatsword
Armor Preference	Appropriate Light Armor
Primary Skills	Hide, Move Silently, Tumble,
Use Magic Devices, Spot, Listen	
Starting Feats	Martial Weapon Prof., Dodge
Additional Feats	Mobility, Spring Attack,
Toughness, Improved Criticals, Knockdown,	
Blind Fighting	

This assassin template does a superlative job when it comes to getting in and out of problems. With Hide in Plain Sight, this character can launch a sneak attack, avoid attacks of opportunity while maneuvering, and disappear to prepare another sneak attack at any point. This PC is evil (quite literally), and players who enjoy this aspect of rogue play will rejoice in the assassin's art.

Taking Knockdown later on adds a little bit of combat control to the mix; something that helps a fair bit when trying to deal with multiple enemies without taking the hit-and-run route.

The balanced attributes for this template are very point efficient early on, and that allows for a very nice spread of bonuses to skills and actions.

BLACKGUARD

- ⊕ Hit Die: d10

- ⊕ Proficiencies: All simple and martial weapons, all types of armor and shields

- ⊕ Skill Points: 2 + Int. Modifier

- ⊕ Required Feat: Cleave

- ⊕ Required Skill: Hide (5 ranks)

- ⊕ Required Alignment: Any evil

- ⊕ Base Attack Bonus: +6

The blackguard prestige class is incredibly powerful. As paladins gain immunity to disease and fear, these dark warriors learn the art of sneak attacks. Instead of holy paladin magic, the blackguard gain damaging spells and the ability to buff their strength. By the final tally, these characters are just as offensively powerful as paladins are solid in defense.

Players who want to deal a fair amount of damage while keeping a high saving throw and superb armor class will be in heaven with the blackguard (well, maybe not heaven). Because this is an evil class, one should avoid trying out a blackguard unless one is absolutely sold on the idea of being a rotten, filthy murderer for the run of the game. There are so many good deeds out there that it takes some ugly work to maintain a proper sense of malice! Skin eating is optional but preferred.

Special Abilities

- ⊕ Smite Good: At second level, the Blackguard can add his Charisma modifier to attack rolls against creatures of good.

- ⊕ Dark Blessing: At second level, the character's Charisma modifier is added to all saving throws.

- ⊕ Bull's Strength: At second level, the blackguard can raise his Strength by 1d4+1, as if he were casting Bull's Strength on himself.

- ⊕ Turn Undead: At third level, blackguards can turn undead.

- ⊕ Create Undead: At third level, these characters can also summon undead to aid them.

- ⊕ Sneak Attack: At fourth level, blackguards begin learning how to make sneak attacks. This starts with a d6 bonus against unwary foes, and will rise by an additional d6 for every three blackguard levels after this point (at 7th and 10th level).

- ⊕ Summon Fiend: Fifth level blackguards can summon a fiend to aid them in battle.

- ⊕ Inflict Serious Wounds: At sixth level, inflict serious wounds can be cast once per day, dealing 3d8 points of damage (+1 point per level of the character).

- ⊕ Contagion: At seventh level, contagion may be cast against the blackguard's foes. This causes a target to be struck down with one of the following debilitating diseases, randomly chosen: Blinding Sickness, Cackle Fever, Mind Fire, Red Ache, Shakes, or Slimy Doom.

- ⊕ Inflict Critical Wounds: At eighth level, the blackguard can also wield this enhanced cause wounds spell. If the caster succeeds in striking an opponent with a touch attack, the target suffers 4d8 points of damage (+1 point per caster level to a maximum of +20).

Blackguard Warrior (Villain)

HUMAN FIGHTER/BLACKGUARD (10/10)

Strength	14 (+3)	Dexterity	12
Intelligence	14	Constitution	14
Wisdom	10	Charisma	14 (+2)

Primary Attributes	Strength and Charisma
Weapon Choices	Bastard Sword (Appropriate)
Armor Preference	Full Plate Suit and a Tower Shield
Primary Skills	Discipline, Heal, Lore, Parry, Hide
Starting Feats	Power Attack, Cleave, Exotic Weapon
Additional Feats	Toughness, Weapon Focus, Weapon Specialization, Expertise, Knockdown, Improved Critical, Improved Knockdown, Improved Expertise, Improved Power Attack, Great Cleave, Improved Initiative

Playing this template is not too far from playing either a Vigilant or an Armsman; this character has a lot of versatility, hit points, damage potential, and nifty tricks.

In parties or with henchmen, rely on knockdown to keep enemies off guard and keep the pressure on casters and missile troops. For defensive battles, turn to expertise and throw the Villain's armor class into the rafters. Very few enemies can break through such an impressive defense.

It's always nice to have Inflict Wound abilities, but they don't come into play very much with this template; there are just too many important things to do (there is never time to reach out and touch people during a brawl). If the blackguards were able to use Harm it might be a different story…but that would be wrong, wrong, wrong!

Note that Divine Might and Divine Shield are not available to this class, even though they can meet the requirements. It's too bad, really, even though it sure would be nice to grab these. Taking a level or two as a cleric (during normal feat levels, such as 15 and 18) would be a fair way to get these. There would certainly be an experience penalty, but some people may find this acceptable for a very nice addition to the character.

If a character is looking for an extra combat feat, the balance can be shifted to a 13 Fighter/7 Blackguard mix. This sacrifices 1d6 points of sneak damage, so it really is a matter of what a person is interested in using.

37

HARPER SCOUT

- ⊕ Hit Die: d6

- ⊕ Proficiencies: Simple Weapons and Light Armor

- ⊕ Skill Points: 4 + Int. Modifier

- ⊕ Required Feats: Alertness, Iron Will

- ⊕ Required Skills: Search (4 ranks), Persuade (8 ranks), Lore (6 ranks), Discipline (4 ranks)

- ⊕ Required Alignment: Any non-evil

Harpers aren't powerhouses when it comes to normal or prestige classes. The point of playing a harper is to go out into the world and make things right for innocent creatures of many races. This is not a job for a coward, because evil often has a nasty reserve of resources to stop such activities.

The harper scout is a bit of everything, though she rarely is a master of anything. Like the bard, these characters can take a huge range of skills without a penalty, but the lack of offensive magic or melee combat capabilities make scouts quite ephemeral as forces of goodness.

These characters are flagged as an expert-only selection. It is recommended that players who have not mastered all of the tricks and tactics of this system stay away from such a choice until they are ready for a trial.

Special Abilities

- ⊕ **Harper Knowledge:** Like a bard, a harper scout has a knack for picking up odds and ends of knowledge. This ability works exactly like the bardic knowledge ability of the bard class. If a harper scout has bard levels, the character's harper scout levels and bard levels stack for bardic knowledge.

- ⊕ **Favored Enemy:** A harper scout selects a favored enemy just as a ranger does. If a harper scout with ranger levels chooses a favored enemy that she already has chosen as a ranger, the bonuses stack. Upon reaching 4th level as a harper scout, the bonus against the harper scout's first favored enemy increases to +2, and she gains a new favored enemy at +1.

- ⊕ **Deneir's Eye:** At 2nd level, the harper scout gains a +2 holy bonus to saving throws against traps. This is a supernatural ability.

- ⊕ **Tymora's Smile:** At 3rd level, once per day, the harper scout or a target receives a +2 saving throw bonus on all saving throws for five turns. This is a supernatural ability.

- ⊕ **Lliira's Heart:** At 4th level, the harper scout gains a +2 holy bonus to saving throws against mind-affecting spells. This is a supernatural ability.

Paladin Harper (Savior)

HUMAN PALADIN/HARPER (15/5)

Strength	14	Dexterity	12
Intelligence	14	Constitution	14
Wisdom	10	Charisma	14 (+5)

Primary Attribute	Charisma
Weapon Choices	Longsword
Armor Preference	Full Plate Suit and a Tower Shield
Primary Skills	Persuade, Lore, Search, Discipline
Starting Feats	Power Attack, Cleave
Additional Feats	Toughness, Expertise,
Improved Critical, Improved Expertise, Knockdown, Improved Knockdown	

This is one of the more survivable harper combinations that a player can choose. A strong paladin background gives the final character a very high spread for her saving throws, nice hit points, and melee training that isn't bad at all. Taking a few harper levels here and there won't cause the character in incur an experience penalty, and it won't dilute the character's power much in the long run.

Apart from a few minor abilities (the harper scout spells and being able to choose two hated foes), this template plays a lot like a softer Vigilant. Using Expertise and Knockdown, this warrior can keep enemies from landing blows.

- ⊕ **Spells:** These spells are cast as arcane spells, so they are subject to arcane spell failure if the harper scout is wearing armor: At 2nd level, the harper scout gains the ability to cast the spell Sleep once per day. At 3rd level, the harper scout gains the ability to cast the spell Cat's Grace once per day. At 4th level, the harper scout gains the ability to cast Eagle's Splendor once per day. At 5th level, the harper scout gains the ability to cast the spell Invisibility once per day.

- ⊕ **Craft Harper Item:** At 5th level, the harper scout gains the ability to create two types of potions. The harper scout can create one potion per day, either Cat's Grace or Eagle's Splendor. To create either potion, the harper scout must spend 60 gold and five experience points. These potions allow a harper scout to better support her agents and allies.

SHADOW DANCER

- Hit Dice: d8

- Proficiencies: Simple Weapons and Light Armor

- Skill Points: 6 + Int. Modifier

- Required Feats: Dodge, Mobility

- Required Skills: Move Silently (8 ranks), Hide (10 ranks), Tumble (5 ranks)

At first glance, the shadow dancer doesn't add a whole lot to a stealthy class: more hiding, some extra concealment, and a summoned shadow. In practice however, this limited selection has a huge effect on the primary class that merges with the shadow dancer.

Hide in Plain Sight is one of the best abilities in the game. Anyone with a decent hide skill can use this to restore his stealth mode protections even when there are enemies just a few feet away. Rogues can make a Sneak Attack, step back, and Hide without taking more than a few moments. Mages can take Silent Spell and cast just ten feet from battle without being engaged. This ability is stunningly powerful.

Shadow Evade is also a critical ability, especially in areas where there are a lot of archers. Having any extra cover will help mages to deal with missile troops (the great bane of casters everywhere). Because this power can be used three times per day, it needn't be applied sparingly on the battlefield.

Special Abilities

- Hide in Plain Sight: The shadow dancer is able to use the Hide skill even while being observed.

- Shadow Daze: Once per day, the shadow dancer may inflict an illusory daze upon a target. This daze lasts for five rounds.

- Summon Shadow: Once per day, the shadow dancer can summon a shadow. This shadow is extremely difficult to turn and becomes more powerful as the shadow dancer gains levels.

- Shadow Evade: Three times per day, the shadow dancer can call upon the shadows in the area to help conceal her. The shadow dancer gains a concealment bonus, damage reduction and an AC bonus that improves with experience.

Wizard Shadow Dancer (Eclipser)
GNOME WIZARD/ROGUE/SHADOW DANCER (18/1/1)

Strength	6	Dexterity	14
Intelligence	18 (+5)	Constitution	16
Wisdom	10	Charisma	8

Primary Attribute	Intelligence
Weapon Choices	No
Armor Preference	Light Armor (later on)
Primary Skills	Concentration, Spellcraft, Move Silently, Hide, Tumble
Starting Feats	Toughness
Additional Feats	Silent Spell, Empower Spell, Maximize Spell, Quicken Spell, Still Spell, Spell Focus, Spell Penetration, Dodge, Greater Spell Focus, Stealthy, Greater Spell Penetration

To gain access to the Shadow Dancer's power, a character can take the rogue level at seventh, the shadow dancer at eighth, then continue along as a wizard until the end of the line. To accomplish this, save the majority of the character's skill points at each level (those not spent on concentration and spellcraft), then use all of these during the rouge's level; this will get Hide, Move Silently, and Tumbling all up to their required ranks.

Playing a wizard with these abilities means that a person can choose when and how to deal with various problems. Area-of-effect spells are a lot easier to manage because the caster can sneak into the best position before launching an assault. Beyond that, Hide in Plain Sight allows the mage to stealth away from his initial spot and start over for even more brutality. Using silent spells will improve on this.

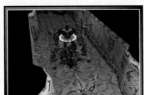

Skills

Skills fill out the peripheral qualities of a character. They identify the things that a person has trained in during her career. Some of these revolve around battle, such as discipline and taunt. Other skills involve various forms of sneaking, trapping, lore skills, and tricks for dealing with non-player characters (NPCs) during adventures.

ANIMAL EMPATHY

Ability: Charisma

Classes: Druid and Ranger

Untrained: No

Check: Animals and dire animals have a DC of 20 + the creature's hit die. For beasts and magical beasts, the DC is 24 + the creature's hit die. If the check succeeds, the creature is charmed, or, if the check exceeds the DC by six or greater, the creature is dominated.

Special: If the character fails its check by five or more, the creature will go hostile.

Use: Select this skill and then select the target creature.

A successful check allows a character to charm or dominate certain creatures. This ability is somewhat limited in scope, depending on where the character is being played. Though *Neverwinter Nights* and *Shadows of Undrentide* offer support for this skill, many modules may not have the same interesting uses for animal empathy (or even the creatures to use it on at all).

APPRAISE

Ability: Intelligence

Classes: All

Untrained: No

Check: None

Special: The higher the skill, the better the deal when purchasing or selling items.

Use: Automatic in stores

The higher the character's skill, the better the price received when selling or purchasing goods. A bit of extra money is especially keen for characters with a constant need for additional items (rogues, archers, and mages are all good examples of this).

CONCENTRATION

Ability: Constitution

Classes: All

Untrained: Yes

Check: The DC is equal to 10 + the damage received + the level of the spell that you're trying to cast. The caster receives a -4 penalty to the check if casting within three meters of an enemy.

Use: Automatic

Concentration checks are made whenever a character is distracted during the act of casting a spell. It is also used to avoid the effects of the Taunt skill. This is a fairly important skill for almost every caster, unless a mage is going to be doing primarily out-of-battle casting for their entire career. Even with a good henchman or a full party, nasty things can and do happen, and being able to get a spell off despite an ogre's "loving" caress can make all the difference.

CRAFT TRAP

Ability: Intelligence

Classes: All

Untrained: Yes

Check: The type of trap being created determines the DC.

Use: Selected

The character using this skill can combine raw components to form various trap kits.

Minor traps require 1 component.

Average traps require 3 components.

Strong traps require 5 components.

Deadly traps require 7 components.

| | | DIFFICULTY CHECK NEEDED TO EXCEED TO MAKE | | | |
| | | MINOR | AVERAGE | STRONG | DEADLY |
	COMPONENT NEEDED	DC	DC	DC	DC
Acid Splash	Acid Flask	15	25	30	35
Electrical	Quartz Crystal	20	25	30	35
Fire	Alchemist Fire	20	25	30	35
Frost	Cold Stone	15	20	25	30
Gas	Choking Powder	30	35	40	45
Holy	Holy Water Flask	15	20	25	30
Negative	Skeleton Knuckle	15	20	25	30
Sonic	Thunderstone	15	20	25	30
Spike	Caltrops	5	20	25	35
Tangle	Tanglefoot Bag	15	20	25	30

DISABLE TRAP

Ability: Intelligence

Classes: All

Untrained: No

Check: There are four progressively difficult actions that a character may perform on a trap. The base DC is determined by the difficulty rating of the trap and the difficulty of the action. Disable trap can be used to: examine the trap to determine the difficulty in disarming it (base DC -7), flag the trap so that other party members know to avoid the trap (base DC -5), recover the trap (base DC +10) or disarm it (base DC).

Special: Only rogues may disarm traps with a DC of 25 or greater. With 5 or more ranks in Set Traps, a character gains a +2 synergy bonus on Disable Trap checks. Disable Trap and Set Trap can be considered subsets of the D&D Disable Device skill.

Use: Assess, Flag, Disarm, and Recover are radial menu options off of a detected trap.

This skill allows the character to perform a variety of actions on a trap. Recovery of traps can be a fine way to pick up a bit of money the next time the character returns to town; some of the higher-level traps sell for a fair bit of coin.

DISCIPLINE

Ability: Strength

Classes: All

Untrained: Yes

Check: The DC is equal to the attacker's attack roll.

Use: Automatic

A successful check allows the character to resist the effects of any combat feat (Disarm, Called Shot, Sap, or Knockdown). Note that discipline is a *Neverwinter Nights* skill. It is not a part of the *Dungeons & Dragons* game experience but is a necessary part of the Aurora Engine technology.

Serious melee warriors need to take this skill. There is so little choice in the matter that it is almost amusing. People without discipline face an uphill battle in the later levels when enemies have tons of feats to knock people around. Take discipline up as high as it will go, and even consider throwing a skill focus into this (especially if you are a fighter).

HEAL

| Ability: Wisdom |
| Classes: All |
| Untrained: Yes |

Check: Must beat the poison or disease DC. If successful, the target is cured, and is healed with a number of hit points equal to the skill roll, plus all modifiers. If the target suffers from no poisons or diseases, it still is healed of damage.

Use: Use Healing Kit on wounded creature.

With this skill, a character can heal hit points and cure poisons and diseases with a Healing Kit. In *Neverwinter Nights* and *Shadows of Undrentide* this is a secondary skill that doesn't get too much use (there are many potions, scrolls, healers, and other ways to get around damage and status ailments). However, this skill is important for certain modules and persistent worlds that are more brutal in the way that they handle rest and healing. People who desire a full character with a balance of skills and attributes will enjoy this skill.

HIDE

| Ability: Dexterity |
| Classes: All |
| Untrained: Yes |

Check: When hidden, a roll is made against an opposing creature's Spot check, applying any penalties your character might receive from wearing armor. Success means that the opposing creature remains unaware as he passes or your character approaches. Characters may not attempt a Hide check if they are within the line of sight of any intelligent non-party member.

Special: Hide and Move Silently are combined into a single modal Stealth action. Movement in Stealth mode is slower than the normal rate. Wearing armor or using a torch inhibits this ability, but low light can provide a bonus. A character is harder to spot if standing still, and/or if small.

Use: Stealth Mode

This skill allows a character to hide from enemies. Taking this skill without move silently isn't too effective, because any motion will give enemies a chance to detect the character based on that skill instead. It is critical for a sincere stealth character to master both of these!

LISTEN

| Ability: Wisdom |
| Classes: All |
| Untrained: Yes |

Check: Listen detects hidden creatures by opposing their Move Silently check. A successful check renders the hidden creature visible and able to be targeted by the listener.

Special: Standing still provides a +5 bonus to a Listen check. A character with the Alertness feat gains a +2 synergy bonus on Listen checks. Rangers gain a bonus when listening against a favored enemy. Elves, gnomes and halflings gain a +2 racial bonus to Listen checks. Half-elves receive a +1 racial bonus.

Use: Detect Mode

Listen alerts a character to hidden creatures that may be nearby.

LORE, KNOWLEDGE

Ability: Intelligence

Classes: All

Untrained: Yes

Check: A roll against an unidentified item's value to determine magical properties that the item may possess.

Special: Bards are able to identify items easier than other classes.

Use: Automatic every time the player inspects an item

Lore allows a character to identify unknown magic items. Various spells and items can also give a character a bonus to their lore skill. Lore is a subset of the D&D Knowledge skill. The following table provides a base for the difficulty in identifying items with the lore skill.

Identifying Items with the Lore Skill

LORE SKILL MODIFIER	ITEM VALUE	LORE SKILL MODIFIER	ITEM VALUE
1	10	19	40000
2	50	20	50000
3	100	21	60000
4	150	22	80000
5	200	23	100000
6	300	24	150000
7	400	25	200000
8	500	26	250000
9	1000	27	300000
10	2500	28	350000
11	3750	29	400000
12	4800	30	500000
13	6500	31 and beyond	Add an
14	9500		extra
15	13000		100,000 gp
16	17000		value per
17	20000		point after
18	30000		30

MOVE SILENTLY

Ability: Dexterity

Classes: All

Untrained: Yes

Check: The DC is the opposing creature's Listen check. If you are successful, the opposing creature remains unaware as your character moves.

Special: Hide and Move Silently are combined into a single modal Stealth action. Movement in Stealth mode is slower than the normal rate. Wearing armor inhibits this ability, but low light can provide a bonus.

Use: Stealth Mode

A character may sneak quietly past an enemy. Taking this skill and hide up to a high level will provide many opportunities to avoid fights or to choose the time and place for initiating battles.

OPEN LOCK

Ability: Dexterity

Classes: All

Untrained: No

Check: The DC is determined by the lock's difficulty rating. A successful check will open the lock.

Special: Thieves' Tools, if used, provide various bonuses to a character's Open Lock attempt, but are destroyed in the attempt whether successful or not.

Use: Select the skill and then target a locked object.

Using this skill allows the character to gain entrance to locked rooms, or to open locked containers. Though containers can be dealt with often as not by heavy fighters and mages, a quiet party needs to be a bit subtle when looking around for goodies. Open Locks provides such an opportunity.

PARRY

Ability: Dexterity

Classes: All

Untrained: Yes

Check: The DC is the modified attack roll of the incoming blow. A successful parry means that the attack does not damage the parrying character. A character may only parry a number of attacks equal to the number of attacks available to the character.

Special: If the parry is successful and the difference between the roll and the DC is ten points or greater, a counterattack occurs, which is a bonus attack made by the character parrying against the parried opponent.

Use: Select the Parry mode. The character will remain in parry mode until the mode is exited.

Parry blocks incoming attacks and occasionally allows for impressive counterattacks. The skill is a more in-depth selection of fighting defensively. It allows the player/character the opportunity to opt for total defense during melee combat. Parry is a *Neverwinter Nights* skill. It is not a part of the *Dungeons & Dragons*® game experience but is a necessary part of the Aurora Engine technology.

Though the parry skill offers a tantalizing option for defensive fighting, it is a dream that is somewhat unrealized. The complexity of this system prevents many warriors from reaching their desired goal of being able to stop anything from getting past them and engaging them in a duel of skill rather than brute force. Instead of spending a great deal of points investing in parry, defensive fighters should look into the feats of expertise in its place.

Those who wish to give parry a try despite the dips in the road should devote themselves entirely over to this skill; a mixed approach will yield nothing short of a character that has lost potential and gained nothing in return. A true parry fighter should focus on dexterity and grab finesse weapons only. Have the character take improved parry (a feat that requires a 13+ intelligence) and skill focus (parry). Combine this with a full set of skill points over the levels, and the character will gain a final skill level that is well into the 30s. For a one-on-one fight, this creates a nasty situation for most attackers! Parry is still somewhat limited against massive groups of attackers, because of the maximum parry limit each round, but this format is as good as it gets.

PERFORM

Ability: Charisma

Classes: Bard

Untrained: Yes

Check: None. The higher the rank in this skill, the better the bardsong.

Use: Select the skill and it will affect a 30-foot radius of allies around the singer.

A Bard using Perform can use his bardsong, which improves his allies' ability to fight in combat and withstand mind-affecting spells. Perform is essential for any Bard who wants to have access to his bardsong and the bonuses it provides.

PERSUADE, DIPLOMACY

Ability: Charisma

Classes: All

Untrained: Yes

Check: The DC is determined by the NPC being spoken to.

Special: The diplomacy skill was broken into two skills, Persuade and Taunt for *Neverwinter Nights* and *Shadows of Undrentide*.

Use: Used in conversation

In conversation, a character has the option to persuade others to reveal additional information about plots or to give bonus treasure. This skill is one of the most rewarding in the game; certain sections of the game and several quests behave very differently when a high persuasion character is thrown forward.

PICK POCKET

Ability: Dexterity

Classes: All

Untrained: No

Check: There are two steps to picking pockets. First, the item must be acquired, and then the targeted creature must not notice the theft. To steal the item, the base DC from a neutral or tolerant creature is 20, and a hostile creature is 30. This roll is affected by armor check penalties. The targeted creature makes an opposed Spot check versus the Pick Pocket check of your character. Hostile creatures get a +10 bonus to their Spot checks against Pick Pocket. If the opposed roll succeeds, they have detected your character's attempt to steal. An NPC who detects the attempt will turn hostile, whereas a PC will be informed that you have attempted to pickpocket them. If, however, both checks succeed for your character, then he or she successfully manages to steal the item without being detected.

Use: Select skill, then select valid target.

Pick Pocket allows a character to remove items from another's backpack. During normal play, this skill doesn't get too much use. Townsfolk and some NPCs around the world have items that are interesting, but it isn't worth the substantial investment of skill points that it takes to safely procure these goodies.

On the other hand, people who play on persistent world servers or just spend time with a lot of human players will find that pick pocketing is a dangerous and still lucrative skill! There is money and power to be made by stealing from the rich and famous of the realm, and making a few enemies here and there might well we worth the issues of bounty hunters and whatever else.

Some people may take theft somewhat poorly, even in an out-of-character fashion. In these cases, it is best to remind everyone involved that a thief is…well, a thief. If some players can't handle that aspect of roleplaying, it is better to give them back their equipment just to avoid being plagued by people who aren't interested in that level of character interaction. Either way, it's only a game, and having a good time as any character is more important than bickering and arguing over who killed who.

SEARCH

Ability: Intelligence

Classes: All

Untrained: Yes

Check: Detecting a trap requires a roll against a DC comprised of the setter's Set Trap skill, plus the strength of the trap. Only rogues may detect traps with a DC greater than 25.

Special: The search range is 5 ft. if passively searching, 10 ft. if actively searching. Elves and dwarves have a +2 racial bonus to their Search checks. Half-elves have a +1 racial bonus.

Search is used to spot traps. Running around and setting off such foul mechanisms can be the death of even a sturdy barbarian. Having a rogue around who can accurately find and disable traps is a blessing.

SET TRAP

Ability: Dexterity

Classes: All

Untrained: No

Check: A roll is made for success when a trap kit is used from inventory. The DC of the task is determined by the power of the trap.

Special: 5 or more ranks in Disable Traps grants a +2 synergy bonus on Set Trap checks. Any party members will be able to see traps that your character has set. Disable Trap and Set Trap can be considered subsets of the D&D Disable Device skill.

Spectacular Failure: If you fail by 10 or more, it triggers the trap in the attempt to set it. This can only occur if you are in combat when trying to set the trap.

Use: Use a trap kit from your inventory. An icon visible to you and your party will appear on the ground to represent the trap.

A character may place trap kits. What better way to say, "I love you" than with the gift of rotating knives and caustic acid?

SPELLCRAFT

Ability: Intelligence	
Classes: All	
Untrained: No	

Check: A successful check means that your character has identified a spell being cast by an opponent. The DC of this check is equal to 15 plus the level of the spell. The character also gains a +1 bonus for every 5 ranks in this skill to all saving throws against spells.

Special: A specialist wizard gets a +2 bonus when dealing with a spell from his specialized school. As well, a successful Spellcraft check is required before your character can attempt to counterspell. The specialist wizard suffers a -5 penalty when dealing with a spell or effect from a prohibited school.

Use: Spellcraft checks are automatic anytime a spell is cast nearby.

Spellcraft is used to identify spells and for performing counterspells. Getting a saving throw bonus for a skill that is often class-related is a huge perk. Spellcraft and concentration are pretty much staple skills for any arcane or divine caster.

SPOT

Ability: Wisdom	
Classes: All	
Untrained: Yes	

Check: The DC is determined by the Hide check of the hidden creature.

Special: The Alertness feat grants a +2 synergy bonus on Spot checks. Rangers receive a bonus on Spot checks against their favored enemy. Elves have a +2 racial bonus on Spot checks, and half-elves have a +1 racial bonus.

Use: Detect Mode

A successful check of this skill can reveal a hidden creature. Characters who are worried about rogues should certainly look into this skill.

TAUNT, DIPLOMACY

Ability: Charisma	
Classes: All	
Untrained: Yes	

Check: The DC is a concentration check made by the target against the character's Taunt skill roll. It is considered an attack. If the taunt is successful, the opponent suffers an Armor Class penalty equal to the difference between the taunt roll and the defender's roll (to a max of a -6 penalty) for 5 rounds. The target will also suffer a 30% chance of spell failure, if they don't resist the taunt.

Special: Taunt penalties are not cumulative. The diplomacy skill was broken into two skills, Persuade and Taunt for *Neverwinter Nights*.

Use: Select skill and then target creature.

Taunt is used to provoke an enemy into dropping his guard for a short time. Most of the time, it isn't worth the time and micromanagement to deal with taunt, especially when dealing with mages (who have concentration perked through the roof). However, a warrior who wants to use improved power attack against a high hit point target could use this to bridge the gap in attack bonuses. This is more of an option for characters that cannot afford feats in the more effective battle abilities (i.e., knockdown, sap, etc.).

TUMBLE

Ability: Dexterity	
Classes: All	
Untrained: No	

Check: None

Special: For every 5 ranks in this skill, the character's armor class is improved by +1.

Use: Automatic

The character with high tumbling is able to roll away from attacks during combat, positioning themselves safely at all times. A good archer, rogue or light fighter could hardly say no to such a pleasant notion.

USE MAGIC DEVICE

Ability: Charisma

Classes: Bard and Rogue

Untrained: No

Check: The DC of this task is determined by the value of the item, if the character is trying to use an item restricted to a specific class. If the character is trying to emulate a specific race, the DC is increased by 5. If trying to emulate a specific alignment then the DC is increased by 10.

Use: Automatically applied whenever a character attempts to use or equip an item that they would normally be unable to.

Skill Requirements for Magical Devices

SKILL VALUE	CLASS RESTRICTED ITEM	RACE RESTRICTED ITEM	ALIGNMENT RESTRICTED ITEM
1	1,000 gp or fewer	Impossible	Impossible
5	4,800 gp or fewer	1,000 gp or fewer	Impossible
10	20,000 gp or fewer	4,800 gp or fewer	1,000 gp or fewer
15	100,000 gp or fewer	20,000 gp or fewer	4,800 gp or fewer
20	100,000 gp or fewer	100,000 gp or fewer	20,000 gp or fewer
25	100,000 gp or fewer	100,000 gp or fewer	100,000 gp or fewer

A successful check grants access to the abilities of a magic item as if your character had the requisite class, race, or alignment to do so. The following table shows what items a character with this skill can use. All items are given a challenge rating based on their value in gold pieces. The categories define whether these magical items are class related (i.e., wizard-only items), race related (i.e., elf-only items), or alignment related (i.e., lawful-character items).

Feats

All player characters are given the chance to take feats. These help to refine a character, giving the PC more abilities than their class alone would allow. Not only is this a fine way to create variety within the system, it also fosters a sense of excitement when it comes time to take another look at the special list.

All characters start out with at least one feat. Humans gain a free feat for being what they are, and fighters gain a free feat at the first level, too. Thus, human fighters start with the most possible feats for a level-one character with three selections! Most classes will only get to pick six more bonus feats over their levels (one every third level, starting at level 3). Fighters, rogues, and wizards are examples of classes that are given extra feats to specialize in their professions.

The following text gives both the general requirements and importance of the selectable feats, and it also explains some of the interesting combinations that are hidden within the system.

Alertness

Type of Feat: General

Prerequisite: None

Use: Automatic

This grants a cumulative +2 bonus to Spot and Listen checks due to finely tuned senses. A rogue with a feat to spare could hardly go wrong with this, nor could any character that plays around rogues and has an investment in either of these perceptive skills.

Ambidexterity

Type of Feat: General

Prerequisite: Dex 15+

Required for: Improved Two-Weapon Fighting

Use: Used automatically when two-weapon fighting.

When fighting with two weapons, this feat reduces the penalty of the off-hand weapon by 4. Rangers receive this feat free at level 1. All dual wielders should work hard to get their dexterity up to 15 so that this feat can be taken. Without Ambidexterity and Improved Two-Weapon Fighting, the entire course of a dual wielder's career is thrown into shadow.

Arcane Defense

Type of Feat: General

Prerequisite: Spell focus in the chosen school

Use: Automatic

Character gains a +2 bonus to saving throws versus the chosen school of magic. This is not a very efficient feat to take, considering that a +2 bonus to Will saves would be a far more common gift. Even characters that plan to take Iron Will can gain bonuses through early feats (such as Luck of Heroes) instead of relying on this overly specific feat.

Armor Proficiency (Heavy)

Type of Feat: General

Prerequisite: Armor Proficiency (Light) and Armor Proficiency (Medium)

Use: Automatic. Fighters, paladins, and clerics receive this feat free.

This feat grants the knowledge to make effective use of heavy armor.

Armor Proficiency (Light)

Type of Feat: General

Required for: Armor Proficiency (Medium)

Use: Automatic. All classes except monks, sorcerers, and wizards have this feat free.

This feat grants the knowledge to make effective use of light armor.

Armor Proficiency (Medium)

Type of Feat: General

Prerequisite: Armor Proficiency (Light)

Required for: Armor Proficiency (Heavy)

Use: Automatic. All classes except monks, rogues, sorcerers, and wizards have this feat free.

This feat grants the knowledge to make effective use of medium armor.

Artist

Type of Feat: General

Prerequisite: Perform skill, can only be taken at 1st level

Use: Automatic

Character gains a +2 bonus on Perform checks. Often, a skill focus in Perform is more efficient, but choosing both of these may be needed for characters who are seeking an exceptionally high Perform rating.

Blind Fight

Type of Feat: General

Prerequisite: None

Use: Automatic

This feat grants the character the ability to fight well, even if blinded or against invisible creatures. The character gets to reroll her Miss chance percentile one time to see if it actually hits. As well, invisible creatures get no bonus to hit the character in melee. This feat carries a lot of weight for those who are interested in fighting mages (especially in player-versus-player combat). Various combinations of darkness and ultravision sorcery are common in the land, and fighters who will face that frequently may enjoy the comfort provided by the Blind Fighting feat.

Blooded

Type of Feat: General

Prerequisite: Can only be taken at 1st level

Use: Automatic

Character gains a +2 bonus on Initiative and a +2 bonus on Spot checks. Initiative is not always the most critical function on the field of battle in *Shadows of Undrentide*, so many warriors should lean toward other feats. A major focus on Initiative and Spot would point toward rogues as a target for Blooded, but rogues are often devoted to automatically gaining Initiative (through sneak attacks and such). This further muddies the waters around this eccentric feat.

Bullheaded

Type of Feat: General

Prerequisite: Can only be taken at 1st level

Use: Automatic

Character gains a +2 bonus on resisting Taunts and a +2 bonus on Will saving throws. A substantial number of characters that take Taunt should look into this feat. Getting a +2 bonus to Will saves while adding to Taunt is a fairly hefty set of boons. The only major disadvantage to Bullheaded is that a character must acquire it during creation.

Called Shot

Type of Feat: General

Prerequisite: Base attack bonus of +1 or higher

Use: Selected

Grants the ability to make a potentially disabling attack against an opponent's arms or legs. Called Shots are made at a -4 penalty. Called Shots must overcome the target's Discipline skill check, and if successful will damage the target based on the location of the Called Shot. A Called Shot against the legs will reduce the opponent's movement rate by 20% and give him a -2 cumulative penalty to his Dexterity. A Called Shot against the arms will apply a cumulative -2 penalty to the creature's attack rolls.

Successful Called Shots last for four rounds.

Circle Kick

Type of Feat: General

Prerequisite: Base attack bonus +3, Dex 15+, Improved Unarmed Strike

Use: Automatic

If the character succeeds in hitting an opponent with an unarmed attack, they get an additional free attack against another, nearby enemy. Could a monk possibly say no to something this wonderful?

Cleave

Type of Feat: General

Prerequisite: Str 13+, Power Attack feat

Required for: Great Cleave

Use: Automatic

If a character with this feat kills an opponent in melee combat, he gets a free attack against any opponent who is within melee attack range. Only one such attack can be made per round with this feat, even if multiple enemies are slain by additional attacks. Once taken, the *Shadows of Undrentide* feat of Great Cleave removes this limitation.

Combat Casting

Type of Feat: General

Prerequisite: Ability to cast 1st-level spells

Use: Automatic

Character is adept at casting spells in combat, removing the standard -4 penalty to Concentration checks when within three meters of an enemy.

Courteous Magocracy

Type of Feat: General

Prerequisite: Can only be taken at 1st level

Use: Automatic

Character gains a +2 bonus on Lore checks and Spellcraft checks.

Deflect Arrows

Type of Feat: General

Prerequisite: Dex 13+, Improved Unarmed Strike

Use: Automatic if not caught flat-footed. Monks receive this feat free at level 2.

Character can attempt to deflect one incoming missile attack per round (Reflex save made against DC 20). Though this feat is extremely flashy and useful, it is hard to find enough free room to afford both this and Improved Unarmed Strike.

Dirty Fighting

Type of Feat: General

Prerequisite: Base attack bonus +2

Use: Automatic

Dirty Fighting gives a character the chance to stop his normal chain of attacks and try for a blow that will inflict extra damage. Though a person can add 1d4 additional points of damage with a successful strike, this negates the character's attacks for the rest of the combat round. As such, this is a feat for very low-level characters.

Characters who are created with low levels in mind (someone who won't likely pass beyond level five or six) will find that this feat is a lot more potent. When a person won't be losing attacks, dirty fighting becomes a fine way to deal extra damage without a penalty to hit or a decrease in armor class. Indeed, people designing templates for intentionally low-level parties should look at dirty fighting in a very different way.

Disarm

Type of Feat: General

Prerequisite: Int 13+

Required for: Improved Disarm

Use: Selected. A Disarm attempt provokes an attack of opportunity.

The character can attempt to Disarm an opponent in melee combat. Attempting a Disarm applies a -6 penalty to the character's attack roll, and the combatant with the larger weapon gains a +4 bonus per size category of difference. A successful hit deals normal damage, and if the opponent fails a Discipline check then the weapon flies from the opponent's hands.

This is a rough feat to take unless Improved Disarm is the intended goal. Having to provoke attacks of opportunity while overcoming a moderate attack penalty is a lot to ask otherwise.

Divine Might

Type of Feat: General

Prerequisite: Turn Undead, Charisma 13 or higher, Strength 13 or higher, Power Attack

Use: Selected

Up to three times per day, the character may add his Charisma bonus to all weapon damage for a number of rounds equal to the Charisma bonus.

If a paladin has Power Attack and 13 Strength, this should be one of the next glimmers in her eye. Doing four to six extra points of damage per attack, depending on level and items, can really add up against the hoards of chaos.

Divine Shield

Type of Feat: General

Prerequisite: Turn Undead, Charisma 13 or higher, Strength 13 or higher, Power Attack

Use: Selected

Up to three times per day, the character may add his Charisma bonus to his armor class for a number of rounds equal to the Charisma bonus.

As if paladins didn't have enough defensive power already, this feat makes it even better for them. Melee-oriented clerics may enjoy this one too, depending on that weight of their Charisma bonus.

Dodge

Type of Feat: General

Prerequisite: Dex 13+

Required for: Mobility

Use: Automatic, though a condition that negates a Dexterity bonus to AC also negates any Dodge bonuses. Multiple Dodge bonuses (different feats, racial bonuses) are cumulative

Increased agility grants a +1 Dodge bonus to AC against attacks from a character's current target (or last attacker). Though this bonus isn't overwhelming by itself, one point could always be the difference between a hit and a miss. On top of that, Mobility and eventually Spring Attack can be taken after this! Spring Attack is a dream within a dream for a hit-and-run character of almost any sort.

Empower Spell

Type of Feat: Metamagic

Prerequisite: Ability to cast 2nd-level spells

Use: Empowered Spells occupy spell slots two levels higher than normal. Saving throws and opposed rolls, such as those made when Dispel Magic is cast, are not affected.

Magical expertise allows certain spells to be cast with a 50% increase in variable numeric effects (number of targets, damage, etc), excluding duration. All arcane casters and most divine ones should take this feat when they have a chance. The best uses for Empower Spell are with bread and butter attack spells or enchantments. Area-of-effect evocation spells (Fireball and its well-wishers) inflict a lot of damage when Empowered. Though a Maximized Spell is often better, there is potential for an Empowered Spell to surpass even those expectations.

Expertise

Type of Feat: General

Prerequisite: Int 13+

Required for: Improved Expertise

Use: Combat mode

A character with this feat can make defensive attacks, gaining a +5 bonus to AC but receiving a –5 penalty to attack rolls.

Expertise is a very interesting combat ability because it won't disengage while a character is fighting, as long as he stands in place. This includes characters that begin spellcasting! Mages, who already have a high intelligence, should strongly consider grabbing this wonderful feat if they are worried about their armor class. Better to stay out of battle entirely, but that isn't always an option.

Extend Spell

Type of Feat: Metamagic

Prerequisite: Ability to cast 1st-level spells

Use: Extended Spells occupy spell slots one level higher than normal Spells with an instantaneous or permanent duration are not affected.

Magical expertise allows certain spells to be cast with a 100% increase in duration. Clerics and druids who rely heavily on buffing themselves and their parties may find this to be one of the more useful feats.

Extra Music

Type of Feat: General

Prerequisite: Bardic Music

Use: Automatic

The character may use bard song four extra times per day.

Extra Stunning Attacks

Type of Feat: General

Prerequisite: Base attack bonus +2, Stunning Fist

Use: Automatic

The character gains three extra Stunning Attacks per day.

Extra Turning

Type of Feat: Special

Prerequisite: Exclusive to cleric or paladin

Use: Automatic

This divine ability allows the character to turn undead six additional times per day.

Great Cleave

Type of Feat: General

Prerequisite: Strength 13+, Power Attack, Cleave, base attack bonus +4 or higher

Use: Automatic

Same as the feat Cleave, except that the character has no limit to the number of times used per round. Though Cleave is a perfect feat for almost every melee character, Great Cleave is not quite as attractive as it sounds. In many cases, a warrior simply cannot chop through multiple creatures in a single round (unless the monsters are extremely weak, and then this feat is a bit of overkill anyway). Great Cleave is more an ability for filling out a character that is a monster in his own right rather than a necessity for easier combat.

Great Fortitude

Type of Feat: General

Prerequisite: None

Use: Automatic

A character with this feat is very hardy, gaining a +2 bonus to all Fortitude saving throws.

Greater Spell Focus

Type of Feat: General

Prerequisite: Spell Focus

Use: Automatic. This feat may be selected multiple times, but the effects do not stack. It applies to a different school of magic in each case.

A character becomes even more adept with spells of a particular school of magic. The character gains a +4 bonus to the spell save DC for all spells of the chosen school.

Greater Spell Penetration

Type of Feat: General

Prerequisite: Spell Penetration

Use: Automatic

A +4 bonus on caster level checks is granted to the character when trying to beat a creature's spell resistance.

Improved Critical

Type of Feat: General

Prerequisite: Proficiency with the chosen weapon, base attack bonus +8 or higher

Use: Automatic. The threat range of a Keen weapon is already doubled, increasing to triple with this feat. This feat can be selected multiple times, applying to a new weapon category each time

Combat ability doubles the critical threat range with a given weapon. A longsword that normally threatens a critical on a roll of 19-20 would now threaten a critical on a roll of 17-20. Every character that plans on using a weapon in a serious way should take this skill. Even weapons with a threat range of 20 benefit greatly from Improved Critical (it still doubles the chance of landing a critical strike).

Improved Disarm

Type of Feat: General

Prerequisite: Int 13+, Disarm

Use: Selected

A character with this feat has learned not to provoke an attack of opportunity when attempting to disarm an opponent. Success knocks the opponent's weapon away from him. The penalty to make a disarm attempt is reduced to -4.

These two substantial bonuses bring disarming techniques up to a roughly equivalent level with Knockdown. Still, this is the weakest of the two because it requires two feats, a 13 Intelligence, and only works against a fairly limited set of enemies. Improved Knockdown works against the vast majority of creatures in the realms, but Disarm can only be a viable technique against armed opponents (obviously). Against human players, Disarm is probably a fair bit better than it sounds, but for most modules and the central storyline, Knockdown is the king of the hill.

Improved Expertise

Type of Feat: General

Prerequisite: Int 13+, Expertise

Use: Combat Mode

A character with this feat can make defensive attacks, gaining a +10 bonus to AC but receiving a -10 penalty to attack rolls. Few things compare to the quality of this feat for defensive characters. Players who accompany powerful archers and mages are heavily encouraged to take this skill. In these cases, it is just as effective to tie up an enemy and let the rest of the party do the talking when it comes to damage.

Improved Initiative

Type of Feat: General

Prerequisite: None

Use: Automatic

The character gains a +4 bonus to Initiative checks. Most characters simply won't have the feats left over to take this, even though a bonus to Initiative would be nice.

Improved Knockdown

Type of Feat: General

Prerequisite: Knockdown, Intelligence 13+, base attack bonus +7

Use: Selected. Monks receive this feat free at 6th level.

Characters with this feat have learned to use the Knockdown ability as if they are one size category larger than they really are. All other Knockdown conditions still apply. Being able to control combat through a melee ability is one of the best tools for any warrior. The more henchmen, summonings, or allies involved in the fight, the better this technique becomes.

Improved Parry

Type of Feat: General

Prerequisite: Intelligence 13+

Use: Automatic

Grants a +4 competence bonus to the character's opposed attack rolls when using the Parry skill. Combined with a skill focus, this opens the way for characters to have a very high Parry even at lower levels.

Improved Power Attack

Type of Feat: General

Prerequisite: Power Attack, Strength 13+

Use: Combat Mode

This feat can be used at a -10 penalty to attack but with a +10 bonus to any damage given. Improved Power Attack is very useful when fighting large numbers of easy-to-hit opponents. This feat is also useful for people who adventure with allies who use Knockdown and other disabling attacks. Improved Power Attack is a true blessing when a character goes after temporarily defenseless targets.

Improved Two-Weapon Fighting

Type of Feat: General

Prerequisite: Two-Weapon Fighting, Ambidexterity, base attack bonus +9 or higher

Use: Automatic. Rangers receive this feat at 9th level, even if they don't meet the prerequisites.

The character with this feat is able to get a second offhand attack (at a penalty of -5 to the attack roll). This penalty does not affect any other strikes that are made during the same combat round; this is a completely free strike.

Improved Unarmed Strike

Type of Feat: General

Prerequisite: None

Required for: Stunning Fist, Deflect Arrows

Use: Automatic. Monks receive this feat free at 1st level.

Armed opponents no longer get attacks of opportunity against the character when you make unarmed attacks against them. Because of this, very few characters will ever need to take Improved Unarmed Strike. Non-monks do not hold their own well without weapons, so this is more a feat for roleplayers and characters on persistent world servers that strip people down on occasion.

Iron Will

Type of Feat: General

Prerequisite: None

Use: Automatic

Focused presence of mind provides a +2 bonus to all Will saving throws. This is a fairly decent feat for characters with a low Will save, especially if fear and various enchantments have been plaguing the character recently.

Knockdown

Type of Feat: General

Prerequisite: None

Required for: Improved Knockdown

Use: Selected. Prone characters cannot attack. Characters receive a +4 attack bonus against prone opponents in melee, but a -4 attack penalty with a ranged weapon. A character can only knock down an opponent that is one size category larger, the same size, or smaller than he is. The opponent gets a +4 bonus for every size category he is larger than the attacker or a -4 penalty for every size category he is smaller. Monks receives this feat free at Level 6.

With this maneuver, a character can attempt to knock an opponent to the ground. An attack roll is made with an -4 penalty to attack and, if successful, an opposed roll is made, comparing your attack roll with the defender's Discipline skill check. If successful, the target is knocked to a prone position.

Lightning Reflexes

Type of Feat: General

Prerequisite: None

Use: Automatic

This feat grants a +2 bonus to all Reflex saving throws, due to faster than normal reflexes.

Lingering Song

Type of Feat: General

Prerequisite: Bardic Music

Use: Automatic

The effects of the bard's songs will last an additional five rounds. Because bardic music is quick to enact and lasts fairly well, this feat is not one of the more potent to choose for the later game. For a low-level bard, however, there might be a reason. This would be even more prominent if the character is playing in modules with slower progression than the main game and expansion pack.

Luck of Heroes

Type of Feat: General

Prerequisite: Can only be taken at 1st level

Use: Automatic

Character gains a +1 bonus on all saving throws. The level-one feats are quite hard to purchase (since there is so much to grab that early and so few points to do it with), but Luck of Heroes is one of the better choices for a character that is interested in any of the saving throw abilities. Many feats only give two points of resistance for saves.

Maximize Spell

Type of Feat: Metamagic

Prerequisite: Ability to cast 3rd-level spells

Use: Maximized Spells occupy spell slots three levels higher than normal. Saving throws and opposed rolls, such as those made when dispel magic is cast, are not affected.

Magical expertise allows certain spells to be cast with all variable numeric effects (number of targets, damage, etc.) applied at their maximum. Some of the game's early level buffs (i.e., Cat's Grace, Owl's Wisdom, etc.) can be used in a maximized form to ensure that a specific bonus is reached.

Mobility

Type of Feat: General

Prerequisite: Dex 13+, Dodge

Use: Automatic, though a condition that negates a Dexterity bonus to AC also negates any dodge bonuses. Multiple dodge bonuses (from different feats or racial bonuses) are cumulative.

A character with this feat has learned to avoid attacks of opportunity more effectively, gaining a +4 dodge bonus to AC against them. Characters that move into and out of battle frequently, such as rogues, use this feat best.

Point Blank Shot

Type of Feat: General

Prerequisite: None

Required for: Rapid Shot

Use: Automatic

Unfazed by close combat, a character with this feat negates the -4 penalty for using missile weapons within melee attack range, and gains an additional +1 to attack and damage with ranged weapons when the target is within 15 feet. This is another feat that all aspiring archers will enjoy. This creates a win-win situation for the bowman; enemies who stay at long range will face the character's best attacks, and enemies who come in close will have to endure even nastier bonuses before getting their precious melee strikes.

Power Attack

Type of Feat: General

Prerequisite: Str 13+

Required for: Cleave, Improved Power Attack

Use: Combat Mode

A character with this feat can make powerful but ungainly attacks. When selected, this grants a +5 bonus to the damage roll, but inflicts a -5 penalty to the attack roll. This power is best used against targets that are fairly easy to hit (large enemies without armor or magical defense). In these cases, the 25% reduction on attack rolls won't make much of a difference. However, this feat should not be used at all when fighting against enemies with a high armor class; the penalty to hit greatly outclasses the mediocre bonus to damage in these circumstances (i.e., don't use Power Attacks against dragons, no matter how scary they look).

Quicken Spell

Type of Feat: Metamagic

Prerequisite: Ability to cast 4th-level spells

Use: Quickened spells occupy spell slots four levels higher than normal.

Magical expertise allows spells to be cast instantaneously, making them invulnerable to counterspells or interruption. A Quickened Spell is cast as a free action, and another action can be attempted within the same round, including the casting of another spell. Only one Quickened Spell can be cast in a round, however.

Rapid Reload

Type of Feat: General

Prerequisite: Base attack bonus +2

Use: Automatic

The character is able to reload so quickly that he gets the same number of attacks with any crossbow as he would get if he were using a normal bow. Serious archers often avoid crossbows for a number of reasons (the need to take this feat, lack of high-end power that composite bows provide, etc.). However, this feat may be useful for back-of-the-party characters that just want to throw a few more quarrels into the mix during their spare time.

Rapid Shot

Type of Feat: General

Prerequisite: Dex 13+, Point Blank Shot

Use: Selected

A character with this feat is quick with ranged weapons, gaining an extra attack per round while using them. When a rapid attack round is attempted, the extra attack is made at the highest base attack bonus, though all attacks within the round suffer a -2 penalty.

All serious archers should take this feat; the trivial penalty to hit can scarcely compare with the extra attack that is granted. At low levels, this is an even greater boon, so many archers will want to take this feat as soon as possible.

Resist Disease

Type of Feat: General

Prerequisite: None

Use: Automatic

The character gains a +4 bonus on Fortitude saving throws to resist the effects of disease.

Resist Poison

Type of Feat: General

Prerequisite: None

Use: Automatic

The character gains a +4 bonus on Fortitude saving throws against poison.

Resistance to Energy

Type of Feat: General

Prerequisite: Base Fortitude save bonus +8

Use: Automatic

The character gains +5 resistance against the chosen type of energy (first five points of damage of this type of energy are ignored).

Shield

Type of Feat: General

Prerequisite: None

Use: All classes except monks, rogues, sorcerers, and wizards have this feat free.

A character with this feat has the basic knowledge of how to effectively use a shield. Most of the time, this feat is worthless or even harmful to the classes that need to take it before using a shield. Consider that mages cannot use shields without some of the worst armor penalties, while rogues and monks need their hands free for many of their own activities (bow use, unarmed fighting, etc.). Only those who have a very distinct plan for what they want to do with a character should take this feat.

Silent Spell

Type of Feat: Metamagic

Prerequisite: Ability to cast 1st-level spells

Use: Silenced Spells occupy spell slots one level higher than normal.

Magical expertise allows the casting of certain spells without using a verbal component. This feat does not pay for itself against most opponents, but casters who are worried about being silenced can't live without having several bread and butter spells "memorized" in silent mode. If enemies begin using anti-magic tactics, this is a feat that will come to the front very quickly.

Also, roguish casters will find use in Silenced Spells because they can be cast without giving away the mage's position. If a mage is already hiding successfully, this can be a good way to gain another round or two before enemies figure out what is going on and organize an effective resistance.

Silver Palm

Type of Feat: General

Prerequisite: Can only be taken at 1st level

Use: Automatic

The character gains a +2 bonus on Appraise and Persuade checks.

Skill Focus

Type of Feat: General

Prerequisite: Able to use the skill

Use: Automatic. This feat may be selected multiple times, but the effects do not stack. It applies to a different skill in each case.

A character with this feat is adept at a certain skill, gaining a +3 bonus on all checks with it. Though many of the skill-enhancing feats grant four points (two points to two skills), this one is beneficial for characters who are driven toward one specific ability. Parry is a fitting example for a skill that benefits from this type of power perking.

Snake Blood

Type of Feat: General

Prerequisite: Can only be taken at 1st level

Use: Automatic

Character gains a +2 bonus on Fortitude saving throws against poison and a +1 reflex saving throw bonus on all saves. This feat is not very powerful, but it is an interesting focus for a character's background that a sincere roleplayer might enjoy.

Spell Focus

Type of Feat: General

Prerequisite: Ability to cast 1st-level spells

Use: Automatic. This feat may be selected multiple times, but the effects do not stack. It applies to a different school of magic in each case.

A character with this feat is adept in a certain school of magic, granting a +2 bonus to spell save DC for all spells that the character casts from that school. This makes it more difficult for enemies to resist the effects of spells of this school when the caster casts them.

Spell Penetration

Type of Feat: General

Prerequisite: Ability to cast 1st-level spells

Use: Automatic

A character with this feat can use magic to better pierce the defenses of his opponents, gaining a +2 bonus to caster level checks to beat a creature's spell resistance. This is a good example of a later-level mage feat. Spell focus and meta-magic feats should come first, but this additional bonus to succeed with aggressive spells is useful for negative enchantments and evocation spells.

Spring Attack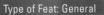

Type of Feat: General

Prerequisite: Dex. 13+, Dodge, Mobility, base attack bonus +4 or higher

Use: Automatic

Moving during combat does not provoke an attack of opportunity. This cannot be used while wearing heavy armor. This feat builds off of Mobility, and it fits very well for characters who move into and around combat with high frequency. Rogues (in their constant pursuits of sneak attacks) are happy to have Spring Attack because it allows people to go for the nasty attacks and retreat when the fighting gets ugly.

Stealthy

Type of Feat: General

Prerequisite: None

Use: Automatic

The character gains a +2 bonus on Hide in Shadows and Move Silently checks. Rogue and roguish classes that are already maxing both their Hide and Move Silently skills are best suited to take this feat. This way, the character can use those skills as if he were two levels higher. Characters who casually use stealth skills are often better served by other feats.

Still Spell

Type of Feat: Metamagic

Prerequisite: Ability to cast 1st-level spells

Use: Stilled Spells occupy spell slots one level higher than normal.

Magical expertise allows certain spells to be cast without gestures, ignoring their somatic component. Any penalties incurred from casting in armor do not apply to a spell that has been prepared by this feat. For mages with a quick multiclass into another field (such as the sorcerer/paladin 18/2 template) this is a wonderful feat. This way, the caster can decide whether to have his best spells memorized and go in without armor, or to don everything and simply cast spells at one level below their normal maximum.

Strong Soul

Type of Feat: General

Prerequisite: Can only be taken at 1st level

Use: Automatic

The character gains a +1 bonus to Fortitude and Will saving throws, as well as +1 bonus to any saving throw versus death magic. For most people, Luck of Heroes would make a lot more sense as a level-one feat. Don't take this unless death magic is a specific fear for a character (or the person can afford two level-one feats for improved saving throws).

Stunning Fist

Type of Feat: General

Prerequisite: Dex 13+, Wis 13+, base attack bonus +8 or higher, Improved Unarmed Strike

Use: Selected. Monks receive this feat free at level 1, even if they do not meet the prerequisites. As well, monks suffer no attack/damage penalties when using this feat and may use it once per day per level. Constructs and Undead are immune to this attack, as are any creatures that are immune to critical hits.

A character with this feat can attempt a disabling strike with a -4 attack penalty and a -4 damage penalty. If successful, they have hit a vulnerable spot, and the target must make a Fortitude save (DC 10 + 1/2 the attacker's level + the attacker's Wisdom modifier) or be held for three rounds. This attack may be used once per day for every four levels of the character.

Thug

Type of Feat: General

Prerequisite: Can only be taken at 1st level

Use: Automatic

The character gains a +2 bonus on Initiative checks and a +2 bonus on Taunt checks. Though Initiative and Taunt have their place in the game, this is a very tough feat to justify since it must be taken so early on.

Toughness

Type of Feat: General

Prerequisite: None

Use: Automatic

A character with this feat is tougher than normal, gaining one bonus hit point per level. Hit points are gained retroactively when choosing this feat. This feat is very powerful for a number of classes, though it obviously has a lot more effect on classes that don't gain a lot of hit points normally (such as wizards, sorcerers, rogues, and bards). Essentially, this is a perfect choice for any character with a free feat to spend.

Two-Weapon Fighting

Type of Feat: General

Prerequisite: None

Required For: Improved Two-Weapon Fighting

Use: The Ambidexterity feat further reduces the attack penalty for the second weapon by 4 (-4/-4). Best results are achieved if the off-hand weapon is light, further reducing the penalty for both the primary and off-hand by 2 (-2/-2). Rangers receive this feat free at 1st level.

A character with this feat reduces the penalties suffered when using a weapon in each hand. The normal penalty of -6 to the primary hand and -10 to the off-hand becomes -4 for the primary hand and -8 for the off-hand. Characters who wish to dual wield are practically forced to take this feat if they want to be useful in battle. The penalties to hit otherwise far outweigh any advantages that a second weapon will provide.

Weapon Finesse

Type of Feat: General

Prerequisite: Base attack bonus +1 or higher

Use: Automatic when using any of the following weapons: dagger, handaxe, kama, kukri, light crossbow, light hammer, mace, rapier, short sword, shuriken, sickle, sling, throwing axe, and unarmed strike.

A character with this feat is adept at using light weapons subtly and effectively, allowing him to calculate attack rolls with his Dexterity modifier bonus instead of his Strength bonus (if his Dexterity is higher than his Strength). Though this won't allow the quick fighter to dish out as much damage as a heavy tank, the high bonus to hit helps to level the playing field for rogue and archer types who can't afford to focus on Strength.

Weapon Focus

Type of Feat: General

Prerequisite: Proficiency with the chosen weapon type, base attack bonus +1 or higher

Required for: Weapon Specialization (fighter only)

Use: Automatic. This feat may be selected multiple times, but the effects do not stack. It applies to a new weapon in each case.

A character with this feat is particularly skilled with a specific weapon, gaining a +1 attack bonus with them. Because this is required for weapon specialization, all classes should take Weapon Focus toward their primary weapons if they ever plan on taking that higher-level feat. As for Weapon Focus's actual bonus, a single point to attack can mean a lot, but other feats should come first for most characters (Rapid Shot for bow users, Power Attack, Knockdown, and other useful skills for melee types).

Weapon Proficiency (Exotic)

Type of Feat: General

Prerequisite: Base attack bonus +1 or higher

Use: Automatic

This feat allows effective use of all exotic weapons. The exotic weapons list includes the dire mace, double axe, kama, katana, kukri, scythe, shuriken, and two-bladed sword.

Weapon Proficiency (Martial)

Type of Feat: General

Prerequisite: None

Use: Barbarians, fighters, paladins, and rangers are automatically proficient with all martial weapons.

This feat allows effective use of all martial weapons. A character cannot equip weapons they are not proficient in using. The martial weapons list includes the bastard sword, battleaxe, greataxe, greatsword, halberd, handaxe, heavy flail, light flail, light hammer, longbow, longsword, rapier, scimitar, short sword, shortbow, throwing axe, and warhammer.

Weapon Proficiency (Simple)

Type of Feat: General

Prerequisite: None

Use: All characters except for druids, monks, rogues, and wizards are automatically proficient with all simple weapons. The spell Tenser's Transformation gives a wizard a temporary proficiency with all simple weapons.

This feat allows effective use of all simple weapons, including club, dagger, mace, sickle, spear, morningstar, quarterstaff, light crossbow, dart, sling, and heavy crossbow. A character cannot equip weapons they are not proficient in using.

Weapon Specialization

Type of Feat: Special

Prerequisite: Four Levels dedicated to Fighter training, Weapon Focus in the chosen weapon type

Use: This feat may be selected multiple times, but the effects do not stack. It applies to a new weapon in each case, so long as that group is already associated with Weapon Focus.

A character with this feat has trained especially hard with a specific weapon group, gaining a +2 damage bonus with that category. Though two extra points of damage are not enough to bring down creatures in a single swipe, this skill has incredible importance even in the later levels of the game. Over multiple attacks, this feat gives an edge to characters that is highly noticeable. Many combat-oriented templates are worth devoting some time and levels into fighter so that weapon specialization becomes available.

This feat is more specific than it used to be in the original *Neverwinter Nights* release. Instead of requiring +4 for a character's Base Attack Bonus and a single level of fighter (chosen when the person wants to grab the feat), Bioware has shored up the system. Now, everyone who wants to take Weapon Specialization must gain at least four levels as a fighter. This is a good limitation and it promotes the intense fighter regimen of training!

Zen Archery

Type of Feat: General

Prerequisite: Base attack Bonus +3, Wisdom 13 or higher

Use: Automatic

Wisdom guides the character's ranged attacks, letting her use her Wisdom modifier instead of her Dexterity when firing ranged weapons. There are some monk and cleric templates that might find substantial use for this skill, though these are classes that are often strapped for spare feats.

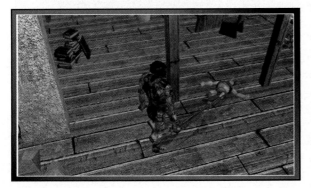

Spells

This section lists all of the spells that are available to casters in *Shadows of Undrentide*. Both the original *Neverwinter Nights* spells and the exclusive expansion pack spells have been provided so that players can get a realistic feel for what each class allows.

BARD SPELLS

Bardic magic covers a number of schools that are taken out of the greater systems of magic. Bards can heal a little, enchant their allies and enemies, and do a very minor bit of battle evocation. This is a good school of magic for people who want to have a bit of everything at their disposal.

0-Level Bard Spells

Cure Minor Wounds: Heal 4 points of damage.

Daze: If 5 HD or less, target is dazed.

Flare: A burst of hot light is fired from the caster to one target, making it suffer a –1 penalty to attack rolls.

Light: Create a small light source.

Resistance: +1 bonus to all saving throws.

1st-Level Bard Spells

Amplify: The caster or a target gains a +20 bonus to Listen checks.

Balagarn's Iron Horn: The caster creates a deep, resonant vibration that shakes all creatures in the area of effect from their feet if they fail a Strength check (as if the caster had a Strength of 20). Every creature that falls will be knocked down for 1 round.

Charm Person: 50% bonus in target's personal reputation to caster.

Cure Light Wounds: 1d8 points of damage + 1/level healed.

Expeditious Retreat: Caster boosts his or her normal movement rate by 150%, allowing him or her to flee from dangerous encounters.

Grease: Slows or knocks down opponents.

Identify: Gain a 25 + 1 per caster level bonus to Lore skill.

Lesser Dispel: Weak version of Dispel Magic.

Mage Armor: +4 AC bonus.

Protection from Alignment: Target receives +2 AC bonus, +2 saving throw bonus against creatures of a particular alignment.

Scare: Causes Fear in weak creatures.

Sleep: Causes 2d4 HD of creatures to fall asleep.

Summon Creature I: Summons a dire badger.

2nd-Level Bard Spells

Blindness/Deafness: The target creature is struck blind and deaf.

Bull's Strength: Target creature's Strength is increased by 1d4+1.

Cat's Grace: The target creature's Dexterity is increased by 1d4+1.

Clarity: Removes sleep, confusion, stun, and charm effects and protects against same.

Cure Moderate Wounds: Heal 2d8 points of damage + 1/level.

Darkness: Cover creatures in a shroud of darkness.

Eagle's Splendor: Target's Charisma increases by 1d4 +1.

Fox's Cunning: Target's Intelligence increases by 1d4 +1.

Ghostly Visage: 10/+2 damage reduction; immune to level 1 spells or lower.

Hold Person: Target humanoid is paralyzed.

Invisibility: Target invisible until attacks or casts a spell.

Owl's Wisdom: Target's Wisdom increases by 1d4 + 1.

See Invisibility: Target creature is able to see all invisible creatures.

Silence: Creates a zone of silence around target creature.

Sound Burst: 1d8 sonic damage to creatures in area.

Summon Creature II: Summons a dire boar.

Ultravision: Darkvision and low-light vision.

3rd-Level Bard Spells

Bestow Curse: Lowers all of the target creature's ability scores by 2.

Charm Monster: 50% bonus in target's personal reputation to caster.

Clairaudience/Clairvoyance: Target gains +10 bonus to Spot and Listen checks.

Confusion: Target behaves erratically.

Cure Serious Wounds: Heal 3d8 points of damage +1/level.

Dispel Magic: Remove magical effects from creatures.

Fear: Make enemies run away.

Find Traps: +10 to Search checks.

Haste: One extra attack action per round and movement is increased by 50%.

Invisibility Sphere: Self and allies hidden in a sphere of invisibility.

Magic Circle Against Alignment: Caster and all nearby allies gain +2 AC, +2 saving throws and immunity to mind-affecting spells from the specified alignment.

Remove Curse: All curses removed from target.

Remove Disease: All diseases removed from target.

Slow: Target movement rate lowered by 50%.

Summon Creature III: Summons a dire wolf.

Remove Paralysis: All paralysis and hold effects removed from target.

Resist Elements: 20/- damage resistance against all elemental forms of damage.

Silence: Creates a zone of silence around target creature.

Sound Burst: 1d8 sonic damage to creatures in area.

Wounding Whispers: The caster is surrounded with whispers that injure any creature that hits the caster for 1d8 points of sonic damage.

4th-Level Bard Spells

Cure Critical Wounds: Heals 4d8 points of damage +1 per caster level.

Dismissal: All associates of target are unsummoned.

Dominate Person: Target temporarily becomes under the caster's control.

Hold Monster: Target monster is paralyzed.

Improved Invisibility: Attack and cast spells while remaining concealed.

Legend Lore: +10 bonus to Lore checks, +1 per 2 caster levels.

Neutralize Poison: Target cured, if poisoned.

Summon Creature IV: Summons a dire spider.

War Cry: +2 bonus to attack and damage for allies; all enemies are stricken with fear.

5th-Level Bard Spells

Ethereal Visage: 20/+3 damage reduction and immunity to spells of 2nd level and lower.

Greater Dispelling: More powerful version of Dispel Magic.

Healing Circle: All friends nearby heal for 1d8 + 1 point per caster level.

Mind Fog: -10 penalty on Will saving throws while in the fog.

Summon Creature V: Summons a dire tiger.

6th-Level Bard Spells

Dirge: The caster's song draws the energies of death and destruction. Any enemies in the area of effect suffer 2 points of Strength and Dexterity ability score damage each round.

Energy Buffer: Target gains damage resistance 40/- against elemental damage.

Ice Storm: 3d6 bludgeoning and 2d6 cold damage.

Mass Haste: All nearby allies gain one extra attack action per round and a 50% increase in movement speed.

Summon Creature VI: Summons a dire bear.

CLERIC SPELLS

Clerics have some of the best enchantment spells in the game (buff magic) and they possess the best healing ability in the land. In addition, clerics even have some decent battle magic. Clerics are usually a few levels behind wizards in terms of inflicting damage with their spells, but the buffs and healing more than make up for this deficiency.

0-Level Cleric Spells

Cure Minor Wounds: Heals 4 points of damage.

Inflict Minor Wounds: If the caster succeeds in striking an opponent with a touch attack, the target suffers 1 point of damage.

Light: Creates a small light source.

Resistance: +1 bonus to all saving throws.

Virtue: 1 temporary hit point.

1st-Level Cleric Spells

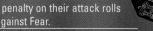

Bane: Caster's enemies are filled with fear and doubt. They suffer a –1 penalty on their attack rolls and on saving throws against Fear.

Bless: +1 attack and damage for all allies near caster.

Cure Light Wounds: 1d8 points of damage + 1/level healed.

Divine Favor: Caster gains a +1 bonus to attack and weapon damage rolls for every three caster levels (at least +1, to a maximum of +5).

Doom: Target receives -2 modifier to attack and damage rolls; saving throws, ability checks, and skill checks are also given a -2 penalty.

Endure Elements: Target creature gains damage resistance 10/– against all elemental forms of damage. The spell ends after absorbing 20 points of damage from any single elemental type.

Entropic Shield: A magical field appears around the caster, granting the caster a 20 percent miss chance against all ranged attacks.

Inflict Light Wounds: Target suffers 1d8 points of damage if the caster succeeds in striking an opponent with a touch attack.

Protection from Alignment: Target receives +2 AC bonus and +2 saving throw bonus against creatures of a particular alignment.

Remove Fear: All fear effects are removed from target.

Sanctuary: Caster's presence is ignored by nearby creatures.

Scare: Causes Fear in weak creatures.

Shield of Faith: Target gains a +2 deflection bonus to his/her armor class, with an additional +1 bonus for every six levels of the caster (maximum of +5).

Summon Creature I: Summons a dire badger.

2nd-Level Cleric Spells

Aid: Target receives +1 bonus to attacks and saving throws versus Fear; +1d8 hit points.

Bull's Strength: Target creature's Strength increases by 1d4+1.

Cure Moderate Wounds: Heals 2d8 points of damage + 1/level.

Darkness: Covers creatures in a shroud of darkness.

Eagle's Splendor: Target's Charisma increases by 1d4 +1.

Endurance: Target's Constitution increases by 1d4 + 1.

Find Traps: +10 to Search checks.

Fox's Cunning: Target's Intelligence increases by 1d4 +1.

Hold Person: Paralyzes target humanoid.

Inflict Moderate Wounds: Target suffers 2d8 points of damage if the caster succeeds in striking an opponent with a touch attack.

2nd-Level Cleric Spells

Lesser Dispel: Weaker version of Dispel Magic.

Lesser Restoration: Removes all effects that apply ability score, AC, attack, damage, spell resistance or saving throw penalties.

Negative Energy Ray: 1d6 points of damage from negative energy ray.

Owl's Wisdom: Target's Wisdom increases by 1d4 + 1.

3rd-Level Cleric Spells

Animate Dead: Summons forth an undead minion.

Bestow Curse: Lowers all of the target creature's ability scores by 2.

Blindness/Deafness: Target creature is struck blind and deaf.

Clarity: Removes sleep, confusion, stun, and charm effects. Also protects against the same.

Contagion: Random disease afflicts target.

Continual Flame: Creates a magical flame that burns until dispelled.

Cure Serious Wounds: Heals 3d8 points of damage +1/level.

Dispel Magic: Removes magical effects from creatures.

Inflict Serious Wounds: The target suffers 3d8 points of damage if the caster succeeds in striking an opponent with a touch attack.

Invisibility Purge: Removes all invisibility from nearby creatures.

Magic Circle Against Alignment: Caster and all nearby allies gain +2 AC, +2 saving throws, and immunity to mind-affecting spells from the specified alignment.

Negative Energy Protection: Target becomes immune to all negative energy attacks.

Prayer: Allies gain +1 to attack, damage, skill, and saving throw rolls; enemies receive -1 penalty to the same.

Protection From Elements: 30/- damage resistance against all elemental forms of damage.

Remove Blindness/Deafness: All nearby allies cured of blindness and deafness.

Remove Curse: All curses removed from target.

Remove Disease: All diseases removed from target.

Searing Light: Undead suffer 1d8/level, Constructs suffer 1d6/level, while others suffer 1d8 per 2 caster levels.

Summon Creature III: Summons a dire wolf.

4th-Level Cleric Spells

Cure Critical Wounds: Heals 4d8 points of damage +1 per caster level.

Death Ward: Target becomes immune to any death spells or effects.

Dismissal: All associates of target are un-summoned.

Divine Power: Cleric gains bonus hit points, Strength becomes 18, and attack bonus improves.

Freedom of Movement: Target becomes immune to paralysis.

Hammer of the Gods: 1d8 damage per 2 caster levels.

Inflict Critical Wounds: The target suffers 4d8 points of damage if the caster succeeds in striking an opponent with a touch attack.

Neutralize Poison: Target is cured if poisoned.

Poison: Inflicts Blue Whinnis poison on target.

Restoration: Removes most effects, including level drain and blindness.

Summon Creature IV: Summons a dire spider.

5th-Level Cleric Spells

Circle of Doom: All enemies within the area of effect are struck with negative energy that causes 1d8 points of damage, +1 point per caster level. Negative energy spells have a reverse effect on the undead, healing them instead of harming them.

Flame Strike: 1d6 fire and divine damage/level.

Healing Circle: All nearby allies heal for 1d8 + 1 point per caster level.

Raise Dead: Returns one target corpse to life.

Slay Living: Target must make Fortitude save or die.

Spell Resistance: 12 +1 per caster level spell resistance.

Summon Creature V: Summons a dire tiger.

True Seeing: Ability to see through Sanctuary and Invisibility spells.

6th-Level Cleric Spells

Banishment: Caster destroys all summoned creatures, familiars, animal companions and Outsiders in the area of effect. Caster can banish the number of creatures equal to twice the caster's level in HD.

Blade Barrier: Creates a wall of blades; 1d6/level damage.

Create Undead: Creates one undead creature.

Greater Sanctuary: Caster becomes ethereal; no other creature can detect the caster. Attacking or performing a hostile action dispels Greater Sanctuary.

Greater Dispelling: More powerful version of Dispel Magic.

Harm: Target reduced to 1d4 hit points.

Heal: Target is fully healed.

Planar Ally: An Outsider is summoned to assist the caster. The type of Outsider varies with the caster's alignment.

Summon Creature VI: Summons a dire bear.

7th-Level Cleric Spells

Destruction: Target must save or die.

Greater Restoration: Removes most temporary and all permanent negative effects.

Regenerate: Restores 6 hit points every round.

Resurrection: Returns a single target corpse to life with full hit points.

Summon Creature VII: Summons a huge elemental of random type.

Word of Faith: Enemies are stunned or killed.

8th-Level Cleric Spells

Aura Versus Alignment: +4 AC, immunity to mind-affecting spells, and SR 25 against creatures of the specified alignment.

Create Greater Undead: Creates a powerful undead creature.

Earthquake: Caster causes a massive earthquake around himself/herself, causing 1d6 points of damage per caster level (to a maximum of 10d6) to all creatures in the area of effect. The earthquake doesn't affect the caster.

Fire Storm: Rain of fire; 1d6 damage/level.

Mass Heal: All nearby allies are fully healed.

Summon Creature VIII: Summons a greater elemental of random type.

Sunbeam: 1d6 damage/level to undead; 3d6 damage to others.

9th-Level Cleric Spells

Energy Drain: Target temporarily gains 2d4 negative levels.

Gate: Summons forth a Balor.

Implosion: Kills all living things within area of effect.

Storm of Vengeance: 3d6 acid damage each round.

Summon Creature IX: Summons an elder elemental of random type.

Undeath's Eternal Foe: All allies in the area of effect receive the following bonuses: immunity to negative damage, immunity to level/energy drain, immunity to ability score decreases, immunity to poisons, and immunity to diseases.

DRUID SPELLS

Druid magic would resemble clerical magic if it were filtered through the realm of nature. Druids still excel at healing and buffing their allies, but their combat magic has a much more elemental and terrestrial base to it. At higher levels, these masters of the land can transform into creatures with incredible power.

0-Level Druid Spells

Cure Minor Wounds: Heals 4 points of damage.

Flare: Caster fires a burst of hot light to one target, making it suffer a −1 penalty to attack rolls.

Light: Creates a small light source.

Resistance: +1 bonus to all saving throws.

Virtue: 1 temporary hit point.

1st-Level Druid Spells

Camouflage: Caster's coloring changes to match the surroundings, gaining a +10 competence bonus to any Hide checks.

Cure Light Wounds: 1d8 points of damage + 1/level healed.

Endure Elements: 10/- damage resistance against all elemental forms of damage.

Entangle: Traps enemies with clinging vegetation.

Grease: Slows or knocks down opponents.

Magic Fang: Strengthens the caster's animal companion, giving it +1 to hit and +1 to damage. It also grants the creature damage reduction of 1/+1 and the ability to strike as if it were a +1 weapon (so it can bypass other creatures' damage reduction).

Sleep: Causes 2d4 HD of creatures to fall asleep.

Summon Creature I: Summons a dire badger.

Ultravision: Darkvision and low-light vision.

2nd-Level Druid Spells

Barkskin: Hardens the target creature's skin, improving Armor Class.

Blood Frenzy: Caster enters a rage similar to that of a Barbarian. Caster gains a +2 bonus to Strength and Constitution and a +1 bonus to Will saves, while suffering a −1 penalty to AC.

Bull's Strength: Target creature's Strength increases by 1d4+1.

Charm Person or Animal: 50% bonus in target's personal reputation to caster.

Flame Lash: 2d6 fire damage + 1d6 per caster level above 3.

Hold Animal: Paralyzes target animal.

Lesser Dispel: Weaker version of Dispel Magic

Lesser Restoration: Removes all effects that apply ability score, AC, attack, damage, spell resistance, or saving throw penalties.

One With the Land: Caster forges a strong link with nature, gaining a +3 competence bonus to Animal Empathy, Hide, Move Silently, and Set Trap skills.

Resist Elements: 20/- damage resistance against all elemental forms of damage.

Summon Creature II: Summons a dire boar.

3rd-Level Druid Spells

Call Lightning: 1d6/level damage from bolt of lightning.

Contagion: Random disease inflicts target.

Cure Moderate Wounds: Heals 2d8 points of damage + 1/level.

Dominate Animal: Caster temporarily gains control of target animal.

Greater Magic Fang: Strengthens the caster's animal companion, giving it +1 to hit and +1 damage for every three levels of the caster (maximum of +5/+5). It also grants the creature damage reduction and enchantment bonus equal to the hit/damage bonus given.

Neutralize Poison: Target is cured if poisoned.

Poison: Inflicts Blue Whinnis poison on target.

Protection From Elements: 30/- damage resistance against all elemental forms of damage.

Quillfire: Caster throws poisonous quills at a target, causing 2d8 points of damage. It also inflicts Scorpion Venom on the target.

Remove Disease: All diseases removed from target.

Spike Growth: Covers the terrain with small spikes. Any creature suffers 1d4 points of damage each round that they remain within the afflicted area. These spikes can damage the victim's legs, so that even when they are free of the spike growth, their movement rate is slowed for a day.

Summon Creature III: Summons a dire wolf.

4th-Level Druid Spells

Cure Serious Wounds: Heals 3d8 points of damage +1/level.

Dispel Magic: Removes magic effects from creatures.

Flame Strike: 1d6 fire and divine damage/level.

Freedom of Movement: Target becomes immune to paralysis.

Hold Monster: Target monster is paralyzed.

Mass Camouflage: All allies in the area of effect gain a +10 bonus to their Hide skill.

Stoneskin: 10/+5 points of damage reduction.

Summon Creature IV: Summons a dire spider.

5th-Level Druid Spells

Awaken: Animal companion is temporarily improved.

Cure Critical Wounds: Heals 4d8 points of damage +1 per caster level.

Death Ward: Target becomes immune to any death spells or effects.

Ice Storm: 3d6 bludgeoning and 2d6 cold damage.

Inferno: Caster causes a target to ignite into flame. Each round, the target suffers 2d6 points of fire damage.

Owl's Insight: Target gains an enhancement bonus to Wisdom equal to half the caster's level.

Slay Living: Target must make Fortitude save or die.

Spell Resistance: 12 +1 per caster level spell resistance.

Summon Creature V: Summons a dire tiger.

Wall of Fire: 4d6 points of fire damage.

6th-Level Druid Spells

Drown: Caster creates water in the lungs of a target creature. Any drowned creature loses all but 1 HP; only living creatures are affected.

Energy Buffer: Target gains damage resistance 40/- against elemental damage.

Greater Dispelling: More powerful version of Dispel Magic.

Greater Stoneskin: 20/+5 damage reduction.

Healing Circle: All nearby allies heal for 1d8 + 1 point per caster level.

Regenerate: Restores 6 hit points every round.

Summon Creature VI: Summons a dire bear.

7th-Level Druid Spells

Aura of Vitality: All allies within the area of effect receive a +4 bonus to Strength, Constitution, and Dexterity.

Creeping Doom: Carpet of insects attacks at caster's command.

Fire Storm: Rain of fire; 1d6 damage/level.

Harm: Target reduced to 1d4 hit points.

Heal: Target is fully healed.

Summon Creature VII: Summons a huge elemental of random type.

True Seeing: Ability to see through Sanctuary and Invisibility spells.

8th-Level Druid Spells

Bombardment: Rocks fall from the sky, inflicting 1d8 points of damage per caster level (max 10d8) to all enemies in the area.

Finger of Death: Target dies.

Nature's Balance: Lowers enemies' spell resistance by 1d4 per 5 levels of the caster; heals allies.

Premonition: Damage reduction of 30/+5.

Summon Creature VIII: Summons a greater elemental of random type.

Sunbeam: 1d6 damage/level to undead; 3d6 damage to others.

Sunburst: A brilliant explosion occurs where the caster directs, causing 1d6 points of damage per caster level to all undead creatures to a maximum of 25d6 (6d6 points of damage to creatures that are not undead). Vampires are destroyed instantly if they fail a Reflex saving throw. All enemies in the area of effect must also make a successful Reflex saving throw or be blinded permanently (the blindness can only be magically removed).

9th-Level Druid Spells

Earthquake: Caster causes a massive earthquake around himself/herself, causing 1d6 points of damage per caster level (to a maximum of 10d6) to all creatures in the area of effect. The earthquake doesn't affect the caster.

Elemental Swarm: One 24 HD Elemental under control of Druid.

Mass Heal: All allies nearby are fully healed.

Shapechange: Ability to transform into a dragon, giant, Balor, slaad, or golem.

Storm of Vengeance: 3d6 acid damage each round.

Summon Creature IX: Summons an elder elemental of random type.

PALADIN SPELLS

Paladins are warriors of faith far more than casters of divine magic. Instead, paladins' magic is supplementary, adding to their ability to stay in battle and inflict more damage against enemies of light and purity.

1st-Level Paladin Spells

Bless: +1 attack and damage for all allies near caster.

Cure Light Wounds: 1d8 points of damage + 1/level healed.

Divine Favor: Caster gains a +1 bonus to attack and weapon damage rolls for every three caster levels (at least +1, to a maximum of +5).

Endure Elements: Target creature gains damage resistance 10/– against all elemental forms of damage. The spell ends after absorbing 20 points of damage from any single elemental type.

Entropic Shield: A magical field appears around the caster, granting the caster a 20% miss chance against all ranged attacks.

Protection from Alignment: Target receives +2 AC bonus and +2 saving throw bonus against creatures of a particular alignment.

Resistance: +1 bonus to all saving throws.

Virtue: 1 temporary hit point.

2nd-Level Paladin Spells

Aid: Target receives +1 bonus to attacks and saving throws versus fear; +1d8 hit points.

Aura of Glory: Bonus to Charisma; cures allies and bolsters them against Fear.

Bull's Strength: Target creature's Strength increases by 1d4+1.

Eagle's Splendor: Target's Charisma increases by 1d4 +1.

Remove Paralysis: All paralysis and hold effects removed from target.

Resist Elements: 20/- damage resistance against all elemental forms of damage.

3rd-Level Paladin Spells

Cure Moderate Wounds: Heals 2d8 points of damage + 1/level.

Dispel Magic: Removes magical effects from creatures.

Magic Circle Against Alignment: Caster and all nearby allies gain +2 AC, +2 saving throws, and immunity to mind-affecting spells from the specified alignment.

Prayer: Allies gain +1 to attack, damage, skill, and saving throw rolls; enemies receive -1 penalty to the same.

Remove Blindness/Deafness: All nearby allies cured of blindness and deafness.

4th-Level Paladin Spells

Cure Serious Wounds: Heals 3d8 points of damage +1/level.

Death Ward: Target becomes immune to any death spells or effects.

Freedom of Movement: Target becomes immune to paralysis.

Neutralize Poison: Target is cured if poisoned.

RANGER SPELLS

Rangers, like paladins, are a class of warriors with a mix of magic in their blood. These characters take a note from the realm of druidic magic, and their enchantments blend a bit of healing with various natural spells.

1st-Level Ranger Spells

Camouflage: Caster's coloring changes to match the surroundings, gaining a +10 competence bonus to any Hide checks.

Cure Light Wounds: 1d8 points of damage + 1/level healed.

Entangle: Traps enemies with clinging vegetation.

Grease: Slows or knocks down opponents.

Magic Fang: Strengthens the caster's animal companion, giving it +1 to hit and +1 to damage. It also grants the creature damage reduction of 1/+1 and the ability to strike as if it were a +1 weapon (so it can bypass other creature's damage reduction).

Summon Creature I: Summons a dire badger.

Ultravision: Darkvision and low-light vision.

2nd-Level Ranger Spells

Cat's Grace: Target creature's Dexterity increases by 1d4+1.

Hold Animal: Target animal is paralyzed.

One With the Land: Caster forges a strong link with nature, gaining a +3 competence bonus to Animal Empathy, Hide, Move Silently, and Set Trap skills.

Protection From Elements: 30/- damage resistance against all elemental forms of damage.

Sleep: Causes 2d4 HD of creatures to fall asleep.

Summon Creature II: Summons a dire boar.

3rd-Level Ranger Spells

Aid: Target receives +1 bonus to attacks and saving throws versus fear; +1d8 hit points.

Cure Moderate Wounds: Heals 2d8 points of damage + 1/level.

Greater Magic Fang: Strengthens the caster's animal companion, giving it +1 to hit and +1 to damage for every three levels of the caster (maximum of +5). It also grants the creature damage reduction and enchantment bonus equal to the hit/damage bonus given.

Invisibility Purge: Removes all invisibility from nearby creatures.

Neutralize Poison: Target is cured if poisoned.

Remove Disease: All diseases removed from target.

Summon Creature III: Summons a dire wolf.

4th-Level Ranger Spells

Cure Serious Wounds: Heals 3d8 points of damage +1/level.

Freedom of Movement: Target becomes immune to Paralysis.

Mass Camouflage: All allies in the area of effect gain a +10 bonus to their Hide skills.

Polymorph Self: Caster can turn into a pixie, troll, umber hulk, giant spider, or zombie.

Summon Creature IV: Summons a dire spider.

SORCERER/WIZARD SPELLS

Sorcerers and Wizards are the damage dealers of the magical world. Through a heavy mix of enchantments to aid allies and beguile enemies, they also are quite adept at confusing and disrupting others while protecting their own. When it comes time to draw upon the elements, these casters can level entire battlefields with spells of legendary power.

0-Level Sorcerer/Wizard Spells

Acid Splash: Caster fires a small orb of acid at the target for 1d3 points of acid damage.

Daze (Enchantment): If 5 HD or less, target is dazed.

Electric Jolt: The caster causes 1d3 points of electrical damage to a target.

Flare: Caster fires a burst of hot light to one target, making it suffer a -1 penalty to attack rolls.

Light (Evocation): Creates a small light source.

Ray of Frost (Conjuration): 1d4 cold damage.

Resistance (Abjuration): +1 bonus to all saving throws.

1st-Level Sorcerer/Wizard Spells

Burning Hands (Transmutation): 1d4/level fire damage from cone of fire.

Charm Person (Enchantment): 50% bonus in target's personal reputation to caster.

Color Spray (Illusion): Blinds, stuns, or knocks creatures unconscious.

Endure Elements (Abjuration): 10/- damage resistance against all elemental forms of damage.

Expeditious Retreat: Caster boosts his or her normal movement rate by 150%, allowing him or her to flee from dangerous encounters.

Grease (Conjuration): Slows or knocks down opponents.

Identify (Divination): Gain a 25 + 1 per caster level bonus to Lore skill checks.

Mage Armor (Conjuration): +4 AC bonus.

Magic Missile (Evocation): 1 missile every 2 levels; each missile causes 1d4 + 1 damage.

Negative Energy Ray (Necromancy): 1d6 points of damage from negative energy ray.

Protection From Alignment (Abjuration): Target receives +2 AC bonus, +2 saving throw bonus against creatures of a particular alignment.

Ray of Enfeeblement (Necromancy): 1d6 Strength damage.

Scare (Necromancy): Causes Fear in weak creatures.

Shield: Caster gains a +4 bonus to AC and a +3 bonus to Reflex saves. The caster is also immune to magic missiles for the duration of the spell.

Sleep (Enchantment): Causes 2d4 HD of creatures to fall asleep.

Summon Creature I (Conjuration): Summons a dire badger.

True Strike: Caster gains a +20 bonus to attack rolls through magical intuition.

65

2nd-Level Sorcerer/Wizard Spells

Balagarn's Iron Horn: The caster creates a deep, resonant vibration that shakes all creatures in the area of effect from their feet if they fail a Strength check (as if the caster had a Strength of 20). Every creature that falls will be knocked down for one round.

Blindness/Deafness (Enchantment): Target creature is struck blind and deaf.

Bull's Strength (Transmutation): Target creature's Strength increases by 1d4+1.

Cat's Grace (Transmutation): The target creature's Dexterity increases by 1d4+1.

Continual Flame: Creates a magical flame that burns until dispelled.

Darkness (Evocation): Covers creatures in a shroud of darkness.

Eagle's Splendor (Transmutation): Target's Charisma increases by 1d4 +1.

Endurance (Transmutation): Target's Constitution increases by 1d4 + 1.

Fox's Cunning (Transmutation): Target's Intelligence increases by 1d4 +1.

Ghostly Visage (Illusion): 10/+2 damage reduction; immune to 0- and 1st-level spells.

Ghoul Touch (Necromancy): Paralyzes target with touch attack.

Invisibility (Illusion): The target becomes invisible until she attacks or casts a spell.

Knock (Transmutation): Ability to unlock doors and containers.

Lesser Dispel (Abjuration): Weaker version of Dispel Magic

Melf's Acid Arrow (Conjuration): Acid bolt inflicts 3d6 damage plus 1d6 per round until spell expires.

Owl's Wisdom (Transmutation): Target's Wisdom increases by 1d4 + 1.

Resist Elements (Abjuration): 20/- damage resistance against all elemental forms of damage.

See Invisibility (Divination): Target creature can see all invisible creatures.

Summon Creature II (Conjuration): Summons a dire boar.

Tasha's Hideous Laughter: If the target fails a saving throw, he will start to laugh. This makes the target unable to move or defend until the spell wears off.

Ultravision (Transmutation): Darkvision and low-light vision.

Web (Conjuration): Traps enemies in a web.

3rd-Level Sorcerer/Wizard Spells

Clairaudience/Clairvoyance (Divination): Target gains +10 bonus to Spot and Listen checks.

Clarity (Necromancy): Removes sleep, confusion, stun, and charm effects and protects against the same.

Dispel Magic (Abjuration): Removes magical effects from creatures.

Displacement: Target gains 50% concealment through the caster's ability to emulate the natural abilities of the displacer beast.

Find Traps (Divination): +10 to Search checks.

Fireball (Evocation): 1d6 fire damage/level.

Flame Arrow (Conjuration): 4d6 damage per fire arrow; 1 arrow every 4 levels.

Gust of Wind: Creates a blast of air that knocks down any creatures failing their saving throws. It is also powerful enough to disperse any area of effect effects (such as Cloudkill) that are in the path of the wind gust.

Haste (Transmutation): One extra attack action per round; movement increases by 50%.

Hold Person (Enchantment): Paralyzes target humanoid.

Invisibility Sphere (Illusion): Self and allies hidden in a sphere of invisibility.

Lightning Bolt (Evocation): 1d6 points of electricity damage/level.

Magic Circle Against Alignment (Abjuration): Caster and all nearby allies gain +2 AC, +2 saving throws and immunity to mind-affecting spells from the specified alignment.

Negative Energy Burst (Necromancy): 1d8 points of negative energy damage + 1 per level.

Protection from Elements (Abjuration): 30/- damage resistance against all elemental forms of damage.

Slow (Transmutation): Lowers target movement rate by 50%.

Stinking Cloud (Conjuration): Creatures are dazed and nauseated.

Summon Creature III (Conjuration): Summons a dire wolf.

Vampiric Touch (Necromancy): 1d6 damage for every two caster levels.

4th-Level Sorcerer/Wizard Spells

Bestow Curse (Transmutation): Lowers all of the target creature's ability scores by two.

Charm Monster (Enchantment): 50% bonus in target's personal reputation to caster.

Confusion (Enchantment): Target behaves erratically.

Contagion (Necromancy): Random disease inflicts target.

Elemental Shield (Evocation): A ring of fire damages attackers and grants 50% cold/fire resistance to caster.

Enervation (Necromancy): Target temporarily gains 1d4 negative levels.

Evard's Black Tentacles (Conjuration): Traps and attacks enemies with tentacles.

Fear (Necromancy): Makes enemies run away.

Ice Storm (Evocation): 3d6 bludgeoning and 2d6 cold damage.

Isaac's Lesser Missile Storm: Each creature in the targeted area of effect is hit by 1 magic missile for every 2 levels of the caster (max of 10 missiles). Each missile causes 1d6 points of damage.

Improved Invisibility (Illusion): Attack and cast spells while remaining concealed.

Lesser Spell Breach (Abjuration): Strips an enemy mage of up to three defenses.

Minor Globe of Invulnerability (Abjuration): Prevents all 3rd-level and lower spells from affecting caster.

Phantasmal Killer (Illusion): Kills the target.

Polymorph Self (Transmutation): Caster can turn himself/herself into a pixie, troll, umber hulk, giant spider, or zombie.

Remove Blindness/Deafness (Divination): All nearby allies cured of blindness and deafness.

Remove Curse (Abjuration): All curses removed from target.

Shadow Conjuration (Illusion): Ability to conjure one of Darkness, Invisibility, Mage Armor, Magic Missile, or Summon Shadow.

Stoneskin (Abjuration): 10/+5 points of damage reduction.

Summon Creature IV (Conjuration): Summons a dire spider.

Wall of Fire (Evocation): 4d6 points of fire damage.

5th-Level Sorcerer/Wizard Spells

Animate Dead (Necromancy): Summons forth an undead minion.

Bigby's Interposing Hand: A giant hand appears over the target, making it difficult for him/her to attack. Target receives a −10 penalty to all attack rolls for the duration of the spell.

Cloudkill (Conjuration): Kills 3 HD or less creatures; 4-6 HD creatures must save or die.

Cone of Cold (Evocation): 1d6 cold damage/level.

Dismissal (Abjuration): All associates of target are un-summoned.

Dominate Person (Enchantment): Target temporarily becomes under the caster's control.

Energy Buffer (Abjuration): Target gains damage resistance 40/- against elemental damage.

Feeblemind (Divination): 1d4 points of Intelligence damage/level to target.

Firebrand: Masses of flame fly from the caster, striking 1 target per level of the caster. Each mass of flame explodes, inflicting 1d6 points of damage per level (max of 15d6) to all targets in the area of impact.

Greater Shadow Conjuration (Illusion): Conjures a shadow variant of a variety of spells.

Hold Monster (Enchantment): Paralyzes target monster.

Lesser Mind Blank (Abjuration): Renders target immune to mind-affecting spells; removes any current mind-affecting spells.

Lesser Planar Binding (Conjuration): Control or summon an outsider.

Lesser Spell Mantle (Abjuration): Absorbs up to 1d4 + 6 levels of spells.

Mind Fog (Enchantment): -10 penalty on Will saving throws while in the fog.

Summon Creature V (Conjuration): Summons a dire tiger.

6th-Level Sorcerer/Wizard Spells

Acid Fog (Conjuration): Slows creatures within fog and deals acid damage.

Bigby's Forceful Hand: A giant hand appears and attempts to stop and knock down one target. The hand gains a +14 bonus on the Strength check.

Chain Lightning (Evocation): 1d6 damage/level; secondary bolts.

Circle of Death (Necromancy): Kills 1d4 creatures/level.

Ethereal Visage: 20/+3 damage reduction and immunity to spells of 2nd-level or lower.

Globe of Invulnerability (Abjuration): Immunity to spells of 4th-level or lower.

Greater Dispelling (Abjuration): More powerful Dispel Magic.

Greater Spell Breach (Abjuration): Strips an enemy mage of up to six magical defenses.

Greater Stoneskin (Transmutation): 20/+5 damage reduction.

Isaac's Greater Missile Storm: Each creature in the targeted area of effect is hit by 1 magic missile for every 2 levels of the caster (max of 20 missiles). Each missile causes 3d6 points of damage.

Legend Lore (Divination): +10 bonus to Lore checks, +1 per 2 caster levels.

Mass Haste (Enchantment): All nearby allies gain one extra attack action per round and a 50% increase in movement speed.

Planar Binding (Conjuration): Summon or control an outsider.

Shades (Illusion): Ability to conjure a shadow variant of Cold of Cone, Fireball, Stoneskin, Wall of Fire, or Summon Shadow.

Summon Creature VI (Conjuration): Summons a dire bear.

Tenser's Transformation (Transmutation): Caster becomes physically powerful.

True Seeing (Divination): Ability to see through Sanctuary and Invisibility spells.

7th-Level Sorcerer/Wizards Spells

Banishment: Caster destroys all summoned creatures, familiars, animal companions and Outsiders in the area of effect. A number of creatures equal to twice the caster's level in HD can be banished.

Bigby's Grasping Hand: A giant hand appears and attacks the target. If the hand hits and succeeds in a grapple check, the opponent is held for the duration of the spell.

Control Undead (Necromancy): Ability to dominate one undead creature.

Delayed Blast Fireball (Evocation): 1d8 fire damage/level; can delay blast until target enters zone.

Finger of Death (Necromancy): Target dies.

Mordenkainen's Sword (Transmutation): Summons a powerful sword-wielding creature.

Power Word, Stun (Divination): Automatically stuns a single target.

Prismatic Spray (Evocation): Random effects ranging from damage to death.

Protection From Spells (Enchantment): +8 bonus on all saving throws against spells.

Shadow Shield (Illusion): Gain +5 AC bonus, 10/+3 damage reduction; immunity to death and negative energy effects.

Spell Mantle (Abjuration): Absorbs up to 1d8 + 8 spell levels.

Summon Creature VII (Conjuration): Summons a huge elemental of random type.

8th-Level Sorcerer/Wizards Spells

Bigby's Clenched Fist: A giant hand appears and attacks the target, once each round for the duration of the spell. Each hit causes 1d8+11 points of damage to the target. If the targets fail their saving throw, they are stunned for that round as well.

Create Undead (Necromancy): Creates one undead creature.

Greater Planar Binding (Conjuration): Paralyzes outsider or summon outsider.

Horrid Wilting (Necromancy): 1d8 negative energy damage per caster level.

Incendiary Cloud (Evocation): 4d6 fire damage to all within cloud.

Mass Blindness/Deafness (Illusion): All nearby enemies are struck blind and deaf.

Mass Charm (Enchantment): All nearby creatures gain a 50% improvement in their personal reputation toward the caster.

Mind Blank (Abjuration): Renders all nearby allies immune to mind-affecting spells and effects.

Premonition (Divination): Damage reduction of 30/+5.

Summon Creature VIII (Conjuration): Summons a greater elemental of random type.

Sunburst: A brilliant explosion occurs where the caster directs, causing 1d6 points of damage per caster level to all undead creatures to a maximum of 25d6 (6d6 points of damage to creatures that are not undead). Vampires are destroyed instantly if they fail a Reflex saving throw. All enemies in the area of effect must also make a successful Reflex saving throw or be blinded permanently (the blindness can only be magically removed).

9th-Level Sorcerer/Wizards Spells

Bigby's Crushing Hand: A giant hand appears and attacks the target. If it hits and succeeds in a grapple check, the target is held fast for the duration of the spell and suffers 2d6+12 points of damage each round.

Dominate Monster (Enchantment): Caster gains temporary control of target monster.

Energy Drain (Necromancy): Target temporarily gains 2d4 negative levels.

Gate (Conjuration): Summons forth a Balor.

Greater Spell Mantle (Abjuration): Absorbs 1d12 + 10 levels of spells.

Meteor Swarm (Evocation): 20d6 damage to all in area.

Mordenkainen's Disjunction (Abjuration): Very powerful version of Dispel Magic.

Power Word, Kill (Divination): Creatures with less than 100 hit points die.

Shapechange (Transmutation): Ability to transform into a dragon, giant, balor, slaad or golem.

Summon Creature IX (Conjuration): Summons an elder elemental of random type.

Time Stop (Transmutation): Caster may attack and cast spells while the rest of the world is frozen in time.

Wail of the Banshee (Necromancy): All enemies in area must save or die.

Weird (Illusion): Kills enemies in area.

The Armory

Though the manual for the original *Neverwinter Nights* game offers a fair bit of information on weapons, armor, and general equipment, this section condenses the various descriptions and tables into one reference. Also, in areas where the original materials do not cover certain rules or exceptions, explanations have been added to clear any confusion.

Weapons

There are dozens of weapons that each character can use for defense. The weapon categories reflect the level of training that it takes to wield the armaments at even a basic level. Thus, simple weapons are intended for the non-battle classes (such as wizards). Martial weapons are given without cost to fighters and other melee classes as a result of their training, but exotic weapons always require an extra level of devotion. People who wish to use any exotic equipment must spend an extra feat to gain proficiency with these extraordinary items.

SIMPLE WEAPONS: MELEE

Unarmed Attacks

These are fist and foot attacks made by characters in melee. Even non-monks can choose to attack without a weapon, though other classes have a hard time doing even moderate damage through this technique. Without the feat of Improved Unarmed Strike, these attacks draw an attack of opportunity.

Club

Weapon Damage:	1d6
Threat Range:	20
Critical Multiplier:	*2
Weapon Type:	Medium
Damage Type:	Bludgeoning
Base Cost:	2 Gold Pieces
Weight:	3 Pounds

This is a heavy piece of wood used for making blunt attacks.

Dagger

Weapon Damage:	1d4
Threat Range:	19-20
Critical Multiplier:	*2
Weapon Type:	Tiny
Damage Type:	Piercing
Base Cost:	4 Gold Pieces
Weight:	1 Pound

This small and easily concealed weapon is a common secondary weapon.

Mace (Light)

Weapon Damage:	1d6
Threat Range:	20
Critical Multiplier:	*2
Weapon Type:	Small
Damage Type:	Bludgeoning
Base Cost:	10 Gold Pieces
Weight:	6 Pounds

A mace is a crushing weapon, made of metal and ideal for smashing opponents. Because the mace can be wielded in one hand, even by smaller creatures, it is an ideal weapon for halflings and such who want to deal bludgeoning damage.

Morningstar

Weapon Damage:	1d8
Threat Range:	20
Critical Multiplier:	*2
Weapon Type:	Medium
Damage Type:	Bludgeoning and Piercing
Base Cost:	16 Gold Pieces
Weight:	8 Pounds

Morningstars are a form of spiked mace.

Quarterstaff

Weapon Damage:	1d6
Threat Range:	20
Critical Multiplier:	*2
Weapon Type:	Large
Damage Type:	Bludgeoning
Base Cost:	2 Gold Pieces
Weight:	4 Pounds

This is a large, stout piece of heavy wood. Because of its damage potential and ease of use, staves are a fair choice for non-battle characters that still want to mix it up in melee now and then (especially with a fair number of buffs enacted). These staves can be used as double weapons in standard third edition rules, but characters wield them as normal weapons in this game.

Spear

Weapon Damage:	1d8
Threat Range:	20
Critical Multiplier:	*3
Weapon Type:	Large
Damage Type:	Piercing
Base Cost:	2 Gold Pieces
Weight:	3 Pounds

Spears are suitable for thrusting attacks.

Sickle

Weapon Damage:	1d6
Threat Range:	20
Critical Multiplier:	*2
Weapon Type:	Small
Damage Type:	Slashing
Base Cost:	12 Gold Pieces
Weight:	3 Pounds

The sickle is nothing more than a farmer's implement, though they can be modified for military use by reinforcing the wood with metal bindings.

Sling

Weapon Damage:	1d4
Threat Range:	20
Critical Multiplier:	*2
Weapon Type:	Small
Damage Type:	Bludgeoning
Base Cost:	2 Gold Pieces
Weight:	Negligible

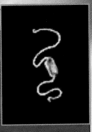

Slings hurl lead bullets.

MARTIAL WEAPONS: MELEE

Battleaxe

Weapon Damage:	1d8
Threat Range:	20
Critical Multiplier:	*3
Weapon Type:	Medium
Damage Type:	Slashing
Base Cost:	20 Gold Pieces
Weight:	7 Pounds

The battleaxe is the most common melee weapon among dwarves. The high critical multiplier for heavy weapons is intended for crushing through damage resistance and other forms of defense to damage.

SIMPLE WEAPONS: RANGED

Dart

Weapon Damage:	1d4
Threat Range:	20
Critical Multiplier:	*2
Weapon Type:	Small
Damage Type:	Piercing
Base Cost:	1 Gold Piece
Weight:	5 Pounds/50 Darts

Darts are small and don't do very much damage, but these slender spikes can be thrown by a wielder who hasn't trained in complex weaponry.

Light Crossbow

Weapon Damage:	1d8
Threat Range:	19-20
Critical Multiplier:	*2
Weapon Type:	Small
Damage Type:	Piercing
Base Cost:	35 Gold Pieces
Weight:	6 Pounds

This weapon requires two hands to use, no matter the size of your character. It fires bolts and does a modest amount of damage. Light crossbows are wonderful for mages and other characters who have almost no skill in ranged or melee combat.

Heavy Crossbow

Weapon Damage:	1d10
Threat Range:	19-20
Critical Multiplier:	*2
Weapon Type:	Medium
Damage Type:	Piercing
Base Cost:	50 Gold Pieces
Weight:	9 Pounds

This weapon requires two hands to use, no matter the size of your character. It fires bolts and does more damage than the light crossbow. Though this is still a simple missile weapon to wield, the increased weight is hardly worth the change from a light crossbow.

Flail, Heavy

Weapon Damage:	1d10
Threat Range:	19-20
Critical Multiplier:	*2
Weapon Type:	Large
Damage Type:	Bludgeoning
Base Cost:	30 Gold Pieces
Weight:	20 Pounds

Heavy flails are two-handed versions of the light flail. These do more damage and are best used in the hands of warriors with a very high strength. The increased threat range for heavy flails also helps to pay for the increased demands on their wielders.

Flail, Light

Weapon Damage:	1d8
Threat Range:	20
Critical Multiplier:	*2
Weapon Type:	Medium
Damage Type:	Bludgeoning
Base Cost:	16 Gold Pieces
Weight:	5 Pounds

A flail is a sturdy wooden handle with a metal ball attached. Using a flail in one hand does a bit less damage, but allows the use of a shield or a second weapon. For characters with many feats, having a light slashing weapon and a flail combine to do vicious things against a wide variety of enemies.

Greataxe

Weapon Damage:	1d12
Threat Range:	20
Critical Multiplier:	*3
Weapon Type:	Large
Damage Type:	Slashing
Base Cost:	40 Gold Pieces
Weight:	20 Pounds

This big, heavy axe is a favorite of barbarians, or anyone who wants to deal out large amounts of damage. Having a triple damage multiplier for criticals is a nice perk for people who are targeting enemies with damage reduction spells or abilities.

Greatsword

Weapon Damage:	2d6
Threat Range:	19-20
Critical Multiplier:	*2
Weapon Type:	Large
Damage Type:	Slashing
Base Cost:	100 Gold Pieces
Weight:	15 Pounds

This reliable and powerful weapon is one of the best melee weapons available. Greatswords are a mainstay for high-strength warriors who desire a fairly high threat range.

Halberd

Weapon Damage:	1d10
Threat Range:	20
Critical Multiplier:	*3
Weapon Type:	Large
Damage Type:	Piercing and Slashing
Base Cost:	20 Gold Pieces
Weight:	15 Pounds

This is a large weapon with both a slashing blade and piercing tip. Though halberds appear to be a weaker two-handed weapon on paper, the ability to deal two forms of damage means that almost no creature is highly resistant to damage from a halberd. Bludgeoning characters could carry around a halberd to pull out when creatures are resistant to them.

Handaxe

Weapon Damage:	1d6
Threat Range:	20
Critical Multiplier:	*3
Weapon Type:	Small
Damage Type:	Slashing
Base Cost:	12 Gold Pieces
Weight:	5 Pounds

This small axe is an ideal off-hand weapon. Handaxes are also good primary weapons for smaller characters.

Light Hammer

Weapon Damage:	1d4
Threat Range:	20
Critical Multiplier:	*2
Weapon Type:	Small
Damage Type:	Bludgeoning
Base Cost:	2 Gold Pieces
Weight:	2 Pounds

This is a small bashing weapon. There are few good things to be said about a light hammer. A light mace is a better weapon in every real way.

Longsword

Weapon Damage:	1d8
Threat Range:	19-20
Critical Multiplier:	*2
Weapon Type:	Medium
Damage Type:	Slashing
Base Cost:	30 Gold Pieces
Weight:	4 Pounds

This is a simple straight blade, a weapon favored by practical warriors. Characters with the ability to use martial weapons that are looking for a well-balanced choice can't go wrong with a longsword. In addition to a fair threat range and damage, longswords are very light. This makes these blades perfect even for weaker characters that don't want to cart around any more gear than they have to.

Rapier

Weapon Damage:	1d6
Threat Range:	18-20
Critical Multiplier:	*2
Weapon Type:	Medium
Damage Type:	Piercing
Base Cost:	40 Gold Pieces
Weight:	3 Pounds

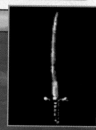

Rapiers are a fine choice for a single weapon, but more than a few people try to dual wield these blades. In these cases, a dueling weapon has been confused for a "dualing" weapon. As a medium weapon, this causes the wielder to incur the full penalty for using a heavier weapon for combat. Characters who require the wonderful threat range of a rapier and a good weapon for dual wielding should take a proficiency in exotic weapons and use kukri instead.

Scimitar

Weapon Damage: 1d6
Threat Range: 18-20
Critical Multiplier: *2
Weapon Type: Medium
Damage Type: Slashing
Base Cost: 30 Gold Pieces
Weight: 4 Pounds

The curve on this blade makes the weapon's edge effectively sharper. Like the rapier, this is a choice for people who desire a high threat range in their diet of combat. Scimitars offer the rapier model of criticals in a slashing format; this makes these blades a fine backup weapon for rapier wielders.

Short Sword

Weapon Damage: 1d6
Threat Range: 19-20
Critical Multiplier: *2
Weapon Type: Small
Damage Type: Piercing
Base Cost: 20 Gold Pieces
Weight: 3 Pounds

This sword is popular as an off-hand weapon, or as a primary weapon for Small characters. A character with a heavy sword (such as a katana or long sword) and a short sword should work wonderfully. This costs many feats, but the end result is a fair threat range, high damage, two damage types, and a nifty bit of style.

Warhammer

Weapon Damage: 1d8
Threat Range: 20
Critical Multiplier: *3
Weapon Type: Medium
Damage Type: Bludgeoning
Base Cost: 24 Gold Pieces
Weight: 8 Pounds

This is a one-handed maul with a large, heavy head. Because blunt weapons are almost critical for fighting against certain enemies, even warriors who specialize in blades should keep something like this around for dealing with resistant foes.

MARTIAL WEAPONS: RANGED

Longbow

Weapon Damage: 1d8
Threat Range: 20
Critical Multiplier: *3
Weapon Type: Large
Damage Type: Piercing
Base Cost: 75 Gold Pieces
Weight: 3 Pounds

You need at least two hands to use a bow, regardless of size. Longbows do more damage than shortbows.

Shortbow

Weapon Damage: 1d6
Threat Range: 20
Critical Multiplier: *3
Weapon Type: Medium
Damage Type: Piercing
Base Cost: 60 Gold Pieces
Weight: 2 Pounds

You need at least two hands to use a bow, regardless of size.

Throwing Axe

Weapon Damage: 1d6
Threat Range: 20
Critical Multiplier: *2
Weapon Type: Small
Damage Type: Slashing
Base Cost: 40 Gold Pieces
Weight: 50 Pounds/50 Axes

The throwing axe has been carefully balanced for flight, sacrificing durability for precision.

EXOTIC WEAPONS: MELEE

Bastard Sword

Weapon Damage: 1d10
Threat Range: 19-20
Critical Multiplier: *2
Weapon Type: Medium
Damage Type: Slashing
Base Cost: 70 Gold Pieces
Weight: 10 Pounds

This is a heavy sword that can be used in one hand. Like the katana, this blade deals an incredible amount of damage for such a compact package.

Dire Mace

Weapon Damage: 1d8/1d8
Threat Range: 20
Critical Multiplier: *2
Weapon Type: Large
Damage Type: Bludgeoning
Base Cost: 80 Gold Pieces
Weight: 20 Pounds

The dire mace is an attempt to combine the versatility of the quarterstaff with the striking power of the mace. This is a double weapon.

Double Axe

Weapon Damage: 1d8/1d8
Threat Range: 20
Critical Multiplier: *3
Weapon Type: Large
Damage Type: Slashing
Base Cost: 60 Gold Pieces
Weight: 25 Pounds

This axe has two heads and is a common weapon among orcs. This is a double weapon.

Katana

Weapon Damage: 1d10
Threat Range: 19-20
Critical Multiplier: *2
Weapon Type: Medium
Damage Type: Slashing
Base Cost: 80 Gold Pieces
Weight: 10 Pounds

This exotic weapon is in many ways similar to the bastard sword. These special weapons do as much damage as a one-handed weapon is capable of dishing out without magical enchantments.

Kama

Weapon Damage: 1d6
Threat Range: 20
Critical Multiplier: *2
Weapon Type: Small
Damage Type: Slashing
Base Cost: 4 Gold Pieces
Weight: 1 Pound

A monk using a kama can strike with his unarmed base attack, incurring a more favorable number of attacks per round.

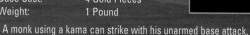

Kukri

Weapon Damage: 1d4
Threat Range: 18-20
Critical Multiplier: *2
Weapon Type: Tiny
Damage Type: Slashing
Base Cost: 8 Gold Pieces
Weight: 3 Pounds

This is a heavy, curved dagger. The threat range of a kukri makes it one of the most lethal weapons in the land, though its base damage is trivial. Kukris are most efficient in the hands of a character with a high strength and power attack. This way, a person can deal fair damage and turn almost every successful strike into a good chance for a critical!

Scythe

Weapon Damage: 2d4
Threat Range: 20
Critical Multiplier: *4
Weapon Type: Large
Damage Type: Piercing and Slashing
Base Cost: 36 Gold Pieces
Weight: 12 Pounds

The scythe is balanced and strengthened for war; it can deliver devastating slashing and piercing attacks. This unique weapon has a critical damage multiplier of four! Though scythes have no useful threat range, do moderate damage for a two-handed weapon, and require a feat to use, it is nice to have such an interesting weapon in one's inventory. Characters who are designed to bring down powerful enemies may prefer this to a greataxe (so long as they can afford the Exotic feat).

Two-Bladed Sword

Weapon Damage: 1d8/1d8
Threat Range: 19-20
Critical Multiplier: *2
Weapon Type: Large
Damage Type: Slashing
Base Cost: 200 Gold Pieces
Weight: 15 Pounds

There are twin blades coming from either end of this sword. This is a double weapon.

EXOTIC WEAPONS: RANGED

Shuriken

Weapon Damage: 1d3
Threat Range: 20
Critical Multiplier: *2
Weapon Type: Tiny
Damage Type: Piercing
Base Cost: 5 Gold Pieces
Weight: Negligible

These are small throwing weapons.

GRENADE-LIKE WEAPONS

Acid

Flasks of acid may be useful to adventures when facing creatures that may be resistant to a large number of more mundane attacks.

Alchemist's Fire

These flasks contain a volatile mixture that bursts into flame upon contact with air.

Caltrops

Caltrops are small, pyramid-shaped spikes that are designed to land facing up no matter how they are tossed onto the ground. These are intended to slow or hobble pursuers.

Choking Powder

Bags of this contain a mixture of pepper and other natural herbs that irritate targets and incapacitate them for a short time.

Holy Water

Flasks of water that have been blessed by a cleric of a benevolent deity can be used against undead. When hurled, these flasks will break and do damage to nearby undead.

Tanglefoot

These bags of stringy material will burst when they are hurled toward enemies. This will snare targets if they are unfortunate enough to be struck by the web-like particles.

Thunderstone
Thunderstones are made with runic inscriptions so that they explode when thrown against a hard surface. This deafening sound is quite disruptive for creatures that are close to the epicenter of this blast.

Weapon Rules and Miscellany

CRITICAL HITS

Every weapon has a threat range, a series of numbers such as 19-20/x2. This is very important as it determines how often the weapon will score a critical hit and how much damage it inflicts when it does. A critical hit is threatened when your die roll for attacking is within the first series of numbers (i.e., 19 or 20 in this example).

To see if this is a critical hit, your character rolls again with all the same modifiers. If they hit again, they score a critical hit. When this happens, damage is rolled as indicated by the second number (in this example, damage is rolled twice: 2x). Different weapons have different threat ranges and critical damage multipliers.

High threat range weapons are very powerful for characters that make a lot of attacks (i.e., a dual-wielding barbarian). The idea for this style of combat is to score criticals often to supplement normal battle damage. Most of these weapons, like rapiers and kukri, are not very lethal by themselves. However, the frequency of criticals can reach a state that also guarantees them during any melee.

On the other hand, high damage multiplier weapons can never rely on scoring a critical. Axes and bows are especially fine examples of this alternative. Instead of going after frequent criticals, characters with these weapons do extremely high damage on the rare attacks when everything comes together. Though this isn't as useful a style for fighting against weak or even moderately powerful enemies, these weapons are wonderful when battling the most vicious creatures in the game. Under these circumstances, a high damage multiplier will power through such things as damage resistance, thus making a triple damage attack *seem* more like quadruple or quintuple damage.

A perfect party will combine both types of weapon so that there is a spread for bringing down light and heavy opponents.

TWO-WEAPON FIGHTING

If you wield a second weapon in your off hand, you can get one extra attack per round with that weapon. You will receive a penalty of –6 to your main hand attack rolls and a penalty of –10 to your off hand attack rolls. There are several ways to reduce these penalties; the feats of Two-Weapon Fighting and Ambidexterity are ideal for this. Additionally, there is the Improved Two-Weapon Fighting feat, which grants a second off-hand attack, with an additional –5 attack penalty.

Without taking the extra feats to master two-weapon fighting, this style of combat is dramatically inferior to almost every other. After all three feats are taken, a character that is dual wielding will be able to hit a *lot* more often and deal a substantial amount of damage to many enemies.

Penalties for Two-Weapon Fighting

CIRCUMSTANCES	PRIMARY HAND'S ATTACKS	SECONDARY HAND'S ATTACKS
Normal Penalties	-6 to Attack	-10 to Attack
Light Off-Handed Weapon	Penalties Reduced by 2	Penalties Reduced by 2
Two-Weapon Fighting Feat Taken	Penalties Reduced by 2	Penalties Reduced by 2
Ambidexterity Feat Taken	No Change to Attack	Penalties Reduced by 4
Optimal Conditions (Both feats + Light)	-2 to Attack	-2 to Attack

OFF-HAND WEAPON DAMAGE

Any weapon used in the off hand only receives one-half your normal Strength bonus for an attack.

DOUBLE WEAPONS

Using a double weapon is the same as using two weapons (consider the off hand as wielding a light weapon). These weapons all fall under the exotic weapon specialization category, so it costs a

feat to wield these properly. The bonus is that dual-wielding characters are able to effectively muster two powerful weapons without incurring attack penalties. An additional perk is that the wielder only needs to spend feats on one weapon instead of two (one heavy and one light).

In the end, this is one of the most cost-efficient forms of dual wielding. The only alternative that surpasses this is to use two light weapons of the same type, thus eliminating the purchase of exotic weapons.

TWO-HANDED WEAPON DAMAGE

Any weapon being used in two hands delivers one-and-a-half times your normal Strength bonus. For characters with a moderate Strength (anything below the high teens), this rarely offsets the substantial loss of a powerful shield or a second weapon. Characters who desire defense should take the route of a single-handed weapon.

However, two-handed weapons are wonderful for characters that plan on having a Strength that will rise above 20. These are also ideal weapons for people who do not wish to use a shield because of arcane spell failure and don't want to deal with swapping items frequently.

WEAPON SIZE

Weapons come in four different sizes. These sizes affect what size of creature can use this weapon and how:

Tiny: Considered a light, one-handed weapon for all creatures of Small size or larger.

Small: Considered a normal one-handed weapon for Small creatures such as halflings and gnomes. Other creatures can use small weapons as a light, off-handed weapon.

Medium: Considered a two-handed weapon for Small creatures such as halflings and gnomes. Medium-size creatures can wield Medium-size weapons with one hand.

Large: Small creatures, such as gnomes and halflings, cannot wield Large weapons. Humans and other Medium-size creatures can wield them with two hands. Larger creatures, such as giants, can wield Large weapons with one hand.

Armor

Shields and armor are used to protect characters from harm in melee and missile combat. The best suits of armor are often quite a bit heavier and more bulky to use, thus inhibiting the Dexterity of the characters that are using them. Thus, a person can only dodge up to a certain point for each type of armor. The table below shows the advantages and disadvantages for the various types of armor in the game.

Defensive Equipment Statistics

ARMOR NAME	ARMOR CLASSIF.	ARMOR CLASS	MAXIMUM DEXTERITY BONUS	ARMOR CHECK PENALTY	ARCANE SPELL FAILURE
Clothing	Non-Armor	0	Full Dexterity	0	0%
Padded Cloth	Light	1	8	0	5%
Hardened Leather	Light	2	6	0	10%
Studded Leather/Hide	Light	3	4	1	20%
Scale Mail	Medium	4	4	2	20%
Chainmail	Medium	5	2	5	30%
Banded/Splint Mail	Heavy	6	1	7	40%
Half Plate Suit	Heavy	7	1	7	40%
Full Plate Suit	Heavy	8	1	8	45%
Small Shield	Shield	+1	Full Dexterity	+1	+5%
Large Shield	Shield	+2	Full Dexterity	+2	+15%
Tower Shield	Shield	+3	Full Dexterity	+10	+50%

This table makes it fairly clear that a person's armor preference should not only be based on the ability to wear heavier equipment. Indeed, a person with a very high Dexterity can be better off in padded cloth compared to a suit of half plate! At a 30 Dexterity (a value that few people reach), armor itself is a hindrance, no matter how light! Characters should always try to find a balance between speed and protection that matches their needs.

Arcane spell failure is not often a problem for purely arcane casters (who often shun armor and would have to take a number of feats to even use such gear). However, bards and multiclassed characters often feel the fear that comes with casting in armor. Having a quickbar that is set up to quickly don and remove armor is a must for these characters. Note that the feat of Still Spell can be used to negate arcane spell failure from armor.

Miscellaneous Items

Amulets/Necklaces

Amulets are necklaces with some form of large decoration or symbol. Most are ornamental, but some are infused with magic. Magical amulets are often given to grant bonuses toward saving throws, elemental harm, and other such attacks.

Belts

Belts are worn about the midsection, but do not add to the protection given by basic armor unless infused with magic or otherwise unusual.

Boots

Boots come in a variety of forms and functions, but they do not add to the protection given by basic armor unless infused with magic or otherwise unusual. Some of the better boots are intended for enchantments like haste, general speed of movement, or protection from negative enchantments to movement.

Bracers

Bracers are a part of most suits of armor and do not increase their suit's protective abilities unless infused with magic. Magical bracers improve the wearer's armor class or skill with things like discipline, appraise, and other such physical abilities.

Cloaks

Cloaks are simple cloth garments used to protect the wearer from ill weather and other hazards of an open road. Cloaks are perfect for imbuing with invisibility and other such dweomers of stealth.

Gauntlets

Gauntlets are a part of most suits of armor and do not increase their suit's protective abilities unless infused with magic. There are magical gloves for monks that are especially powerful (sometimes increasing the power of monk hand-to-hand attacks by a substantial margin). Other gauntlets are good for increasing strength for dedicated melee types.

Healer's Kits

Healing kits allow your character to use the Heal skill on themselves or others. The Healing Kit may restore hit points, cure disease, or remove poisons. These tools are perfect for characters that do not have access to a healer or healing magics.

Helmets

Helmets come in a variety of styles, but all offer basic protection to the head at the cost of slightly reduced perception. There are a number of powerful helms for mages, so arcane casters should always be on the lookout for these; some such items add spells for certain levels of casting.

Rings

Rings are commonly worn on the fingers as ornamentation, but some are infused with powerful magic. Rings can carry almost any type of enchantment. The classic rings of protection are good for armor class bonuses and saving throws, but there are rings of invisibility, elemental rings, and almost anything else that the mind can imagine. These artifacts are indeed precious.

Thieves' Tools

These picks, files, and other assorted tools allow the character to unlock locked chests and doors.

Trap Kits

These unique items allow any character skilled in setting traps to place deadly contraptions. There are a variety of traps, ranging from fire explosions to gas clouds.

Bags and Boxes

There are a variety of containers that can be carried in your inventory. These help keep similar goods together. Simply drag items into the container. You can access the contents of the container by selecting the "Open" option from the radial menu.

Magical containers decrease the weight of items that are stored within them. This makes such items desirable for almost all characters in the game. Any PC with a low strength will find that these make it possible to carry a lot more equipment and treasure around, thus reducing the number of times a person has to trek back from a dungeon or adventure.

Belladonna

Ingesting this herb grants a +5 AC bonus against shapechangers, such as werewolves and wererats.

Garlic

Eating this strong-smelling herb grants a +2 attack bonus against undead for one minute. However, it also inflicts a -1 penalty to Charisma for the duration of its effects.

Battle Strategies: The Ways of War

No matter how well designed a character is, the test of battle can shake even the best adventurer. Having a specific set of tactics and strategies will make almost every encounter quite a bit easier. *Shadows of Undrentide* is very good at rewarding intelligent gameplay. Though hack n' slashers will still be able to pound through a lot of the opposition, the ideas in this section of the guide will especially aid character templates that rely on creative skills and feats. Defensive warriors, archers, casters, and skill classes will want to pay extra attention!

Art of Melee

These are techniques for melee-centered characters. Though high hit points and a great armor class are the first steps to success in this role, there are many rungs on the ladder to victory.

BE AGGRESSIVE, BUT NOT TOO AGGRESSIVE

Good tanks have to engage enemies a fair bit of the time, especially if they have ranged magic or missile capabilities. Yet, a warrior who is constantly repositioning loses a number of advantages that are inherent to defenders. Attacks of Opportunity (AO) are the first example of this; running into a defender's attack range provokes an attack. The same is true if enemies charge into the player's range. This makes it a lot better to provoke enemies into making the first move.

The best way to handle this mix of problems is to engage archers or mages if they are the ones in the front line. It is a joyous day when this happens because the enemies have stumbled into a terrible attack formation. Engaging the softer members of the enemy party forces the tanks on the other side to do most of the legwork and deal with any opportunity strikes that arise. Beyond that, archers and mages are terrible in melee, thus forcing them to flee or sustain a losing fight.

Of course, most enemies will try to keep this scenario from occurring. Instead, expect enemy warriors to take the front lines and leave their archers and mages in the relatively safe rear. That is fine, too! Back away and find shelter when this happens. Force the tanks on the opposing side to endure any allied missile fire while making an approach. If they come forward without support, the group can engage them at their weakest.

SPECIAL ATTACKS ARE YOUR FRIENDS

Not every ability will work against every creature. For that matter, many abilities won't work all of the time, even against the same types of foes. That said, a melee character still survives on special attacks. Knockdown is a key example of a move that keeps enemies from engaging in effective combat. In a two-on-two fight, the side that uses combat control abilities like this will come out on top almost every time.

If a character has a henchman or a few party members who are capable of inflicting even a bit of damage, special attacks really come into their own. Once a melee battle is engaged, the primary combat control tanks can start to move between targets, knocking opponents down as they go (or using disarm, stun attacks, etc.). The rest of the group, henchman or fellow PCs, is then given free rein to savage the disabled targets. This process sounds simple and fairly obvious, but mastering this takes a bit of practice.

The sacrifices to gain these techniques are not profound, but it does take some planning to create a character that will have everything he needs when the time comes. Many of the special melee abilities require a warrior to have a 13+ Intelligence; no one wants to make a halfling expertise paladin and get to level 9 with only 10 Intelligence. Before a character goes beyond a concept, it is wise to consider all of the feats that are desired for that PC's career. Some people have trouble doing that in their heads, but there are several alternatives. Firstly, writing characters down can be useful and fun, especially for paper-and-pencil gaming types. For the more electronically inclined, there are modules that allow characters to instantly progress through their career and choose which skills/feats/etc. to take. These modules are a blessing for shaking down complex templates!

Art of Bowry & General Missile Combat

Archers and many of the skill classes (Rogues, Bards, etc.) depend on their ability to soften enemies before melee combat begins. There are many ways to make sure that this is a productive process—choosing the right area, tools, and techniques for the fight at hand. This section covers many of the basics and more than a few of the higher-level skills that are needed to survive at range.

SHOOT AND SCOOT

Archers don't get a lot of free shots off unless there are at least two or three allies wandering around to soak up the enemies who advance during a large battle. When an archer is playing alone or even with a single henchman, it is often the case that enemies will peel off to engage the archer directly. This is understandable; most creatures don't enjoy spikes of wood and metal being driven into their flanks, especially when the aggressor doesn't even have the decency to come and introduce himself first.

Of course, archers don't have a very good time of things once those nasty beasties close the gap, so it is imperative that an archer stays mobile throughout an engagement. Having magical items that increase movement speed will aid in this, as will barbarian or monk levels, or the ability to cast buffs such as Expeditious Retreat. By whatever means an archer gains a bit of extra speed, efficient movement is necessary for getting the most out of each combat round. When pursued, an archer should be able to fire a shot or two, reposition, and then continue peeling off arrows. This is obnoxious, rude, and unfair to one's enemies. Archers are trained to be all of these things on the field of battle. Honor is for the dead and the victor, not for the combatants.

Archers with a complement of spells should focus on anything that will either speed them up or slow their enemies down. Grease the floor, darken the corridor, and do whatever else is needed to sow chaos. The more time melee types eat up doing nothing, the greater the chance that bowry will win the day!

WHAT TO BUY, WHEN TO TOSS IT, AND WHO GETS THE LOVE?

Grenade-like items have been added in this expansion pack, and these are especially useful for many of the skill classes. Harper Scouts, Rogues, and other magical item users should keep a stash of these around for many occasions. Tanglefoot bags and caltrops are very effective in tight corridors for delaying the enemies' advance. The longer and more painful the process is for the melee enemies, the more time all of the ranged allies will have to use arrows, scrolls, and other grenades.

If an encounter begins in a large chamber, it is often better to retreat until more of a bottleneck is found. This way, enemies won't simply have the option to skirt the edge of the hazard and engage without paying the price of admission.

Sometimes these items are useful for melee types as well. If there are a lot of mages or archers in an area, it is very hard for the grunts to do their job without getting torn up by evocation, negative enchantments, and arrows. A warrior can use these disruptive grenade items to lay a trap around a corner. This will limit the ability of mages and archers to get into a proper position for their work. If they hold back, it will give the allied grunts a chance to slice down enemy warriors without enduring ranged attacks; if the whole enemy group closes, it will damage or slow the archers and mages, thus exposing them fully at the beginning of the fight. This is a win-win situation.

CLICK ON A DESTINATION, CHOOSE SKILLS ON THE WAY

Feats like Rapid Shot are integral to an archer's daily fighting routines. At first, it seems that selecting these feats during a battle can be somewhat difficult. If a character moves after beginning a combat feat, that feat will disengage. This is doubly troublesome to archers, flying in the face of their need to cover a lot of ground. To counter this, note that it is possible for a player to click on a skill while the character in en route to a location. This will allow the feat to engage once the character reaches his target. For proper use of Rapid Shot, click on a distant and somewhat defensive area, select Rapid Shot during transit, and then enjoy the fun.

Art of Shadows

Rogues can fight, cast spells (one way or another), and generally do a bit of what everyone else is doing. Still, these characters have their own way of going about things, and some of the most rewarding techniques in the game can only be pulled off by rogues. The majority of good stealth work is dedicated to keeping enemies from doing anything effective against rogues. Monsters can kill a person's henchmen, friends, town, and whatever else is nearby, but a rogue always has the option to slip away and find a new set of henchmen, friends, towns, etc.

SNEAK ATTACKS

Sneak attacks are one of the great equalizers in the game. Barbarians, mages, and archers alike fear this dreadful power because it can come at any time and from any direction. Rogues stink if they get pinned out in the open, but they are invincible against the unwary or uninformed.

Sneak Attacks aren't always done through surprise. If a target is engaged in battle with another creature, a rogue can walk up from behind and deal multiple Sneak Attacks until the victim realizes that it's long past time to turn around. Thus, moving silently and hiding in the shadows need not precede every Sneak Attack. Incapacitated enemies are good targets for this too; using scrolls of various binding spells will make the work of a rogue far easier.

It is always nice to have a henchman or party around to distract enemies. A hidden rogue should stay at the front of a group as often as possible. This way, approaching enemies will move past

the point of ambush and give the rogue an opportunity to strike at the most exposed and least able member of their foes. Shamans, mages, and archers meet their end this way all too often. Even in smaller brawls, a rogue should wait for enemies to close on another target (have a tough henchman around if this person is meant to survive). Rogues should go in for a Sneak Attack against one enemy, and then back away and repeat this with another target. This keeps the enemy group from splitting evenly and attacking everyone (if the rogue sticks to one target, that will indeed be the result).

Note that a rogue should tell henchmen or party members to stay behind while doing most exploring; it isn't always good to have allies around while remaining hidden. Half-orc warriors in chain-mail tend to give the group's position away.

Taking all the feats that lead up to Sneak Attack makes it a lot easier for rogues to get into a fight, make a sneak attack or two, and then retreat until it is safe to return for further evilness. Without these feats, rogues stand to endure many attacks of opportunity over their careers.

Magical weapons that stun or otherwise disable enemies are wicked; they are also highly prized by rogues. Sonic traps can be used for many of the same benefits; enemies who are stunned by these offer little resistance to a swift stiletto.

STEALTH

Outside of a fight, Hide and Move Silently are nice for moving about without drawing attention or aggression. In a dungeon or wilderness environment, this gives roguish types that chance to see what creatures and treasure are present before committing to any direct action. For groups, this presents an even greater opportunity, because they can plan ambushes and all sorts of fun things.

Rogue/mage combinations are more powerful than almost any alternative arcane multiclass hybrid. Using the feat Silent Spell, an arcane caster with a high skill in Hiding can stay in the shadows and cast at the same time. A hidden mage is a fairly safe mage! The potential of this combination should not be underestimated in the least.

Art of the Arcane

Mages are the heavy guns of fantasy worlds, but they often have to apply a delicate hand to their art. Undefended mages tend to get snipped by a random archer or lucky tank. Even worse, a mage without a sense of timing can be a *huge* detriment to his allies. Knowing when to buff, when to hurl fire, and when to run is essential to saving one's skin as a caster. They call mages paper dolls with good reason!

THE BEAUTY OF BUFFS

Buffs enhance characters in one way or another. Extra hit points and bonuses to attack are certainly nice, but attribute-increasing spells, shapeshifting, and tons of other enchantments lie on the path to greatness. There are a few good things to consider when selecting and casting these wonderful party-friendly spells.

First, timing is everything. Always keep an eye on the duration for buff spells. One hour per level would sure be nice for even the most powerful buffs, but it just doesn't work out that way very often. Indeed, some of the more brutal transformation and enhancement spells only last for a few rounds. This makes it critical that a mage understand when and where each buff should be used. Anything with 10 turns per caster level or more can be handled casually; these are good to use outside of combat, perhaps when first entering each dungeon area. Buffs with a tight duration should be held until there is a full engagement that threatens the party; if the group can handle a situation without any risks, a powerful buff would be wasted.

There are some buffs that have no place in certain regions. When a mage is dealing with goblins and orcs, there usually isn't much reason for saving throw enhancers and element resistance spells. Yet, there are dungeons with a vicious spread of traps and elemental creatures. These are obvious places for a mage to swap a new spread of spells into his quickbar. This type of area-specific buffing is extremely effective. It just isn't possible or fun to use every buff for each character in every area, so figuring out how to counter the greatest threats will limit what must be memorized. In general, adventures with a lot of large, physical creatures are best countered with attribute buffs, hit points, and combat

bonuses. When traps and mages start to turn up, switch to saving throws, elemental resistance spells, and anything that will speed allied movement (buffs to speed or attacks, or spells that prevent impeded movement).

There are some interesting uses for buffs that have nothing to do with direct combat. For instance, most mages have a horrible time carrying things back to town. A gnomish wizard just doesn't have the strength to cart around five suits of magical armor. Using Bull's Strength can increase the weight capacity of a character by a nice margin. Other attribute buffs can be used to improve the chance of a critical skill check (raising Charisma before a really important conversation, Dexterity for an overly pesky lock, etc.). These are things to keep in mind when dealing with skill and logistic problems that demand everything a character has to offer.

DON'T CRISP YOUR BUDDIES

The short and direct suggestion is to avoid casting area of effect spells when allies are close to the epicenter. Yet, this is a whole lot more difficult than it sounds. There are always complications when a mage wants to use the big spells without having a lot of room to spare.

The more bland way of avoiding this problem is to turn down the difficulty of the game (lower difficulty levels prevent allies from taking damage when area of effect spells are cast by party members). Though this will extend the lifespan of more than a few henchmen and PCs, this makes mages dramatically overpowered. Beyond that, the challenge and joy of effective magic use is mocked by such a simple solution.

The second level of avoidance is to shun area of effect evocation after both sides have initiated melee. This gives the casters a chance to lob a fireball before everyone is intermixed. For a middle ground, this is a fair solution. There isn't too much of a chance that an ally will be hit, and mages still have a lot of potential to deal damage early in the battle against everyone before turning to targeted spells.

Of course, in more complex engagements, a mage has to be on alert for opportunities. It isn't uncommon for enemies to receive reinforcements in some of the larger skirmishes. These are wonderful times to unleash something foul and beautiful.

Finally, there are some evil tricks to open a few doors later on in levels. With the right gear or spells, mages can prepare their parties for area of effect magic. Using some of the more powerful elemental resistance spells will dramatically soften the blow from many evocation spells. If the mage and his henchman or allies get into trouble during a fight, a mage can pull out a spell of fair power without setting his own party back. This tactic can be a great way to get out of ugly situations.

Tactics and Strategy

No matter what profession(s) a person takes, there are certain things that everyone must learn. This section explains a lot of the common tricks for avoiding a foul end.

SHOULD YOU STAY OR SHOULD YOU GO?

There are times when a fight just isn't in one's favor. This can be for a number of reasons (triggering the wrong encounter, not having enough hit points because of a previous fight, etc.). Whatever the cause, there are ways to get out of trouble without resorting to the old Load Game spell. Instead, prepare for a bit of legwork.

Often, a person's chance of survival in fleeing an engagement hinges on when they realize that things are going sour. If a character is already low on hit points and surrounded, there just isn't much hope unless the person teleports back to town (as you can in the first chapter of *Shadows of Undrentide* with Drogan's ring). If teleportation isn't an option, people who wait that long usually end up in someone's stew pot.

It is far better to read the writing on the wall long before things get dire. Signs of a turning battle include: a huge number of gibbering evil creatures charging down the hallway, the loss of party members at the front of the group and a continuing trend toward the rear, and the disappearance of any allied rogues. More seriously, a player should keep a wary eye on the number of creatures involved in each fight. Most of the time, it is the addition of

a few fresh monsters that tips the balance. This is especially the case with casters or enemies with Sneak Attack; these foes can ravage the party if it lacks the people to deal with the new aggressors.

If more enemies are joining the fray and it seems unlikely that the henchman or allies will hold, it is best to leave sooner rather than later. When playing with other people, this can lead to a premature cascade of fleeing PCs, but that is the nature of morale! No one wants to be the last person to flee in the face of unbeatable odds—it tends to be rough on the organs.

Obviously, there are ways to improve on one's running skills, though you should be a bit nervous around anyone who has to practice this too much. Spells like Expeditious Retreat are divine for getting out of trouble. Taking corners as efficiently as possible helps more than most people would think, too. Instead of relying on pathfinding to do all of the work, managing a character closely will cut a lot of wasted time off of most routes out of an area. Combine these with anything that will slow pursuers. Tanglefoot bags, hold spells, and obviously things like Slow or Darkness will assist in this.

USES AND ABUSES OF LACKEYS, MEATSHIELDS, AND NPCs

Having a henchman around is never going to be as nifty as wandering through the world with a party of true allies who are animated and intelligent. Still, there are many tactical uses for a henchman, and they are certainly fun to use and abuse. No matter how a player looks at it, there is a place for henchman in the game, and each PC has a different need for them.

Controlling a henchman is the toughest part of the issue. Though the AI for these NPCs is robust enough to keep them somewhat active, it is extremely rare that they will do exactly what is needed at any given point. Because the player is meant to lead the party, there are some innate problems with NPC tanks; they stay behind the player and wait for the action to come to them. Wizards and Sorcerers tend to have problems with this. The first rule of henchman use in combat boils down to this: "Better him than me." Remember that, unless the character is a virtuous paladin, few people want to get stuck in the gut because their ally is composing poetry on the back lines.

Non-warriors should move quickly at the beginning of a fight to get behind the NPC. This makes it a lot easier for the henchman to figure out what is going on and how to respond. Even characters who don't get hit a lot of the time should have healing potions on their quickbar for saving the henchman from certain death.

One of the best ways to improve henchman control is to master the shortcuts that are involved with them. Right clicking on henchmen will open a radial menu with the vast majority of the common commands. This is perfect for getting the NPCs to do roughly what is needed without taking a whole lot of time.

Also, the henchmen inventory system is now available! This opens the door for trading weapons, armor, and magical equipment to NPCs. Or, for characters with low Strength, henchmen can be used as mules for extra carrying space. Either way, this keeps henchmen from being completely outclassed as characters move up through the levels. Make sure to talk with henchmen and look at their equipment to keep it from getting too pathetic.

KITING: NOT JUST FOR KIDS ANYMORE

Some enemies are smart enough to stay near their lairs, but most creatures are driven to take a bit out of adventurers. A seasoned player can use this against the foul beasts. Kiting is the technique of luring enemies out of one place and drawing them away for various purposes. The term kite is used because the character doing the work often looks like he is stringing a kite along behind him—these kites look like hideous monsters, but the metaphor is a good one nonetheless.

Kiting can be used to lead monsters into an ambush (web spells in a tight area, tanglefoot bags, a room of tanks with a small doorway, etc.). For that matter, kiting can do almost anything to put players in a better spot for dealing with the challenges of an adventure. A rogue might have an ally kite a room of bandits off into the sunset while he runs in to steal their loot. Why not?

Fighting is fun, but solving problems in creative ways is even better.

Archer and mage kiting can be especially effective and brutal. With spells or items to increase speed (Expeditious Retreat, Haste, Boots of Speed, etc.), these characters can run faster than the majority of enemies. This gives the ranged PCs a chance to fire, retreat, fire again, and repeat. Melee and even many ranged monsters will be torn to ribbons by this technique, though a person must avoid backing into a hallway without exits or running into another group of enemies.

MAKING THE MOST OF TRAPS

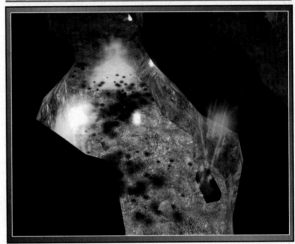

Traps offer a chance to deal damage or otherwise harm a group of enemies without taking action directly. This leaves the character open to flee, cast spells, or do anything else during the event. Traps that stun or deal damage over time (sonic and acid traps, for example) disrupt enemies. The goal of these devices is not to kill enemies on contact (most just aren't powerful enough to do that); rather, they are intended to slow creatures down, hurt them a little, and allow the player to even the odds against an often larger force.

The most basic trap ambush starts when a character recognizes that there are enemies farther down a tunnel. This can be done outside, but it is a lot easier in constrained locales. Out of sight, the player chooses a spot for the trap to be set, and then orders the PC to follow through. With a missile weapon or otherwise ranged attack, the character should then attack the group of enemies and kite them back toward the trapped area. The person who set the trap can move over the location without harm, but the enemies will soon spring the device. Traps that stun are wonderful because they give the PC time to turn and begin inflicting even more damage without taking much fire.

Rogues can even pair this trick with melee Sneak Attacks, although it takes speed and practice to do this without getting nailed with a melee slice or two.

TERRAIN, OBSTACLES, AND AMBUSHES

Archery, spell work, and other ranged activities are fun. What makes them even better is that there are places with a full view over an area that take a long time to approach. Missiles plus counterattacks are decent, but missile attacks without reprisal are better! Archers should keep an eye out for ledges, awkward tunnels, and anything else that may give them a vantage point that will take time to reach. Especially when playing alone, these can provide a safe point for fights that are too tough to handle otherwise.

If there is such a spot, but it isn't close to a battle that keeps causing trouble, use kite techniques to pull the enemies back to the ambush.

THE SPACEBAR IS THERE TO HELP YOU

Complex battles or very developed characters (such as high-level mages) should use the spacebar to pause battles for proper decisions and peace of mind. Some players don't like slowing things down like this because it distances them from the action, but other people find that this brings a level of tactics and strategy to Bioware games. Each person should try this out enough to deter-mine whether pausing is something that improves the game or takes something away from it.

A character that lives or dies because of his henchman is likely to enjoy the pause feature. Henchmen are very tough to deal with during large battles, and it is very helpful to stop everything to ensure that one's henchman isn't totally squirreling out.

USING YOUR QUICKBAR

Each character has three possible quickbars to set up. This allows for a huge number of spells, special moves, and items to be used without pausing the game or wasting time in battle. In general, almost everything that a character does should be placed down on the quickbar.

For greater efficiency and enjoyment, players should organize things in an intuitive way; have a quickbar for the most common moves that is always on top. Use the Shift and Control quickbars for things that aren't used every battle. A mage might put a crossbow and a nice selection of evocation spells on her main bar, buffs on a second, and odd out-of-battle spells (like Identify) on the third. This makes it a lot easier to remember where every-thing is. During multiplayer sessions, this is invaluable.

Warriors are better off if they keep a spare equipment quickbar at the ready. It is often useful to be able to jump into and out of armor; wielding and removing weapons and shields can be even better. Use this to have a bludgeoning weapon to swap for a char-acter's primary slashing blade if resistant enemies take the field. Rogues also need to switch out of equipment frequently (for skill checks and such). Ultimately, the game would have a lot more micromanagement if not for the glory and versatility of the quickbars!

Notice that there are even some nifty emotes and text commands that can be placed in spare slots. When roleplaying with other PCs, these can be fun, not to mention useful during times when it would take too long to type what is needed.

Bestiary of Monsters, Demons, and the Unliving

Although there are many specific creatures and people who will oppose an adventurer, it always helps to have an idea of the general races that wander the land. This bestiary is intended to provide the statistics and background information for the major groups that characters will encounter in *Shadows of Undrentide*. You'll find more specific entries in relevant sections of the walk-through, but this central bestiary will explain more about the various beings rather than listing only their core statistics.

ASABI

Alignment:	Lawful Evil
Creature Type:	Humanoid, Druid
Strength:	11
Dexterity:	13
Constitution:	12
Intelligence:	12
Wisdom:	16
Charisma:	10
Fortitude Save:	7
Reflex Save:	2
Will Save:	5
Base AC:	13
Base HP:	37

Asabi are large creatures that dwell in harsh desert conditions. They often serve (willingly or otherwise) as warriors for evil creatures of greater power. Fully grown, these beasts are over seven feet in length and stand several feet above a human. The color of their thick skin is either brown or gray, although this is lighter on their lower bodies.

Asabi are very aggressive and defend their territory with considerable malice. Few people are able to barter or converse with such beings.

BUGBEAR

Alignment:	Chaotic Evil
Creature Type:	Humanoid
Strength:	15
Dexterity:	12
Constitution:	13
Intelligence:	10
Wisdom:	10
Charisma:	9
Fortitude Save:	3
Reflex Save:	1
Will Save:	1
Base AC:	14
Base HP:	16

Oddly enough, these large creatures are distantly related to goblins, although any obvious resemblance takes the finest scholars in the world to discern. These bearish humanoids often stand over seven feet in height and are well muscled. Found underground in caverns and other defensive locations, bugbears survive by scavenging and raiding. It is quite common for bugbears to attack other intelligent creatures.

These predators have a keen sense of smell and a lust for combat and killing. It is extremely hard to engage a bugbear in anything short of battle. Even their goblin relatives are far from safe when it comes time to fill the stewpot.

DOMESTIC ANIMALS

Alignment:	True Neutral
Creature Type:	Animal
Strength:	15
Dexterity:	11
Constitution:	15
Intelligence:	3
Wisdom:	12
Charisma:	6
Fortitude Save:	3
Reflex Save:	3
Will Save:	0
Base AC:	10
Base HP:	15

There are many creatures that have been domesticated for village use around Hilltop and the other settlements in the Silver Marches. Chickens, cows, oxen, dogs, and other beasts are used for food, clothing, brute muscle, and transport. Most of the time, this is not something that adventurers need trouble themselves with; there are greater duties to attend to, whether for good or ill.

ELEMENTAL

Alignment:	True Neutral
Creature Type:	Elemental
Feats:	Darkvision
Strength:	12
Dexterity:	17
Constitution:	14
Intelligence:	4
Wisdom:	11
Charisma:	11
Fortitude Save:	1
Reflex Save:	1
Will Save:	4
Base AC:	16
Base HP:	26

Elementals most commonly take their form from one of the primary elements (earth, air, fire, or water). It is somewhat difficult to harm these magical creatures because of their attachment to a respective elemental plane. Powerful mages and creatures with summoning powers can draw elementals into the world and force them to obey certain commands. As such, elementals can be servants of good or evil, depending on what drew them (although there is never an innate sense of duty or purpose within these spirits).

It is always a futile task to use an elemental's own powers against it. Fighting fire with fire is not a wise suggestion at times. Instead, using opposing magic or powerful physical attacks poses a greater threat against elementals.

FORMIAN

Alignment:	Lawful Neutral
Creature Type:	Outsider
Strength:	17
Dexterity:	16
Constitution:	14
Intelligence:	10
Wisdom:	12
Charisma:	11
Fortitude Save:	4
Reflex Save:	4
Will Save:	4
Base AC:	18
Base HP:	26

Formians live in vast hives of their fellows, giving away a sense of self in the pursuit of the collective's needs. This makes the formians an extremely dangerous community to attack; they respond with a single-minded drive to defend their territory. Although fast, these ant-like monsters are also very powerful, making them twice as dangerous for even a wary adventurer.

The lawful nature of formian society makes them seem quite unlike humans and indeed many other humanoids. Rather than dealing with issues of goodness or evil, the formians only act when the order of their homes is at risk. People who are in line with the hive's needs are certainly able to interact and bargain with the formians, while the hive's warriors meet others with brutal suicide rushes.

GHOUL

Alignment:	Chaotic Evil
Creature Type:	Undead
Feats:	Darkvision
Strength:	13
Dexterity:	15
Constitution:	10
Intelligence:	13
Wisdom:	14
Charisma:	16
Fortitude Save:	1
Reflex Save:	1
Will Save:	3
Base AC:	14
Base HP:	21

Undead take many forms, and ghouls are certainly one of the more vile abominations in those ranks. These beings, often human by birth, turn into flesh-eating monsters after their deaths. Instead of searching out the living, as some of the other undead creatures do, ghouls feed on the bodies of the dead for their pleasure. If anything comes near, ghouls will certainly attack and try to find more food for themselves, but they do not stray very far from an existing source of bodies.

GNOLL

Alignment:	Chaotic Evil
Creature Type:	Humanoid
Strength:	15
Dexterity:	10
Constitution:	13
Intelligence:	8
Wisdom:	11
Charisma:	8
Fortitude Save:	4
Reflex Save:	0
Will Save:	0
Base AC:	11
Base HP:	11

Gnolls are a hyena-like humanoid race. These tall and strong warriors form tribes that survive by raiding and scavenging through the tundra, desert, and forest alike. While many gnolls are selfish and somewhat evil, their tribal structure makes it possible to negotiate with leaders to avoid bloodshed. Because leaders are chosen for their strength and prowess in battle, gnolls are faster to understand and accept strength before wisdom or guile.

GOBLIN

Alignment:	Neutral Evil
Creature Type:	Humanoid
Feats:	Darkvision
Strength:	10
Dexterity:	14
Constitution:	13
Intelligence:	17
Wisdom:	12
Charisma:	10
Fortitude Save:	1
Reflex Save:	1
Will Save:	4
Base AC:	14
Base HP:	19

There are not many goblins in the Hilltop area of the Silver Marches, although an occasional wanderer will appear. In some cases, goblin wizards have been seen in the area, perhaps trying to uncover some of the many artifacts that have been stowed away in this remote part of Faerun.

Goblins can be many things when it comes to temperament. Alone, most goblins are cowardly, selfish and feeble. In larger groups, or when supported by magic or distance, goblins can be cunning foes with a surprising ability to trick or outflank opponents. The versatile nature of goblin morality ensures that goblins are found in many cultures, environments, and lifestyles.

GOLEM

Alignment:	True Neutral
Creature Type:	Construct
Feats:	Darkvision
Strength:	17
Dexterity:	9
Constitution:	10
Intelligence:	3
Wisdom:	11
Charisma:	3
Fortitude Save:	2
Reflex Save:	2
Will Save:	2
Base AC:	16
Base HP:	60

Golems were once a common sight in the land of Netheril. The creation of these constructs reached the point where they could be given magical powers, intelligence, and even a sense of self and purpose. Sadly, those times have long since faded into memory and then on into legend, but some of the beings remain. Trapped in sand and lost to the ages, these golems burn with a patience that outlives the bones of their creators.

Because golems are given intelligence by their masters, it is impossible to say whether any golem is good or evil without discovering its intended purpose.

HILL GIANT

Alignment:	Chaotic Evil
Creature Type:	Giant
Feats:	Darkvision
Strength:	25
Dexterity:	8
Constitution:	19
Intelligence:	6
Wisdom:	10
Charisma:	17
Fortitude Save:	8
Reflex Save:	4
Will Save:	8
Base AC:	17
Base HP:	102

Although humans and dwarves have battled with giants many times over the decades, these dull brutes are not always bent on violent conflict. In the Silver Marches, there are even lone giants who settle somewhat close to populated communities without meeting a grim end. When left alone, these solitary giants will often be just as happy to keep to themselves and stay in their caves, coming up with wise ideas—some have even learned to count past 21, a feat of greatness among their kind.

HORROR

Alignment:	True Neutral
Creature Type:	Construct
Feats:	Darkvision
Strength:	20
Dexterity:	13
Constitution:	10
Intelligence:	10
Wisdom:	16
Charisma:	12
Fortitude Save:	4
Reflex Save:	4
Will Save:	4
Base AC:	11
Base HP:	71

The horrors are a form of magical construct, somewhat like golems in their creation. Still, these beings are used for war far more often than normal golems, and people who spot battle horrors and their various relatives are soon engaged.

KOBOLD

Alignment:	Lawful Evil
Creature Type:	Humanoid
Feats:	Alertness
Strength:	6
Dexterity:	13
Constitution:	11
Intelligence:	10
Wisdom:	10
Charisma:	10
Fortitude Save:	2
Reflex Save:	0
Will Save:	0
Base AC:	13
Base HP:	2

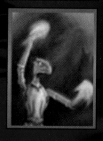

Kobolds are an eccentric lot, having properties of hounds and lizards. A pairing of opposites, it surprises few that the culture of these tiny monsters is filled with contradictions. Kobolds are violent yet comic, nervous and still brave. It is a wonder that kobolds have not been able to further themselves through Faerun, but the continued enslavement of their tribes by more powerful beings is no doubt a factor.

MANTICORE

Alignment:	Lawful Evil
Creature Type:	Magical Beast
Strength:	20
Dexterity:	11
Constitution:	19
Intelligence:	7
Wisdom:	12
Charisma:	9
Fortitude Save:	6
Reflex Save:	6
Will Save:	2
Base AC:	18
Base HP:	80

Manticores are creatures of myth and nightmares. Not many people believe that these monsters even exist, and those who do wonder how such a thing could come into being through natural means. The answer is that each manticore is partially steeped in magic; their rare appearance and powerful abilities owe a great deal to this.

The wicked, spiked tails of the manticore can throw waves of bitter darts into a force of attackers, and the accuracy of such moves is impressive. Entire groups of unlucky adventurers have been driven away with a sweep of a manticore's tail, and those are sometimes the fortunate ones! People who close with a manticore still have to face the creature's massive girth, sweeping claws, and voracious appetite. Those slain by a manticore are seldom found, beyond an abandoned bone or two.

MEDUSA

Alignment:	Lawful Evil
Creature Type:	Humanoid
Feats:	Gaze (Petrification)
Strength:	10
Dexterity:	15
Constitution:	12
Intelligence:	12
Wisdom:	13
Charisma:	15
Fortitude Save:	5
Reflex Save:	2
Will Save:	2
Base AC:	15
Base HP:	33

Of all the ancient tales, the stories of medusas are easily some of the most disturbing. As twisted beings of arrogance and vanity, the monsters that have taken this name are horrific to behold. Even the barest sight of these serpent-haired women can turn the living into stone. Battling these women is made more desperate by the interest in magic that many medusas share; thus, they are rarely defenseless, even when people protect themselves from the deadly gaze.

Worst of all, the cunning and wise nature of these long-lived monsters gives them a chance to manipulate other creatures into doing their biding. From the shadows, these priestesses of darkness move their forces across the land as a king would pieces in a game of chess. No one can say when and where a medusa will appear until it is too late.

MEPHIT

Alignment:	Neutral Evil
Creature Type:	Outsider
Feats:	Darkvision
Strength:	10
Dexterity:	17
Constitution:	10
Intelligence:	12
Wisdom:	11
Charisma:	15
Fortitude Save:	3
Reflex Save:	3
Will Save:	3
Base AC:	17
Base HP:	13

Mephits are a lot like elementals, but these spirits take on more properties of living animals than their fellows. Looking a lot like demonic imps, these elemental creatures are often summoned by wizards or areas with powerful magical energies. Although not terribly difficult to control with dark sorcery, mephits are dangerous enemies. Most mephits are able to create a blast of elemental energy from their home plane; this breath attack covers a fair arc, and entire groups of mephits inflict a lot of damage with this, even to powerful opponents. Because the mephits are immune to damage from their base element, there isn't even the risk of hurting similar spirits in the area, making mephit packs even more deadly.

MUMMY

Alignment:	Lawful Evil
Creature Type:	Undead
Feats:	Darkvision
Strength:	15
Dexterity:	8
Constitution:	10
Intelligence:	6
Wisdom:	14
Charisma:	15
Fortitude Save:	2
Reflex Save:	2
Will Save:	5
Base AC:	17
Base HP:	48

There is a powerful drive for a spirit to live beyond death in many cultures. Mummies are brought into existence when disturbed souls are given a sense of ceremony and ritual in their death. Wearing the wrappings of their death shrouds, these undead wander near the areas where they were entombed, cursing any living who enter with fear, disease, and the danger of combat.

Most mummies have little remaining intelligence, having become mere shadows of their former selves. This makes it impossible to deal peacefully with such creatures. Clerics and paladins are doubly driven to rid the world of these abominable things, for everyone's sake (and the originally deceased).

ORC

Alignment:	Chaotic Evil
Creature Type:	Humanoid
Strength:	15
Dexterity:	10
Constitution:	11
Intelligence:	9
Wisdom:	8
Charisma:	8
Fortitude Save:	2
Reflex Save:	0
Will Save:	0
Base AC:	10
Base HP:	4

An adventure wouldn't be an adventure without orcs. From Baldur's Gate to Waterdeep, Neverwinter to Anauroch, orcs are the mainstay of barbaric tribes, perhaps as humans are the most common and versatile members of the "civilized" races. Orcish raiders in the Hilltop area of the Silver Marches have mostly been eliminated, although there is a particularly cautious and resilient band to the south that hasn't been routed yet. A few elves in the area have taken up the task of stopping this group.

One of the problems in dealing with orcs is that they have a warrior's code that is hard for outsiders to understand. Loss of honor in battle is something that cannot be tolerated by orcs, even young adolescents. This makes it thoroughly vicious to force orcs out of their homes; almost all of them will fight to the death. Female orcs are no less dangerous really, and that effectively bolsters their numbers when fighting on their own turf.

PIXIE

Alignment:	Neutral Good
Creature Type:	Fey
Strength:	7
Dexterity:	18
Constitution:	11
Intelligence:	16
Wisdom:	15
Charisma:	16
Fortitude Save:	0
Reflex Save:	2
Will Save:	2
Base AC:	16
Base HP:	3

Pixies and their racial cousins are sylvan spirits who are most often found in magical areas of forests or in the company of mystics. Distinctly good and kind by nature, there is still an element of mischief and eccentricity to pixies. Jokes, riddles, and games are frequent points of interest for these spirits, and adventurers who come across them will seldom get what is needed without taking part.

SHADOW LICH

Alignment:	Chaotic Evil
Creature Type:	Undead, Wizard
Feats:	Darkvision
Strength:	8
Dexterity:	13
Constitution:	15
Intelligence:	24
Wisdom:	16
Charisma:	6
Fortitude Save:	5
Reflex Save:	5
Will Save:	11
Base AC:	11
Base HP:	82

Not all undead are mindless or display reduced intelligence from their former lives. Indeed, liches are most often created when mages are driven to magic at a level that transcends mortality. Instead of giving in to death when the time comes, some mages destroy their bodies and place their souls into a state of protection. Unfettered then by death's childish pawing, these masters of arcane spellcraft can continue their research.

Adventurers who cross the path of a lich are not in any way safe. Liches can use a full range of magic, and the protections of undeath keep a knife in the back or stray arrow from doing them in.

SKELETON

Alignment:	Neutral Evil
Creature Type:	Undead
Feats:	Darkvision
Strength:	10
Dexterity:	11
Constitution:	10
Intelligence:	10
Wisdom:	10
Charisma:	11
Fortitude Save:	0
Reflex Save:	0
Will Save:	2
Base AC:	10
Base HP:	6

These are the most basic variety of undead, if such a thing can be said. Although extremely negative emotions and events can cause some dead to return, skeletons are almost always animated by magic. With intention, necromancers of various sorts use the skeletons of the dead to do many chores. Skeletons can be used as protection, especially for underground lairs and dungeons. Few people dare to enter when the bones of the dead rally against them. Although rusted blades and armor may not be very effective, these tools are rather intimidating when held by the warriors who brought them into battle centuries ago!

Skeletons have only a moderate amount of energy to their existence, and usually adventurers can destroy them in droves. Clerics are especially happy to do this, and divine power is able to shatter the bonds of these undead with little trouble.

SLAAD

Alignment:	Neutral Evil
Creature Type:	Outsider
Feats:	Darkvision, Hold Person x6, Summon Slaad x1
Strength:	19
Dexterity:	15
Constitution:	17
Intelligence:	6
Wisdom:	6
Charisma:	10
Fortitude Save:	6
Reflex Save:	6
Will Save:	6
Base AC:	18
Base HP:	60

Manravon "The Lisp" Ildonsber was the first sorcerer to discover the existence of slaads. As a specialist in summoning, Manravon was given to all manner of strange activities. Instead of hiring a servant to fetch things for him, Manravon used special summoning magic for even little things. Sadly, this great sorcerer met his end one day by trying to summon a salad from his kitchen. Forgetting how badly his lisp could affect certain spells, Manravon threw out his arms and summoned "Slaad." This didn't end well for him.

Although slaads have a basic level of intelligence, very little is known about their nature, culture or way of living. In Faerun, slaads are summoned by powerful mages to help with critical battles or very heavy labor. Slaads are powerful and vicious, and their skill in battle is matched only by highly trained bladesmen.

SPIRIT

Alignment:	Chaotic Evil
Creature Type:	Undead
Feats:	Darkvision
Strength:	10
Dexterity:	12
Constitution:	10
Intelligence:	11
Wisdom:	11
Charisma:	18
Fortitude Save:	1
Reflex Save:	1
Will Save:	4
Base AC:	11
Base HP:	26

Spirits cover the nightscape, rising from their places of rest to wander the world. These dead are usually somewhat cognizant of their surroundings, and many search for certain changes that will bring them closer to peace. The loss of a beloved item could bring a spirit forth, as could a nearby tragedy that reminds a spirit of something from its own experience. Adventurers can put these undead to rest temporarily with violence, although this rarely "kills" the undead. For final sleep, spirits should be given what they seek or convinced that there is no longer a reason to suffer.

STINGER

Alignment:	Neutral Evil
Creature Type:	Humanoid
Strength:	16
Dexterity:	14
Constitution:	14
Intelligence:	10
Wisdom:	10
Charisma:	12
Fortitude Save:	4
Reflex Save:	1
Will Save:	1
Base AC:	15
Base HP:	26

The Anauroch desert is dangerous even without monsters, but stingers make the area worse for almost everyone who passes through. Large underground tunnels protect the breeding pits where stingers are raised, and only the powerful archers and warriors of the hive go up to the surface for raiding. The ability to burrow through both sand and rock makes it even harder for people to know where stingers will appear. A safe campsite one year could be a den of pitfalls and slashing blades the next time a caravan passes.

Stingers are fairly religious as a society. The priests have greater power than even the most powerful warriors in the den, and the animalistic gods of these beasts are not without power. Given to sacrifices and complex rituals, some stingers even have control over the dead. Entire mercenary bands have failed to clear out stinger dens when faced with such terrors.

WILD ANIMALS

Alignment:	True Neutral
Creature Type:	Animal
Strength:	10
Dexterity:	11
Constitution:	10
Intelligence:	3
Wisdom:	12
Charisma:	10
Fortitude Save:	2
Reflex Save:	2
Will Save:	0
Base AC:	10
Base HP:	5

Out in the wild, animals are unpredictable. One bear can be cute and friendly while the next might be looking for supper! Rangers and druids have the power to calm and control many of these feral beasts, and they can also be a source of protection for such characters. Others, however, should stay away from even calm animals unless they are looking for a fight. Respect an animal's territory and it might be willing to tolerate your passage. Another note for the wise: stay away from animal burrows. Babies that are soft and cuddly often have parents that are sharp and chompy.

WINTER WOLF

Alignment:	Chaotic Neutral
Creature Type:	Magical Beast
Feats:	Darkvision
Strength:	17
Dexterity:	13
Constitution:	15
Intelligence:	9
Wisdom:	13
Charisma:	10
Fortitude Save:	4
Reflex Save:	4
Will Save:	1
Base AC:	13
Base HP:	34

Areas with substantial magic can give rise to beasts with exceptional powers. Winter wolves are a good (and scary) example of this. Somewhat like hellhounds, these wolves are indigenous to Faerun. The increased strength and toughness of winter wolves is noteworthy by itself, but these canines also have a cold breath attack that must be heeded. Fortunately, adventurers do not run into packs of winter wolves on many occasions, so parties can gang up on these lone hunters.

WORG

Alignment:	Chaotic Neutral
Creature Type:	Magical Beast
Feats:	Darkvision
Strength:	17
Dexterity:	15
Constitution:	15
Intelligence:	6
Wisdom:	14
Charisma:	10
Fortitude Save:	4
Reflex Save:	4
Will Save:	1
Base AC:	14
Base HP:	30

Worgs are also magical beasts appearing in cool and temperate climates. These large, wolf-like beasts are a lot more docile than one might expect, and that has led to their domestication by several barbaric races, including goblins and orcs in certain areas. This should not let adventurers be lulled into the sense that worgs are safe to approach; undomesticated worgs are still a grave threat to anyone who lets his guard down.

Human hunters who hunt worgs to protect their cattle often use reinforced spears to pin the monsters to the ground. Even then, it takes several warriors with a steady hand to kill a worg without losing a person or two. It isn't uncommon to see a worg drive itself all the way up a spear just to rend the hapless hunter at the other end. Tough doesn't even begin to cut it when describing such brutes.

WYRMLING

Alignment:	Chaotic Evil
Creature Type:	Dragon
Feats:	Immunity to Sleep, Darkvision
Strength:	11
Dexterity:	10
Constitution:	13
Intelligence:	6
Wisdom:	11
Charisma:	6
Fortitude Save:	3
Reflex Save:	3
Will Save:	3
Base AC:	13
Base HP:	22

"What is small, soft, and fun to play with?"

Not Wyrmlings, that is for sure. Young dragons may not be even remotely dangerous when compared with their elders, but anything remotely related to wyrms should be given a wide berth or at least full attention. The only reason an adventurer would want to brave the developing scales and ripping claws of wyrmlings would be to find ingredients for very potent magics. Dragon eggs, blood, and body parts can sell for a great deal of money in Thay and other places of arcane study. At most stores, dragon parts are just junk, but to the right dealer there is a lot of money to be made.

Wyrmlings are too young to come up with plots of their own. Without guile, they attack almost anything that comes near their caves. Until they reach early maturity, wyrmlings will be surprisingly gentle with each other, meaning that such caves can have as many as a dozen individuals. The litter of bones, smell of blood and excrement, and flapping of wings will at least alert spelunkers that they are getting into trouble. It just might be too late to escape by then.

ZOMBIE

Alignment:	Neutral Evil
Creature Type:	Undead
Feats:	Darkvision
Strength:	13
Dexterity:	8
Constitution:	10
Intelligence:	10
Wisdom:	10
Charisma:	3
Fortitude Save:	0
Reflex Save:	0
Will Save:	3
Base AC:	9
Base HP:	15

Zombies are almost the opposite of most undead. Instead of having a spirit return to the world after its body has passed on, zombies are the presence of a body without any spirit to speak of. Without a true mind, these undead attack anything that lives without any sense of self-preservation. Zombies are slow and witless, but they absorb a fair bit of damage before returning to a natural state of death.

One scary thing about zombies (beyond the obvious) is that they often rise in huge packs. Although a normal human could avoid or outrun a single zombie, it is pretty hard to dodge a wall of broken hands, fingers, and teeth. Being torn apart by a band of these wandering dead summons such a strong image of fear to most adventurers' minds that it shows true courage to stand one's ground in the face of zombies. Beware the shambling hordes of the undead!

Chapter One: Humble Beginnings

Drogan's manor has been a place of learning and importance for many students over the years. Although it's a far cry from a formal academy of magic, the house serves an incredible variety of students. Instead of taking only mages as apprentices, Drogan teaches human and half-orc, paladin and sorcerer alike. This openness may be what draws the hero to such a strange place. Or it could be rumors of intrigue and hidden artifacts that piques the character's interest. Either way, the story begins in the midst of an attack on the manor…

Drogan's Manor

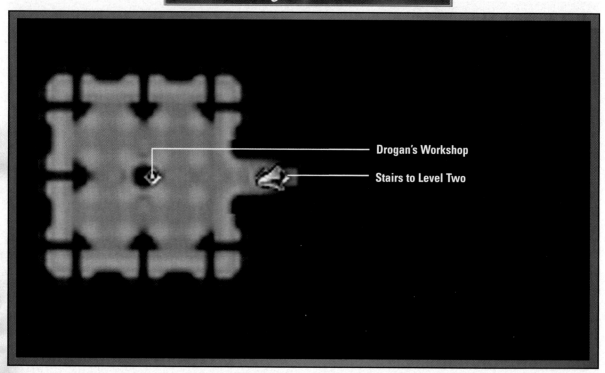

Drogan's Workshop

Stairs to Level Two

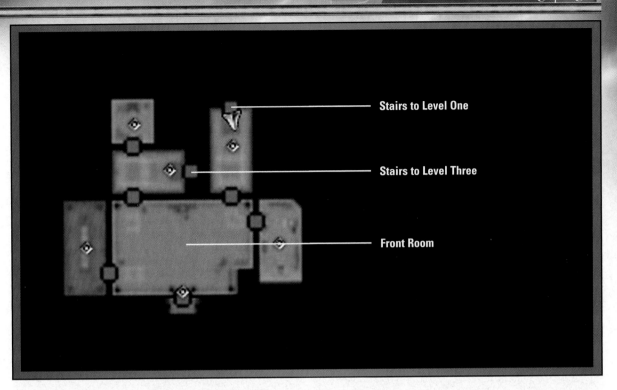

Stairs to Level One

Stairs to Level Three

Front Room

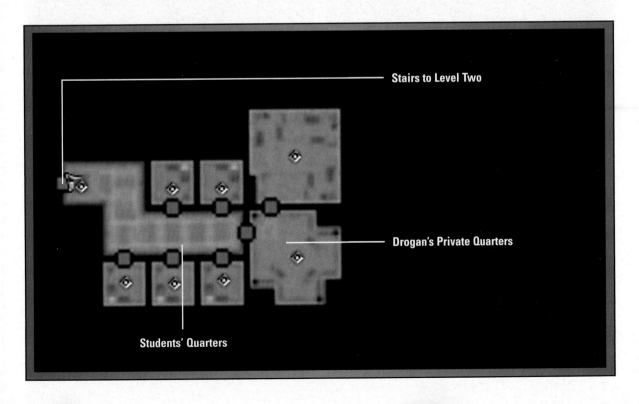

Stairs to Level Two

Drogan's Private Quarters

Students' Quarters

KOBOLD

Alignment:	Lawful Evil
Creature Type:	Humanoid
Fortitude Save:	2
Reflex Save:	0
Will Save:	0
Base AC:	13
Base HP:	2

KOBOLD SHAMAN

Alignment:	Lawful Evil
Creature Type:	Humanoid, Sorcerer
Fortitude Save:	2
Reflex Save:	0
Will Save:	2
Base AC:	13
Base HP:	10

KOBOLD FOOTPAD

Alignment:	Lawful Evil
Creature Type:	Humanoid, Rogue
Fortitude Save:	2
Reflex Save:	2
Will Save:	0
Base AC:	14
Base HP:	12

KOBOLD THUG

Alignment:	Lawful Evil
Creature Type:	Humanoid, Barbarian
Fortitude Save:	4
Reflex Save:	0
Will Save:	0
Base AC:	13
Base HP:	13

KOBOLD HEALER

Alignment:	Lawful Evil
Creature Type:	Humandoid, Cleric
Fortitude Save:	4
Reflex Save:	0
Will Save:	2
Base AC:	13
Base HP:	10

UPSTAIRS BEDROOMS

Your character's room in the manor is fairly small and has only a few items of importance. Look inside the unlocked chest against the wall to collect the protagonist's possessions.

Inside the chest are 50 gold pieces, a Focus Crystal, a magic ring, a journal, and a small magical item that is intended to reflect something about your character.

The ring is called Mystra's Hand. If your character is in trouble and has a Focus Crystal, the ring's unique power can be used to teleport the character back to Drogan's manor. This item can be dragged down onto the quickbar for faster and more efficient use. One especially nice feature is that this ring needn't be worn for its power to be available. Characters only have to carry a Focus Crystal (which will be destroyed during the magical event).

The magical item you find in your chest is based on your character's class, and it will serve to boost one skill once per day for most of the items. A fighter can get a discipline buff, for example.

The journal will give players a fairly quick rundown on the other members of the manor. Other students have been training under Drogan, and it sounds like they cover a wide range of professions and philosophies.

The Gem Grinder can be used for more powerful alchemical processes. Combining the following ingredients will produce interesting items for characters that are interested.

GEM GRINDER

INGREDIENT1	INGREDIENT2	RESULT
Quartz	Green Spore	Ring of Disease Resistance
Quartz	Shadow Hart	Lesser Amulet of Health
2 Fenberries	Empty Bottle	Potion of Barkskin
Quartz	Practice Sword	Timonen Great Sword

After reading the journal and taking everything, close the chest and walk out into the hall. All three of the other students are waiting there and will talk to you about the upcoming trial. It seems that Drogan wants to give you a fairly complex test before graduation.

This is a good chance to begin roleplaying, because there are a number of ways to deal with the other students. You can be cocky or humble, devoted to Drogan or scrambling to get away from him. Whatever the case, there are no major changes to the game or your character no matter what choices you make.

ATTACK ON THE MANOR

The conversation breaks up when there are screams and howls from the floor below. Drogan seems to have gotten himself into dire trouble, and the other students use their rings to rush to the dwarf's aid. This is the noble thing to do, but you can follow the hallway and proceed through the door downstairs to save a Focus Crystal. For that matter, real roguish sorts may want to look through a few of the students' chests before heading down there—never a better time to look, eh?

Chaotic Tip

Blowing chests apart, bashing them, or picking the lock quietly will lead to the same end; your character will have his alignment shifted one point toward chaos.

There is a Minor Sonic Trap Kit and a set of Thieves Tools +1 in Dorna's room. Xanos has scrolls of Light and Daze, and a few other odd items. Mischa has a Training Sword in her chest.

A brave band of kobolds is going after Drogan, and things aren't looking so great for the old dwarf. Even with a wide range of spells at his disposal, there are too many kobolds for Drogan to take down. You arrive just a fraction too late to do anything more than mop up the crude host of jabbering monsters.

The fight isn't a very difficult one for melee, missile, or magical characters. Many of the kobolds will engage the other students and a newcomer who arrives to aid everyone against the attackers. Go forward as aggressively as your character's class warrants; barbarians can charge straight in, rogues can practice sneak attacks, etc.

Speak with Ayala when the battle is over. She claims to be from the Harpers and to have come with good intentions. Perhaps this is true, but she can do little for Drogan at the moment. The woman's spells of healing seem to have no effect; a poison has been used against the dwarf. To make matters worse, the kobolds have managed to get away with four artifacts that the wizard was safeguarding for his organization. With Ayala tied up protecting Drogan, yours is the only character with a chance to succeed in retrieving the items.

No matter how greedy you try to be, there isn't a single coin to start things off. Ayala won't even offer healing until Drogan is at least stabilized. Before exploring the rest of the manor, make sure to ask Ayala if there is anything else that can be done. She will give you a quest.

Also, don't try to pick up Drogan's walking stick. Even though this magical item is quite interesting, it is enchanted with the ability to drain the life from anyone, aside from Drogan, who touches it.

Quest Tip

A CURE FOR DROGAN

To begin curing Drogan, Ayala needs three ingredients that can be found in Hilltop: Tressym Tongue, Charcoal, and Helmthorn Berries.

The first two can be taken from the herbalist in town. He can be convinced to give these up without money or hassle—Drogan is a very important man in Hilltop. The berries can be taken from a cauldron inside the town tavern.

Return to Ayala with all three items to complete the quest.

It's completely up to the player whether to take a henchman along for the ride. Xanos and Dorna are perfectly willing to travel with you, so it's mostly a decision of need. Players who want to take their character through the adventure alone will have a harder time of things, but it can be done. Those who desire magical aid will enjoy Xanos, although he doesn't come into his own for at least a few levels. Dorna has a nice mix of abilities, but her penchant for paired weapons doesn't blend with her cruddy dedication to melee combat.

DON'T LOSE TRACK OF KEY ITEMS

As with most plot-based games, someone who can't find the critical items in the story won't be able to advance. There is a divining pool at the back of the main floor in the manor. Under certain circumstances, these arcane structures can draw key items from far and wide. If a player loses or drops one of the game-critical items in the world, that item will eventually wind up in the divining pool.

RIDDLE ME THIS

To get a few more useful items, use the door in the back wall to go downstairs. Drogan's lab was protected from invasion by magical enchantments, although it seems like the kobolds were able to avoid this problem. Riisi, Drogan's familiar, is down there and will explain what happened. The small creature is pretty shaken up by the recent events. She can't say for certain whether your character is an illusion or real. Answering three short riddles will convince Riisi that everything is okay and that you aren't a kobold in disguise.

If you start off the riddles on a good note (without threatening or yelling at Riisi), the first question will ask whether a woman can have five children with half of them as sons. The answer is yes (you gain a small XP award for the correct answer).

The first riddle is different if things start poorly: How many nines does it take to reach the number 100? The answer is 20, because every nine counts during the final stretch from 90-100, thus beefing the total up considerably (small XP award for the correct answer).

The second riddle queries the fate of a condemned man. A truthful answer will be the man's death by drowning; a false one will get him hanged. Saying that he will be hanged gets the guy off the hook because it creates a logical paradox: he can't be hanged because it would make the statement truthful; he can't be drowned because that will cause the statement to be false. Apparently, executioners are extremely literal in some places (small XP award for the correct answer).

The final riddle is a standard one; it forces a person to consider four trees that are used in pairs, but each pair must be unique. How many pairings are there? The answer is six: three for the first tree, two for the second, and one for the third (small XP award for the correct answer).

Chaotic Tip

Characters who lie to Riisi, saying that Master Drogan is fine, will shift one point toward chaos.

Answering all of the riddles correctly will get the PC several Focus Crystals, a Scare scroll, the key to Drogan's room, and a small XP award.

Use Drogan's key to head upstairs and take what is lying around in his chambers. There are helms, some decent missile weapons, a blade, and an axe. Take as much as your character can carry, and sell what isn't needed at the blacksmith's shop in town.

The table at the center of the side room can be used to make Focus Crystals, even if the character doesn't know a darn thing about alchemy or wizardry. A tiny manual will explain the process; a Quartz Crystal and one of several gems can be placed in the Grinder to accomplish this.

Rest and equip any new and useful items before slipping out the door into Western Hilltop.

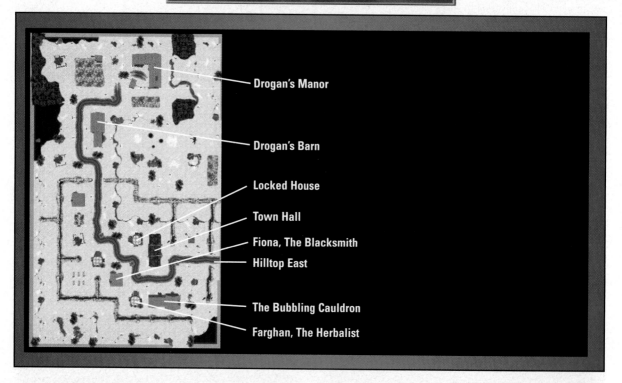

- Drogan's Manor
- Drogan's Barn
- Locked House
- Town Hall
- Fiona, The Blacksmith
- Hilltop East
- The Bubbling Cauldron
- Farghan, The Herbalist

CHICKEN

Alignment:	True Neutral
Creature Type:	Animal
Fortitude Save:	2
Reflex Save:	2
Will Save:	0
Base AC:	10
Base HP:	4

KOBOLD

Alignment:	Lawful Evil
Creature Type:	Humanoid
Fortitude Save:	2
Reflex Save:	0
Will Save:	0
Base AC:	13
Base HP:	2

DOG

Alignment:	True Neutral
Creature Type:	Animal
Fortitude Save:	3
Reflex Save:	3
Will Save:	0
Base AC:	10
Base HP:	15

KOBOLD FOOTPAD

Alignment:	Lawful Evil
Creature Type:	Humanoid, Rogue
Fortitude Save:	2
Reflex Save:	2
Will Save:	0
Base AC:	14
Base HP:	12

KOBOLD THUG

Alignment:	Lawful Evil
Creature Type:	Humanoid, Barbarian
Fortitude Save:	4
Reflex Save:	0
Will Save:	0
Base AC:	13
Base HP:	13

RAT

Alignment:	True Neutral
Creature Type:	Animal
Fortitude Save:	2
Reflex Save:	2
Will Save:	0
Base AC:	14
Base HP:	1

OX

Alignment:	True Neutral
Creature Type:	Animal
Fortitude Save:	2
Reflex Save:	2
Will Save:	0
Base AC:	9
Base HP:	6

There are several mangy dogs walking around the barn, but they are relatively friendly unless anyone tries to take a swing at them. Walk along the path the leads into the main part of town, but look inside the barn on the left for a quick battle against two hiding kobolds. It seems as if the attack has spread kobolds throughout the village. The defenders will have their work cut out for them if they intend to root out all of the savages. All the more chances to help out or make some spare coins.

Neutral Tip

THE PATH OF NATURE

Rangers and Druids who use animal empathy are able to speak with various creatures in and around Hilltop. The guard dogs can explain some of the recent occurrences, the chickens have noticed a bit of treasure, and so forth. For extra experience and a few meager items, characters with this talent should contact as many animals as possible.

There is a side quest for people who speak with the dogs in Hilltop. These hounds will tell you about Bethsheva, the Druid's Wolf; anyone who spends a fair bit of time in the herbalist's store will notice that his dog is by no means a normal mutt.

Bethsheva can be persuaded to reveal a magical ring; she buried this to test the dogs of the town. If they can find the ring, she will take them as a mate. This ring is hidden in the stones behind the smithy. Telling one of the town dogs where the ring is will finally get Bethsheva a mate. Or, you could take the ring and tell the dog where it used to be.

The ring itself grants the wearer a bonus to animal empathy, which is certainly a nice thing to have for characters that embark on this type of quest.

There are many places where you can rest safely, so there is no harm or shame in taking a nap after any of the fights that follow.

LOCAL ATTRACTIONS

Fiona, the blacksmith, has her shop open. Hurry down there before doing too much inside Hilltop. There, you can unload some of the extra items that you took from Drogan's room or from the other students.

Make sure to grab a better weapon, at least one that suits your character and skills. Also consider the armor selection at the shop and take a better suit before you leave. The trivial amount of gold that you throw away now will be made up exponentially, so there is no reason to save.

Just to the side of Fiona's store is the herbalist's eccentric abode. Farghan is a fairly good man and will help you out with a number of things. Telling him the truth about Drogan will get you two of the three herbs for the "A Cure for Drogan" quest. Using persuade makes it possible to glean 100 gold and possibly some equipment, too; the second persuade is made at moderate difficulty for a level-one character.

The city hall is on the other side of the street, guarded by a few armored men of Hilltop. Go inside and speak with Gilford, a noble priest of Ilmater. This cleric not only sells a decent number of items, including more armor and a few magical trinkets, but he also accepts donations for those in need.

Good Tip

GOLD FOR ILMATER

You can donate gold to Ilmater, and it certainly is needed. This will shift your character's alignment toward good. The first donation that you give will determine the extent of the shift, so players who desire a strong alignment shift should wait until the full 100-gold-piece limit can be donated.

Chaotic Tip

KOBOLD DEFENSE TAX

There are several people in town that can be duped into believing that there is a tax for the defense of Hilltop. Gilford can be tricked into donating 10 gold this way. Fiona, the blacksmith, can also be tricked, although she will hold onto her money and simply complain about the whole affair. This shifts your player's alignment toward chaos.

Evil Tip

BEING THIS EVIL IS RARELY COMPLEX

It is easy to gain points of evil for anyone who is interested. What's the shocking strategy for accomplishing this? Murder...sweet, luscious murder! Killing the people of Hilltop will invariably lead your character down a path of darkness with considerable speed. The more innocent the target, the more evil is gained.

Thus, killing the mayor is practically a favor to the town (only one point toward evil), while it's much worse to kill innocents like the old man in the tavern or Nora Blake (five points toward evil for every innocent victim).

Haniah, the Mayor's advisor, is really the person in charge at town hall. In times of crisis, the Mayor seems to put his faith in the bottom of a bottle rather than the gods or good efforts. Haniah is a stronger person and a good woman, so she is organizing things to free Hilltop of the kobolds. Among other problems, she even has to deal with a few villagers who are beginning to make trouble. A helpful player is always welcome at such times.

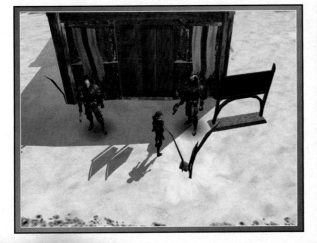

Quest Tip

AN EXCESS OF PROPHET

Piper is a local misfit who has been making odd predictions for some time. Nobody really paid the guy much mind until recently; the attacks gave him his first piece of luck. Now, the man's words of doom and gloom are gaining some credibility. You have to take care of this, but how?

Killing Piper directly, without even stopping to speak with him, is evil and dangerous. People around town will not approve of having a citizen struck down in front of them, even if it is Piper.

Getting Piper to attack your character during a conversation takes only a couple lines of direct threats. Piper will strike at you, but this is ultimately a mismatched encounter. The followers will disperse from this sound beating, but the event will leave a sour taste in everyone's mouths.

Discredit Piper by showing that he has committed crimes of his own, simply to make his omens come to light. This will turn the community away from him, thus saving the town from Piper's foolery.

Get Piper to leave town and spread his "philosophy" elsewhere by suggesting that other, larger towns are in need of a prophet. Whether you send him to Neverwinter or Silverymoon, Piper will try to get some money for making the trip. A modest persuasion will convince the lunatic that the gods will provide for him instead.

Get Piper his blade and convince him to defend Hilltop for a truly righteous conclusion. This way, the town doesn't lose anyone, and indeed it gains a defender to replace a few of the men that were killed in the fighting. Do this by bringing up the need for good and honest defenders for Hilltop. Piper will explain that he had to sell his blade to Fiona; you can then go to Fiona and convince her to just give the blade back (it's hardly worth anything). One point of chaos can be gained by telling the lie that Piper accused Fiona of thievery during this event. Either way, giving the sword back to Piper will end the crisis in a peaceful way.

After Piper has left, try looking on the other side of the street. There is a sign by a large building that announces a tavern. Some shouting can be heard from inside, and there certainly could be trouble.

The Bubbling Cauldron is the main inn and tavern of Hilltop. Normally, there are men and women enjoying drink and each other's company in the inn's large common room, but a number of kobolds are currently barricaded in the kitchen. As you enter, a standoff rages between the terrified kobolds and the angry villagers who are ready to tear them apart. The only thing stopping the mob is the kobolds' hostage, the inn's cook Mara.

Quest Tip

KOBOLDS IN THE KITCHEN

Lodar, the innkeeper, wants Mara to get out of this alive. There is coin to be made during this encounter, one way or another. For a crafty character, there are many ways to deal with this problem. If you question the importance of saving Mara or hold out on assisting, there will be alignment ramifications. Your character shifts one point toward evil for saying each of the following: "I don't see this as my problem," "Losing Mara wouldn't be such a bad thing," asking why it is important to help, and for pondering whether to help the kobolds instead.

Before attending to the kobolds, you can threaten to rob the old man in the corner. The bum smells of whiskey and useless dreams, so why not take everything he has? You'll shift one point toward chaos just for threatening to do this, and going through with it adds three more points to chaos for robbing an old man in the middle of a kobold attack.

Using persuade, you can take Mara's place, dramatically improving the chance for a peaceful resolution. Persuasion and intimidation can also be used to get the kobolds out of the barricade, either to flee or surrender. Lawful or Good characters should work toward letting the kobolds surrender and then keep the mob from murdering the invaders. Chaotic types enjoy breaking promises, so they should lure the kobolds out and set the mob on them.

If the kobolds are allowed to leave with Mara, they will eventually kill her and leave her body in the Foothills outside Hilltop.

Helping the kobolds by killing the mob of humans will take your character almost all the way toward evil, a massive alignment shift for anyone who isn't already there. Still, there is a dagger that the kobold leader will offer as a reward if this action is taken. Hurc's Dagger has vampiric regeneration.

Bards and mages with a Sleep spell are given an extra option to use their talents on the kobolds. This will keep the creatures distracted while your character destroys the barricade and gives the mob room to rush into the breech.

Characters without a decent persuade or any of the listed abilities won't have much of a choice. The kobolds won't listen to reason, so the time comes for you to kick down the barricade. Mara will die from this; the kobolds guarding her take less than a second to end Mara's life. There won't be an alignment penalty for this ending, but it is certainly upsetting that the cook could not be saved.

If the kobolds are killed and Mara is saved, Lodar will be happy to pay a small reward. This is normally 50 gold pieces, but persuasion or threats can double this; forcing Lodar to pay more will shift your character one point toward evil. Mara can be threatened for 10 additional gold pieces; this will also shift your character one point toward evil.

There are Helmthorn berries in a pot at the back of the inn. After the kobolds are gone, these are quick to take and no one will be upset about the loss. Most of the people are just happy to be alive (unless, of course, everyone got killed in the fighting, but there really won't be any complaints then).

Once all of the quests for this area have been attended to, go to the eastern edge of the map and proceed through the gates into Eastern Hilltop. You're needed there as well.

Eastern Hilltop

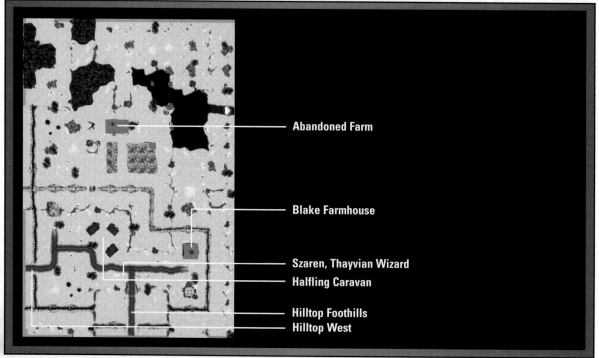

- Abandoned Farm
- Blake Farmhouse
- Szaren, Thayvian Wizard
- Halfling Caravan
- Hilltop Foothills
- Hilltop West

DEER

Alignment:	True Neutral
Creature Type:	Animal
Fortitude Save:	2
Reflex Save:	2
Will Save:	0
Base AC:	10
Base HP:	5

KOBOLD FOOTPAD

Alignment:	Lawful Evil
Creature Type:	Humanoid, Rogue
Fortitude Save:	2
Reflex Save:	2
Will Save:	0
Base AC:	14
Base HP:	12

DOG

Alignment:	True Neutral
Creature Type:	Animal
Fortitude Save:	3
Reflex Save:	3
Will Save:	0
Base AC:	10
Base HP:	15

KOBOLD HEALER

Alignment:	Lawful Evil
Creature Type:	Humandoid, Cleric
Fortitude Save:	4
Reflex Save:	0
Will Save:	2
Base AC:	13
Base HP:	10

KOBOLD SHAMAN

Alignment:	Lawful Evil
Creature Type:	Humanoid, Sorcerer
Fortitude Save:	2
Reflex Save:	0
Will Save:	2
Base AC:	13
Base HP:	10

KOBOLD THUG

Alignment:	Lawful Evil
Creature Type:	Humanoid, Barbarian
Fortitude Save:	4
Reflex Save:	0
Will Save:	0
Base AC:	13
Base HP:	13

There is a caravan of halflings not far into the east side of town. These traders have chosen a poor time to pull into Hilltop, and they were recently attacked by the kobolds. Speak to Furten to find out a bit more about the fighting, and then talk to Torias and Katriana. These two will tell you about some cards that were stolen from the mystic of the troupe; the kobolds fled to an abandoned farm north of the caravan site.

Good Tip

HEALING THE WOUNDED

There are injured halflings in the caravan. Using healing spells or abilities will restore them. This will also cause your alignment to shift toward goodness by one point. A slight XP bonus will also be awarded. Repeating this for other wounded people and creatures, such as those in the town center, will continue this process.

Quest Tip

NOT PLAYING WITH A FULL DECK

If you're tracking down the stolen cards, it doesn't take long to find the farmhouse. Walk west down the road until you come to a slope that rises into the upper plateau of the region. Follow the tracks in the snow and go into the main building of the farmhouse beyond. Those tracks lead all the way into the root cellar of the house; several kobolds are hiding within. There is also a box on the top floor with a Gold Ring, a Quartz Crystal, and some pieces of gold. You may catch a disease from opening this box, but you'll otherwise be unharmed; it isn't too vile a disease, and it is fairly easy to resist.

The beasts below won't give anyone a chance to talk things out. These are vicious and desperate kobolds, and they need to be brought down by magic or steel. The fight isn't difficult and the leader at the back of the room has the halflings' cards. Take those back for a special reading, or turn down the reward and receive three points toward goodness.

If you choose the reading, Daschnaya will tell a vague tale about a creature that is frightened and in trouble nearby, hiding in a town to the east. Your duty is to find and protect this creature if the artifacts are to be returned. Who or what caused the kobolds to attack the village is still a mystery.

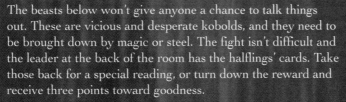

Further along the road is a red mage of Thay; his name is Szaren. This wizard has been sent by his superior to set up a magic shop in the region of Hilltop. This is not as simple a proposition as it could be because few people enjoy the presence of Thay wizards. Szaren wants the protagonist to speak with the mayor on his behalf and convince him that a magic shop would be mutually beneficial.

Quest Tip

THAYVIAN ENCLAVE

Szaren may be able to act the part of a diplomat, but that doesn't mean that he is a nice man in the least. In fact, many of the rumors about Thay wizards are based in truth; they aren't a nice group of people. Running the creep out of town after hearing his argument will shift you toward goodness and chaos by one point.

On the other hand, having a store in town with such potential is hard to ignore. You should listen to Szaren and go to the mayor if this is your goal. Characters with a good reputation (those who haven't murdered Piper and other townsfolk) can use some guile to convince the mayor that the Thay wizards would be useful allies. Considering the recent attack, everyone is feeling a bit exposed. Drawing on these anxieties will make it far easier to land the deal. Szaren will give you some money and promise substantial discounts when the store is finished.

If the mayor refuses to see the light about the matter, he and his advisor can be killed. Szaren is completely comfortable with this arrangement as well, and he will reward you without missing a beat. Obviously, this will shift your alignment toward evil by several points.

When Szaren returns, he will set up his shop in Toman's old house—nobody wants to cut the old guy any breaks after his failure to join everyone during the attack. Not only is this new store a good place to buy items, but Szaren also has a taste for the exotic. There are several items that the Thayvian will purchase from you, including:

ITEM	PRICE PAID
Dragon Egg	700 gold pieces or a cloak with +1 to AC, fire resistance, and light
Mask	1,000 gold pieces or 1,200 if persuade succeeds
Mummified Hand	1,000 gold pieces—persuade is hard to use
Dragon's Tooth	500 gold pieces, 700 with persuade

Before leaving town, one final person approaches in need of a hero. Nora Blake lives with her husband Adam on the east edge of Hilltop. When you see her, she is running down the road with fear in her eyes. Kobolds have attacked her house, and both Adam and her child remain inside. It may already be too late to save her family.

Quest Tip

SAVE MY FAMILY

Spare no time in entering the house. Two kobolds wait near the door, perhaps ready to ambush Nora as she returns. They are not expecting someone as well armed as your character, so the fight should turn against them very quickly. Take the gem from the floor nearby before walking up the steps.

In the master bedroom on the second floor, there is a cunning kobold that has taken the baby hostage. It wouldn't take the kobold long to kill Tynan, so jumping for the child is unlikely to succeed. No matter how powerful your character, the situation must be dealt with carefully.

Any direct attack on the kobolds will be the death of Tynan, and intimidation doesn't work either. This vermin is only smart enough to realize that he has the upper hand; he isn't smart enough to know what that could cost him.

To save Tynan's life, give the kobold the gem from below. At that point, the beast will hand over Tynan. For a brief moment, while the dialogue box is still open, it is your choice whether to strike down the kobold in retribution. There are no alignment changes whether the kobold lives or dies.

Outside, Nora will be frantic. She wants to know what has happened. Telling her the truth and giving Tynan to her is the right thing to do. Instead of a reward, give her some money as well to make sure that she can feed herself and her child while getting back on her feet. Refusing Nora's reward shifts you toward goodness; giving her some money furthers this.

Of course, it was dangerous inside the house, and there wasn't a lot of treasure to be gained. You can demand a reward (for three points toward evil and chaos). This won't get you much, but threatening recent widows is a good thing…if you are cruel, evil, sadistic, and foul. Budding assassins should think of this as "morality" training.

Also, you can simply refuse to return Tynan to his mother. This will cause the distraught woman to attack you. Her death will ensure that people in the village will treat you with a new air of respect and fear (this shifts your character toward evil by five points).

Lying to Nora and saying that her family is alive and well inside the house is a tough persuade to make, but it can be done. This is a chaotic action and will gain you nothing.

With everything quiet again in Hilltop, there is finally a chance to track down the kobolds. Walk to the southern gate and talk with the guard before leaving; he doesn't sound too enthusiastic about having anyone go into the wilderness, even with Xanos or Dorna coming along. Still, no one else is volunteering to help.

Hilltop Foothills

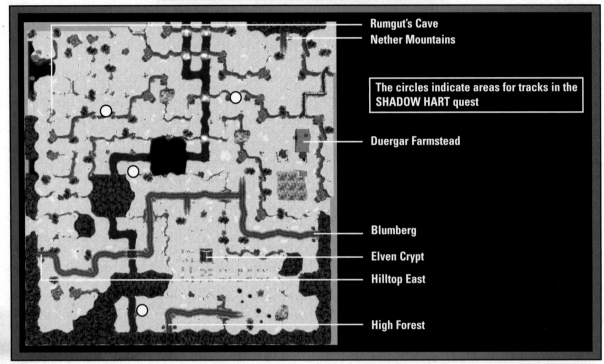

Rumgut's Cave
Nether Mountains

The circles indicate areas for tracks in the SHADOW HART quest

Duergar Farmstead

Blumberg

Elven Crypt

Hilltop East

High Forest

BROWN BEAR

Alignment:	True Neutral
Creature Type:	Animal
Fortitude Save:	5
Reflex Save:	5
Will Save:	2
Base AC:	15
Base HP:	51

GNOLL

Alignment:	Chaotic Evil
Creature Type:	Humanoid
Fortitude Save:	4
Reflex Save:	0
Will Save:	0
Base AC:	11
Base HP:	11

DEER

Alignment:	True Neutral
Creature Type:	Animal
Fortitude Save:	2
Reflex Save:	2
Will Save:	0
Base AC:	10
Base HP:	5

GNOLL SHAMAN

Alignment:	Chaotic Evil
Creature Type:	Humanoid, Sorcerer
Fortitude Save:	3
Reflex Save:	0
Will Save:	3
Base AC:	11
Base HP:	24

HILL GIANT

Alignment:	Chaotic Evil
Creature Type:	Giant
Fortitude Save:	8
Reflex Save:	4
Will Save:	8
Base AC:	17
Base HP:	102

KOBOLD

Alignment:	Lawful Evil
Creature Type:	Humanoid
Fortitude Save:	2
Reflex Save:	0
Will Save:	0
Base AC:	13
Base HP:	2

KOBOLD FOOTPAD

Alignment:	Lawful Evil
Creature Type:	Humanoid, Rogue
Fortitude Save:	2
Reflex Save:	2
Will Save:	0
Base AC:	14
Base HP:	12

KOBOLD HEALER

Alignment:	Lawful Evil
Creature Type:	Humandoid, Cleric
Fortitude Save:	4
Reflex Save:	0
Will Save:	2
Base AC:	13
Base HP:	10

KOBOLD SHAMAN

Alignment:	Lawful Evil
Creature Type:	Humanoid, Sorcerer
Fortitude Save:	2
Reflex Save:	0
Will Save:	2
Base AC:	13
Base HP:	10

KOBOLD THUG

Alignment:	Lawful Evil
Creature Type:	Humanoid, Barbarian
Fortitude Save:	4
Reflex Save:	0
Will Save:	0
Base AC:	13
Base HP:	13

OX

Alignment:	True Neutral
Creature Type:	Animal
Fortitude Save:	2
Reflex Save:	2
Will Save:	0
Base AC:	9
Base HP:	6

There is a campsite on top of a small rise, not far down the road into the foothills. An elf loiters there, and he is more than happy to offer the warmth of his fire to anyone who comes along. Ferran Valiantheart is the archer's name; he is one of the elves who have mastered arcane archery. You may wish to speak with Ferran about his profession, but he knows of other things as well.

YOU CALL THAT A BOW?

It will shift your character three points toward chaos if you threaten the elf. Being an arcane archer, the bowman isn't likely to heed the threat either, so thieves who desire the elf's possessions are looking at a fight. Melee characters are the best bet for bringing Ferran down. Stay on the elf from the beginning of the fight and hope for good things.

The arcane archer has an Amulet of Natural Armor +1, a full set of Ice Arrows, and a special Longbow with a +1 enchantment and +2 to search.

The kobolds that left Hilltop ran into a bit of an ambush not far from Ferran's camp. A nasty pack of Gnolls came out of the trees and put the fear of the reaper into the tiny beasts. Many of the kobolds were killed, but some fled into the crypt to the south. To learn more about the attack on Hilltop, that seems like the best place to look.

Quest Tip

HORNS OF THE SHADOW HART

Asking Ferran about the strange deer tracks in the snow will get him to explain his presence in the area. The elf's wife has a foul illness that few normal means can cure. To save her, the arcane archer is looking for a creature known as the Shadow Hart. This beast is magical and can teleport short distances; this makes it quite hard to track. Ferran asks you to bring the horns of Shadow Hart to him if the creature ever turns up.

Finding the beast takes a fair bit of time, and this quest isn't worth the trouble for people who aren't driven to complete all possible missions. Before the Shadow Hart can appear, you must find several sets of its tracks. These tracks are even hidden from view until you walk almost on top of them. Look for these tracks in the following locations: at the southern exit of the map that leads to the High Forest (by the treeline to the west); in the northeast, when moving on the area above the dwarven farm; on the path to Rumgut's cave; and in the secluded area that is close to Ferran's campsite.

You will be informed when the Shadow Hart appears. A message says that a loud noise is overheard. Look near the track locations at this point, and the creature will be standing near one of them. Speaking to the beast gives the character a chance to scare it away, thus earning a few points of goodness. People with animal empathy can use their skills to get close to the Shadow Hart before attacking, should they wish.

If the Shadow Hart is killed quickly, before it can flee, the horns can be taken back to Ferran to complete the quest.

A veteran warrior has made a homestead for himself on the northeastern edge of the Hilltop Foothills. Nathan Hurst is his name, and the dwarven fighter looks like he has seen more than a fair share of battles. Despite that, he needs someone to help rescue his daughter from a moronic hill giant to the west. This giant, Rumgut, is not terribly violent, but he has kidnapped Nathan's daughter. Because the dwarf is taking care of his wife, who is about to go into labor, he desperately needs you to deal with Rumgut. None of Nathan's farmhands appears up to the challenge. Even though this warrior is a Duergar, it seems that he can be trusted.

Quest Tip

RUMGUT NEEDS A WIFE

Rumgut's cave is very easy to find—not every cave has a 16-foot entrance. On the western side of the foothills, up near the northern edge, is a cave with an unguarded entrance. There is something strange about the rocks along the backside of the cliff, but those are of little consequence at the moment.

Rumgut is inside the cave, and so is Becka. The dull giant believes that Becka is a young giant and will eventually grow up to be a fine wife for him. There are so many logical problems with this that it isn't even funny. The trick is to convince Rumgut to behave without getting him upset. He is drunk beyond repair, so that could be easier said than done.

The direct way to deal with a rogue hill giant often involves a dozen archers and a sensible ambush. Lacking those things, it isn't very wise to go after Rumgut directly, unless your character is of fairly high level and is playing through the game a second time. In almost any fight, Rumgut will mop the floor with anyone of modest level, whether a melee character, missile wielder, or spellcaster. Rumgut does have an Amulet of Natural Armor +1.

To be safer, try to persuade the giant that Becka will never grow any taller or make a good wife for him. This isn't too easy to pull off, but paladins or bards can do it. Convinced of this, Rumgut will simply let Becka go.

If talking to the dull giant doesn't get Becka out of her cell, offer to join her. This will give you a chance to discover the passage that leads out of the cell. Taking Becka out through that route doesn't take long and it gets her home safe and sound.

Return to Nathan for his sincere thanks and a modest reward. Threatening Becka at this point will cause the entire farm to attack you, shifting your character many points toward evil and chaos in the process.

Before moving on to the next village, seek the elven crypt. The kobolds that sought refuge in the elves' place of rest may still have an artifact. Beyond that, they likely have some information about the attack and why Drogan was targeted in the first place.

Elven Crypt

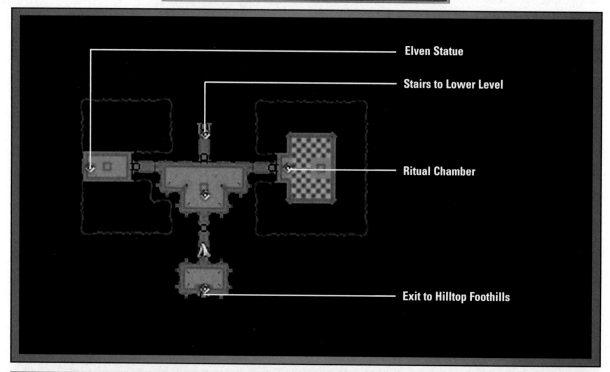

- Elven Statue
- Stairs to Lower Level
- Ritual Chamber
- Exit to Hilltop Foothills

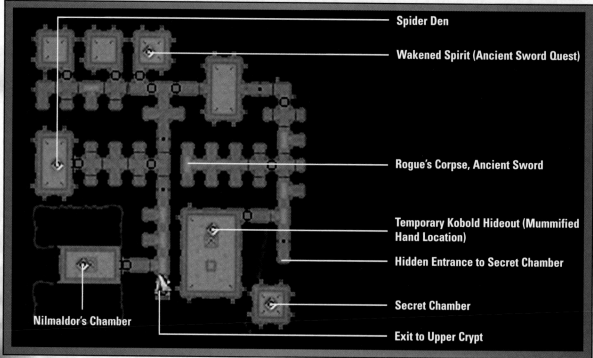

- Spider Den
- Wakened Spirit (Ancient Sword Quest)
- Rogue's Corpse, Ancient Sword
- Temporary Kobold Hideout (Mummified Hand Location)
- Hidden Entrance to Secret Chamber
- Secret Chamber
- Nilmaldor's Chamber
- Exit to Upper Crypt

GIANT SPIDER

Alignment:	True Neutral
Creature Type:	Vermin
Fortitude Save:	2
Reflex Save:	0
Will Save:	0
Base AC:	14
Base HP:	4

KOBOLD

Alignment:	Lawful Evil
Creature Type:	Humanoid
Fortitude Save:	2
Reflex Save:	0
Will Save:	0
Base AC:	13
Base HP:	2

KOBOLD SERGEANT

Alignment:	Lawful Evil
Creature Type:	Humanoid, Rogue
Fortitude Save:	2
Reflex Save:	2
Will Save:	0
Base AC:	14
Base HP:	8

RAT

Alignment:	True Neutral
Creature Type:	Animal
Fortitude Save:	2
Reflex Save:	2
Will Save:	0
Base AC:	14
Base HP:	1

SKELETON

Alignment:	Neutral Evil
Creature Type:	Undead
Fortitude Save:	0
Reflex Save:	0
Will Save:	2
Base AC:	10
Base HP:	6

SKELETAL ARCHER

Alignment:	Neutral Evil
Creature Type:	Undead
Fortitude Save:	2
Reflex Save:	2
Will Save:	5
Base AC:	18
Base HP:	20

SPIRIT

Alignment:	Chaotic Evil
Creature Type:	Undead
Fortitude Save:	1
Reflex Save:	1
Will Save:	4
Base AC:	11
Base HP:	26

Everything is quiet in the crypt's entrance chamber. In fact, it's almost serene. Yet, the smell of dank and dust only hint at the true horrors of these dungeons. The trails of blood that lead deeper into the structure are more direct clues that this place offers neither rest nor safety.

Beyond the first gate is a hoard of diseased rodents. A lone kobold straggler stands at the center of the room, beset by the rats. He doesn't stand a chance whether he falls to them or succumbs to your blade. Either way, heavy warrior types can stand and take the rats (especially with Cleave), while archers or mages can stay back at the door to keep too many from attacking at once.

The room on the left from the main chamber holds a statue of an elven warrior. Faithful prayers will grant healing and a slight shift toward goodness for injured characters. Spitting on the statue will curse your charcter; this is not recommended for even evil characters. Of course, pretending to pray isn't such a good idea either.

The door on the right is locked on the first attempt and can be dealt with later.

RESTLESS SPIRIT

The door on the far side of the main chamber leads to stairs. Descend these and proceed through the first door on the left in the lower crypt. The spirit of Nilmaldor is entombed there. His restlessness stems from a pack of spiders that lives in the next chamber over. These foul creatures offend the elven spirits and were left there by an interloper, a mage who has since passed. Nilmaldor will help you deal with the kobolds if you can clear out the spiders.

If you instead ask about treasure when speaking with Nilmaldor, the ghost will present you with the key to the upstairs ritual chamber. The spirit won't be very pleased with you after that point. Also, nasty characters on a quest for treasure can kill Nilmaldor's spirit and take the Longsword and Longbow from his tomb, along with the ritual key. Both of the weapons boast a +1 enchantment. Killing Nilmaldor shifts you three points toward evil and chaos.

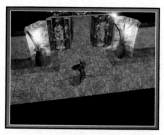

Two kobolds with crossbows have erected a barricade partway to the next chamber. A melee character can strike at them over the crates, so this isn't a very good plan for the monsters. Bash the crates to remove them from the path after the kobolds are dead. Mages and missile characters should have an even easier time with this fight, because there are no melee enemies to deal with.

THE EXTERMINATOR HAS ARRIVED

The next chamber contains the offending spiders. There are a fair number of the arachnids, so it is best to lure a few out at a time using spells or missile weapons. The spiders' poison is not terribly brutal, but it can make the ongoing battle more difficult through moderate penalties.

When all of the spiders are dead, walk to the back of the burial chamber and destroy the clutch of eggs that the spiders have left. This will complete the process and ensure that the crypt is free of the creatures for some time. The sarcophagus in the room is trapped and has little of value, but three of the cocoons have treasure. Several suits of normal Chainmail are available. A magical Cloak of Elvenkind and some Gauntlets of Animal Handling are present too!

Nilmaldor will do two things to reward you for dispatching the spiders. First, the spirit will describe a trap that has been laid in the room where the kobolds are hiding. This will make it a lot easier to handle the large group if a fight is necessary. Next, Nilmaldor will give you a key to the room on the upper level. There is a small magical item to be gained there for most player characters (a simple cloak or amulet), but paladins will *love* what they find. Characters who have paladin levels, even if they multiclass, will receive a set of Full Plate, a shield, and a helm. All of these are magical and of great value!

To complete the test without taking damage, look at the path of red beams that leads to the center of the chamber. Follow this path without stepping onto the normal tiles. Take the magic item(s) from the center, but find the path back without stepping on the red tiles. This ends up taking you onto the tile in front of the monument and a bit to the right. Move from there to the edge of the tiles and return to the front of the room from there. It's very easy to complete this and gain the Valiant Armor. Non-paladins can still do this for the quick XP.

Evil Tip

THE HEAD BONE IS CONNECTED TO THE TREASURE

Stealing from the living is a touchy thing; they can fight back, seek justice, or plead for compassion. It's a difficult matter and should only be dealt with by professionals. Stealing from the dead, however, is a good time all around. Sure, you'll shift one point toward evil with every item that you steal from the crypt cubbies along the walls, but money and a few magical trinkets should pay for a nice bath afterward.

This is considered to be a tempered evil action; that means that neutral or evil characters won't suffer an alignment shift from doing it. Only good characters will shift toward evil from robbing the dead. Everyone else is just being pragmatic.

A skeleton will pop up after each item is taken, but these can be killed (again) quickly for fast experience points and practice.

At the end of the tunnel is a fight between skeletons and another kobold. Holding back will make the fight easier to handle, as the enemies weaken each other. But bold players will prefer the rush of a chaotic melee. The door to the left contains a hallway where some of the more important elves were buried. The first of these rooms has a restless spirit who burns to see his blade returned to its rightful place.

Quest Tip

THE LOST SWORD

A human rogue of some sort came in and took the blade some time past. The best hope for finding the weapon again is that the cretin didn't make it out of the dungeon alive. Sure enough, the rogue's body is on the eastern side of the dungeon. A trap in the first room of the east corridor killed him. Take the sword from his body and return it to the spirit for a reward.

You can choose one of the following from the spirit's chest: a Sapphire, a Potion of Speed, or a magical Amulet of Cold Resistance.

You can break down the other two doors along the hallway. The spirits in those chambers have not been woken and their crypts are intact. Stealing even a single item from these will cause the warrior spirits to wake and attack; it will also shift a good character's alignment toward evil.

Kilrav's Ring

Search the bones across from the doors in the west hallway to find an interesting ring. This item, Kilrav's Ring, is especially wonderful for rogues because it grants a bonus point to many skills: Appraise, Craft Trap, Disable Trap, Hide, Lore, Move Silently, Open Lock, Pick Pocket, Search, Set Trap, and Use Magical Device.

Four kobolds are hiding behind the pillars down the right hallway that leads east. These crossbow wielders are not particularly tough, and you can use the pillars for partial cover as you deal with each rascal. There are skeletons as well, once the corridor turns south. Clerics and paladins can certainly practice the art of turning undead, but even lay characters shouldn't have much of a challenge in putting the beings to rest.

The first room off of the eastern passage has the body of the rogue who stole the spirit's ancient sword. There is a trap by the body that is easily detected and disarmed. A group without a rogue can walk over the trap without too much fear of dying—the blades that rise don't inflict a lot of damage.

WELL, HAVE A LOOK HERE!

Ignore the second door for a moment and walk to the end of the hall. Use the Spot ability until the secret door is detected. Inside that small room are several racks and a chest. Take a helm or two from the chest to protect your character and any allies from the gas trap that you will soon use. Arm this trap by pulling the lever on the right side of the room (it still won't go off until a pressure plate in the kobold's room is pressed). The second weapon rack has a Longbow +1, and many characters will be more than happy to take that before leaving.

Return to the second door and knock on it. A kobold's nervous voice will bark through the metal, asking what you are and what you are doing. With a bit of persuasion, you will be allowed to enter with your weapon sheathed. Disarm, don the helm as protection from the trap's affects, and go inside. You can choose whether to activate the trap immediately or to speak with the kobold leader first. Most people will appreciate the information gained from talking.

The kobolds do have the Mummified Hand, one of the four stolen artifacts. To gain this, persuade the kobolds that you will protect them from the gnolls outside. This takes a fair bit of doing, so a high-Charisma character with a well-perked persuasion is needed. Otherwise, the kobolds will explain what happened but remain guarded about giving up their only bargaining chip. If all negotiations fail, it is time to bring out the gas.

Stepping on the pressure plate near the door will trigger the gas trap quickly. This will affect many of the kobolds in the room, and they won't be able to fight very well until the entire trap has run its course—this takes many rounds. You are nearly free to wipe the floor with the disabled kobolds, so long as you wear the protective helm. Some would call this justice for everything that happened in Hilltop.

You can return to Ayala with the Mummified Hand, but it's equally important to stop at the blacksmith and get everything identified, sold, or equipped. This will relieve a lot of encumbrance for further treasure gathering! Your character won't gain much from returning the first artifact. After all is done, it's off to Blumberg.

Chaotic Tip

WHAT ARTIFACT?

You can keep the first three artifacts for yourself by lying to Ayala. Pretending not to have the artifacts will shift your character's alignment three points toward chaos. The artifacts can then be sold for around 1,000 gold pieces each.

Blumberg

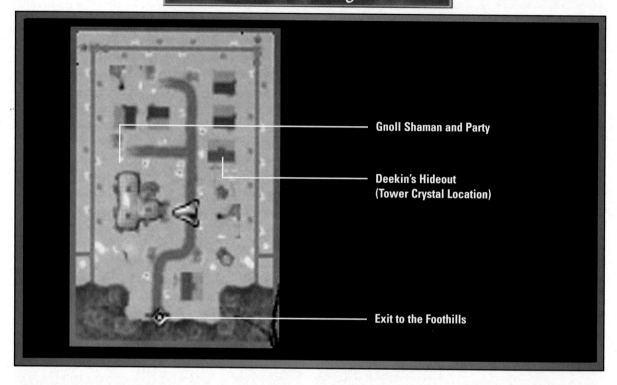

- Gnoll Shaman and Party
- Deekin's Hideout (Tower Crystal Location)
- Exit to the Foothills

COW

Alignment:	True Neutral
Creature Type:	Animal
Fortitude Save:	2
Reflex Save:	2
Will Save:	0
Base AC:	7
Base HP:	5

GNOLL

Alignment:	Chaotic Evil
Creature Type:	Humanoid
Fortitude Save:	4
Reflex Save:	0
Will Save:	0
Base AC:	11
Base HP:	11

DOG

Alignment:	True Neutral
Creature Type:	Animal
Fortitude Save:	3
Reflex Save:	3
Will Save:	0
Base AC:	10
Base HP:	15

GNOLL SHAMAN

Alignment:	Chaotic Evil
Creature Type:	Humanoid, Sorcerer
Fortitude Save:	3
Reflex Save:	0
Will Save:	3
Base AC:	11
Base HP:	24

OX		
Alignment:	True Neutral	
Creature Type:	Animal	
Fortitude Save:	2	
Reflex Save:	2	
Will Save:	0	
Base AC:	9	
Base HP:	6	

RAT		
Alignment:	True Neutral	
Creature Type:	Animal	
Fortitude Save:	2	
Reflex Save:	2	
Will Save:	0	
Base AC:	14	
Base HP:	1	

Things seem a bit trashed for a village that is supposed to be a beautiful gem of the Silver Marches. The gnolls who attacked the kobolds must be going after the people of Blumberg as well. Although it looks like you have arrived after the fighting is over, there are plenty of warriors left from the gnoll tribe. It's almost impossible to save even a single villager—there is only one to be seen, and he won't last very long.

Most of the gnolls are common warriors who are neither well trained nor well armed. Maneuver through the buildings and draw one or two of the fiends at a time to keep the fighting simple. Rogues and ranged characters will be especially happy because the terrain is so good for hit-and-run tactics. A shaman is guiding the actions of the raiding band, and he is in the northwest part of town with the gathered loot. Kill him for a bit of gold and some mediocre items.

One of the gnolls is trying to pound its way into a shop on the east side of town. The yelps of a kobold inside make the scene all the more interesting. Slay this gnoll and look inside the store after the rest of the raiders have been killed. The kobold Deekin is in there, and he will explain more about the attack on Hilltop and the loss of the artifacts. In fact, the conniving creature has hidden one of the four items nearby. He is wise enough to keep it concealed until you return with proof that the kobold's freedom and safety are ensured.

A white dragon of fair power is behind the kobolds' prevalent magic and aggression. This wyrm lives in the northern mountains, at the top of the foothills. Although it sounds foolhardy to travel to the beast's lair, this is the only way to retrieve the rest of the artifacts. For now, that is where you should head.

Nether Mountains

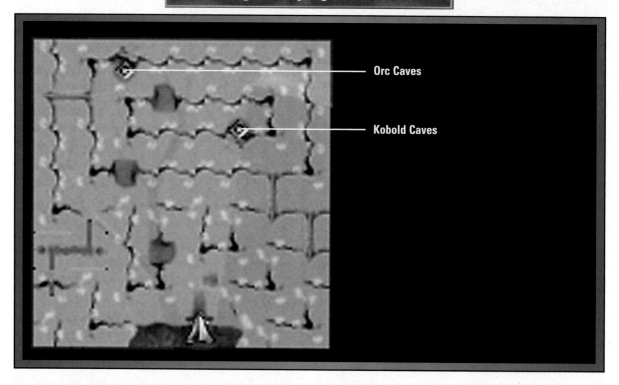

Orc Caves

Kobold Caves

BADGER

Alignment:	True Neutral
Creature Type:	Animal
Fortitude Save:	2
Reflex Save:	2
Will Save:	0
Base AC:	10
Base HP:	6

GRIZZLY BEAR

Alignment:	True Neutral
Creature Type:	Animal
Fortitude Save:	6
Reflex Save:	6
Will Save:	2
Base AC:	15
Base HP:	76

DEER

Alignment:	True Neutral
Creature Type:	Animal
Fortitude Save:	2
Reflex Save:	2
Will Save:	0
Base AC:	10
Base HP:	5

KOBOLD

Alignment:	Lawful Evil
Creature Type:	Humanoid
Fortitude Save:	2
Reflex Save:	0
Will Save:	0
Base AC:	13
Base HP:	2

KOBOLD THUG

Alignment:	Lawful Evil
Creature Type:	Humanoid, Barbarian
Fortitude Save:	4
Reflex Save:	0
Will Save:	0
Base AC:	13
Base HP:	13

WOLF

Alignment:	True Neutral
Creature Type:	Animal
Fortitude Save:	3
Reflex Save:	3
Will Save:	0
Base AC:	10
Base HP:	15

There isn't much to explore in the Nether Mountains. Walk around the perimeter of the area, and you will come across two caves. The northern cave is higher in the mountains and is inhabited by a tribe of orcs. The lower cave is the kobold's place of breeding and rest. It is easier to explore the orc's cave first, as it is smaller and less intense.

Orc Caves

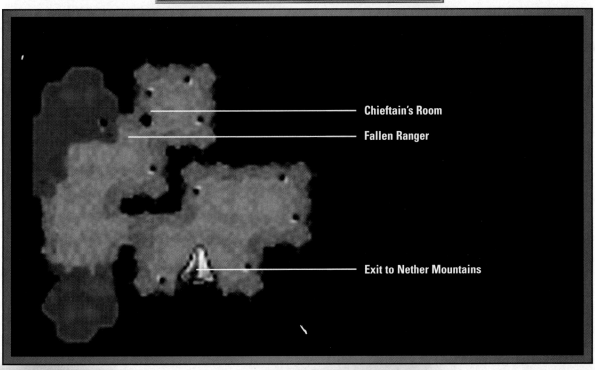

Chieftain's Room

Fallen Ranger

Exit to Nether Mountains

ORC	
Alignment:	Chaotic Evil
Creature Type:	Humanoid
Fortitude Save:	2
Reflex Save:	0
Will Save:	0
Base AC:	10
Base HP:	4

ORC CHIEFTAIN	
Alignment:	Chaotic Evil
Creature Type:	Humanoid, Ranger
Fortitude Save:	6
Reflex Save:	1
Will Save:	1
Base AC:	11
Base HP:	18

Several warriors guard the cave's inner entrance. Mages will have the hardest time with this because the orcs are effectively on top of you once you enter the cavern. Go into the area with summonings or a henchman to distract the orcs; that should give you enough room to use your normal battle tactics.

The loot in the lair is not very impressive, but the spare gold could be helpful. There is a Potion of Invisibility in a box on the right side of the cave; stash that away for future use. The chieftain has a magical Longbow as well, gained from an elven ranger who tried in vain to end the orcs' raiding. This bow has a bit of a somber history, being known as Eliak's Vengeance. Just as Eliak once sought the trolls who killed his parents and was eventually killed, the ranger who died here has fallen to the orcs he strove to destroy. Because the Longbow is only usable by a Ranger, many characters will take this simply to sell it.

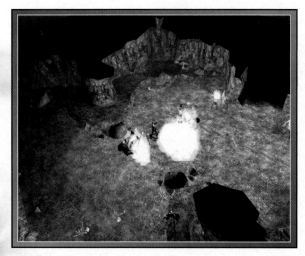

With the orcs slain, there is no reason not to advance on the kobold caves.

Kobold Caves

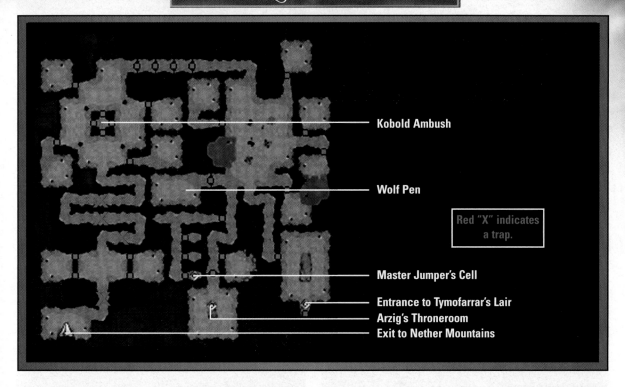

Kobold Ambush

Wolf Pen

Red "X" indicates a trap.

Master Jumper's Cell

Entrance to Tymofarrar's Lair
Arzig's Throneroom
Exit to Nether Mountains

BOAR

Alignment:	True Neutral
Creature Type:	Animal
Fortitude Save:	3
Reflex Save:	3
Will Save:	1
Base AC:	16
Base HP:	23

KOBOLD SERGEANT

Alignment:	Lawful Evil
Creature Type:	Humanoid, Rogue
Fortitude Save:	2
Reflex Save:	2
Will Save:	0
Base AC:	14
Base HP:	8

KOBOLD ADEPT

Alignment:	Lawful Evil
Creature Type:	Humanoid, Cleric
Fortitude Save:	4
Reflex Save:	0
Will Save:	2
Base AC:	13
Base HP:	6

KOBOLD SHAMAN

Alignment:	Lawful Evil
Creature Type:	Humanoid, Sorcerer
Fortitude Save:	2
Reflex Save:	0
Will Save:	2
Base AC:	13
Base HP:	10

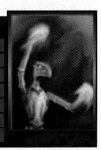

KOBOLD SLASHER

Alignment:	Lawful Evil
Creature Type:	Humanoid
Fortitude Save:	2
Reflex Save:	0
Will Save:	0
Base AC:	18
Base HP:	2

KOBOLD WARDEN

Alignment:	Lawful Evil
Creature Type:	Humanoid, Rogue
Fortitude Save:	2
Reflex Save:	2
Will Save:	0
Base AC:	14
Base HP:	12

KOBOLD SLINGER

Alignment:	Lawful Evil
Creature Type:	Humanoid
Fortitude Save:	2
Reflex Save:	0
Will Save:	0
Base AC:	16
Base HP:	2

RAT

Alignment:	True Neutral
Creature Type:	Animal
Fortitude Save:	2
Reflex Save:	2
Will Save:	0
Base AC:	14
Base HP:	1

KOBOLD SNIPER

Alignment:	Lawful Evil
Creature Type:	Humanoid
Fortitude Save:	2
Reflex Save:	0
Will Save:	0
Base AC:	13
Base HP:	2

WOLF

Alignment:	True Neutral
Creature Type:	Animal
Fortitude Save:	3
Reflex Save:	3
Will Save:	0
Base AC:	10
Base HP:	15

KOBOLD SORCERER

Alignment:	Lawful Evil
Creature Type:	Humanoid, Sorcerer
Fortitude Save:	2
Reflex Save:	0
Will Save:	2
Base AC:	13
Base HP:	4

WINTER WOLF

Alignment:	Chaotic Neutral
Creature Type:	Magical Beast
Fortitude Save:	4
Reflex Save:	4
Will Save:	1
Base AC:	13
Base HP:	34

The light is dim and the smell of kobolds fills the entry cavern, but things are quiet. Walk slowly and use Spot to locate the traps that line the hallway to the east. Kobolds wait in the next chamber to attack any who fall prey to those traps.

There are two side rooms that serve as barracks for the many kobold snipers on the top level. Open the doors to these but let the snipers inside come out to engage you directly; this will make it harder for them to gain sneak attacks. Some may hide back in the room; that still leaves them with less support when the time to rush arrives.

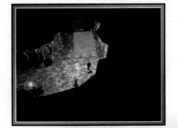

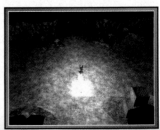

The room on the eastern side of the chamber has a set of armor (Leather Armor +1) and a magical Shortbow +1, among other light gold and treasure.

There are more traps along the passage to the north. These are more dangerous because there are kobolds who will exploit your party's failures.

The first trap is connected to a large crossbow at the other end of the hallway (it's more of a small ballis-tae)! It isn't easy to skirt this trap, so a rogue will have to disarm the trigger unless you are willing to run the risk of taking a hit. If you're willing to spend some time, you can destroy the automated crossbow from a distance, before crossing the trigger's threshold, by using missile weapons, such as a Longbow

Around the next bend are some barrels that will explode when the archers at the other end of the hall make their missile attacks. Hurry past these to avoid the effects of darkness and fire that ensue. Even less militant characters will have better luck moving with haste through this part of the hall.

A final word of caution involves the crates through the dungeon. Starting at the next hall, there are crates you can search through for treasure. There isn't much of value to uncover, and there are kobold slashers inside a few of these containers.

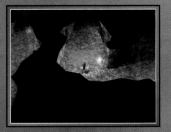 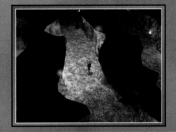 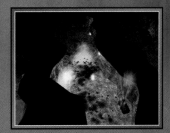

MAIN CHAMBER TRAP AND LOCK PUZZLE

The massive cavern at the end of the twisting hallway is host to a gigantic locking mechanism, as well as an obvious trap. To clear the room safely and slowly, pick the locks or bash open the doors to each of the four smaller rooms, one in each corner. Kill the kobolds in each, making the closest ones come out to fight when possible. This takes a bit of time but preempts a single massive fight.

The alternative is a lot more fun. Rush into the center of the cavern and open the chest that has arrows pointing to it. Of all the clever tricks, the kobolds have made a trap out of this—they are used to fighting against orcs, so this type of thing works pretty well. Gates will rise to close off the center of the room. Bash these open with all speed as the doors to each of the four side rooms open. All of the kobolds will charge into battle. Anyone with Great Cleave will be in absolute heaven, although it's hard to have such a nifty feat at this stage of the game.

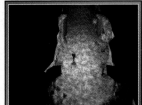

Either way, the four side rooms are intended to keep the path into the lower level safe. The locking levers must be pulled in perfect order to open the northeastern hallway. Pull each lever in the fol-lowing order: red circle (northeast room), black-and-white checkers (southwest room), blue chevrons (southeast room), and yellow rectangle (northwest room). All four of the security doors that lead to the kobold city will open if this is done correctly. If you make a mistake and pull a lever out of order, all of the doors will close and the process must be started from the beginning.

A host of kobolds will make a last-ditch effort to stop you from advancing down the hall. There is a sorcerer with them, and this little guy will be one of the most dangerous. Use magic or archery to take down the sorcerer quickly. Melee characters should use basic missile attacks to lure lesser kobolds down the hall; deal with them, out of range of the others, and then make a rush for the sorcerer.

> ### Ill-Gotten Gains
>
> *The kobolds have gained most of their meager wealth by raiding and stealing from other creatures (orcs, humans, and elves). Thus, there isn't much of a moral dilemma in taking back these treasures. There is a magical shield in the north-west room of the kobold city. A tired kobold (who opens the door to the wolf pen) has a couple of potions. A nice piece of jewelry is in the weapon room in the northeast.*

THE KOBOLD COMPOUND

There isn't too much fighting inside the kobold city; the diminutive creatures don't want you to wreck all of their precious filth. Be wary, however, of the tired kobold. After he opens the door to the wolf pen, several of the half-domesticated canines will rush out and attack. There is nothing more than a gem back inside the pen.

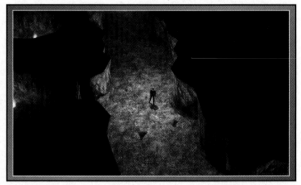

A long corridor in the southwest leads into the prison area. The kobold chieftain has imprisoned the Master Jumper there. The clever guy will agree to let you into the dragon's area of the dungeon if the chieftain can be properly dealt with. Considering that the chief isn't likely to enjoy all of the fighting inside his city, this isn't a very rough deal to make.

The central passage south leads toward the chieftain himself. A small side room marks the place of worship and training for the city's shamans. Be very careful when clearing that room; there are several casters and a Winter Wolf. It is a lot safer to lure the first few casters out into the hall before engaging anything else in the room. Use missile weapons or blast-radius items and stay back from the door to avoid the casters' line of sight.

There is a magical ring in the room, worn by the head shaman. Other treasure includes some magical gauntlets and a healthy spread of useful potions.

Arzig, the chief, will wait in his throne room. If you released the kobolds from the tavern back in Hilltop, the leader will not attack until he hears what you have to say. Players can convince Arzig to settle things with the Master Jumper. This simply takes a bit of time and an ox-load of patience. The process ends as a Shakespearian comedy or a tragedy. Keep everyone happy, and all of the kobolds get married. Insult Arzig, and everyone dies in a flurry of carving.

To ensure that negotiations go well, always choose the middle ground between what Arzig and the Master Jumper want. Don't let the Master Jumper insult his leader, nor should Arzig be allowed to dictate when he gets to see the dragon. Visits should be allowed once a month. This will keep either side from feeling slighted.

More militant characters will find that there are several tricks for this battle. Using missile weapons will soften Arzig's soldiers while pulling them back down the main hallway. Mages can use area-of-effect spells early on and run back through the dungeon while peeling off kobolds here and there. If you have very high poison resistance, the trap on the chest to the left can be triggered. The poisonous cloud from this may assist you by disrupting the kobolds.

A massive boulder blocks the passage into Tymofarrar's (the white dragon) quarters. The kobolds will move it out of your way. Tell the Master Jumper that everything is ready and he will set things in motion. If the Master Jumper was killed during any fighting, it is possible to use the rod that Arzig has on a machine that will take care of the boulder. Look to the right of the obstructed doorway; there is a secret area that houses this machine. Obviously, Arzig won't give up the rod willingly, but a few blows to the head can persuade him.

Dragon Caves

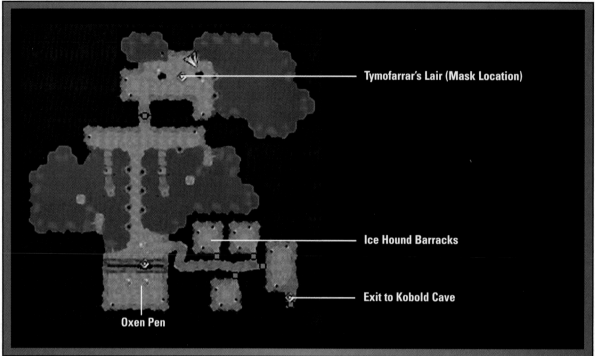

Tymofarrar's Lair (Mask Location)

Ice Hound Barracks

Exit to Kobold Cave

Oxen Pen

BOAR

Alignment:	True Neutral
Creature Type:	Animal
Fortitude Save:	3
Reflex Save:	3
Will Save:	1
Base AC:	16
Base HP:	23

OX

Alignment:	True Neutral
Creature Type:	Animal
Fortitude Save:	2
Reflex Save:	2
Will Save:	0
Base AC:	9
Base HP:	6

KOBOLD ICE HOUND

Alignment:	Lawful Evil
Creature Type:	Humanoid, Rogue
Fortitude Save:	3
Reflex Save:	3
Will Save:	1
Base AC:	12
Base HP:	18

WHITE DRAGON

Alignment:	Chaotic Evil
Creature Type:	Dragon
Fortitude Save:	11
Reflex Save:	11
Will Save:	11
Base AC:	25
Base HP:	189

The kobolds in the lower caves are a lot more aggressive than those in the kobold city. These elite "Ice Hound" archers have arrows that deal extra cold damage when they strike. Spells of elemental resistance will reduce their effectiveness tremendously. If everything ended peacefully upstairs, it is possible to bypass the kobold archers without drawing their attention.

Several rooms of Ice Hounds guard the front area. Each of these warriors has access to Ice Bolts. Characters with low hit points must be even more careful of going out in the open around such enemies. Move slowly and be wary of traps, for there is a nasty one in a pool of water beyond the first door.

THE RUNNING OF THE BULLS

Klonk is the head of the Ice Hounds. He is a kobold with experience and cunning. This archer will wait for the party to engage him before running deeper into the cavern. Following Klonk will subject you to bolts from almost all directions. The simple way to solve this is to open the ox pen and let the huge creatures clear a path for the party. It is slower to move forward and use missile weapons to pick off the kobolds, but that can be done too.

Klonk's Ice Blade is a short sword that inflicts an extra d6 of ice damage when it strikes. For this stage of your character's career, that is certainly a lot of elemental pain for the victim. Keep this around if you have the carrying capacity to spare.

The final door opens into Tymofarrar's private room. Although the dragon is evil, it is willing to listen and see what you have to offer it. Because battle is unlikely to succeed, even good characters should talk things out and try to placate the mighty wyrm. The wisest bet is to explain about Deekin and then agree to seek J' Nah for Tymofarrar. The dragon will provide some powder to weaken the foul sorceress. Use the key that Tymofarrar gives you on the rock formation nearby. This will teleport the party out of the dungeon without delay.

High Forest

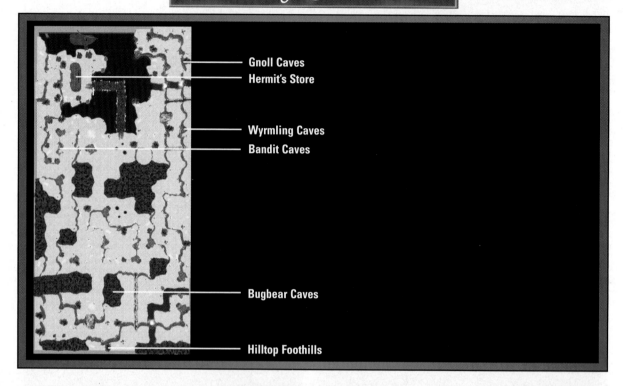

- Gnoll Caves
- Hermit's Store
- Wyrmling Caves
- Bandit Caves
- Bugbear Caves
- Hilltop Foothills

BANDIT

Alignment:	Chaotic Evil
Creature Type:	Fighter
Fortitude Save:	2
Reflex Save:	0
Will Save:	0
Base AC:	11
Base HP:	12

DEER

Alignment:	True Neutral
Creature Type:	Animal
Fortitude Save:	2
Reflex Save:	2
Will Save:	0
Base AC:	10
Base HP:	5

BROWN BEAR

Alignment:	True Neutral
Creature Type:	Animal
Fortitude Save:	5
Reflex Save:	5
Will Save:	2
Base AC:	15
Base HP:	51

TROLL

Alignment:	Chaotic Evil
Creature Type:	Giant
Fortitude Save:	5
Reflex Save:	2
Will Save:	5
Base AC:	18
Base HP:	63

The bandits in the center of the forest have a Fire Opal, some magical boots, and a bit of light treasure beyond that. The boots are Boots of Reflexes +1. Somewhat higher-level characters will encounter trolls and bears throughout the region; it is imperative to have good equipment when dealing with these ferocious monsters.

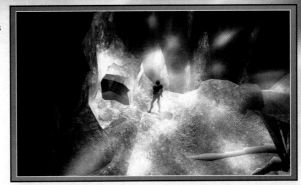

Across the piers of the north shore is a large building. Inside is a store run by an eccentric hermit. Nobody knows just how this person got such an exceptional stash of magical items, but he is willing to part with more than a few of them. This is a great place for buying scrolls, magical rings, extra bags (not bags of holding, but still enchanted to hold extra equipment), and other goods. It's quite difficult to get the codger to spill anything about himself, but his services are superb. Beyond the store he runs, the hermit can teleport you to Hilltop, Blumberg, the Kobold Caves, or the Foothills for 500 gold pieces. If you are carrying Drogan's artifacts, those can be sold to the hermit as well.

Bandit Cave

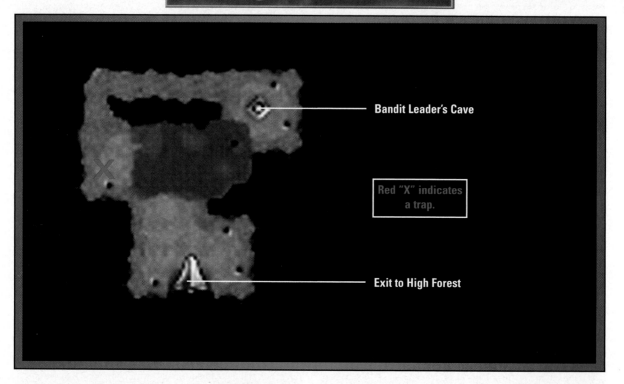

Bandit Leader's Cave

Red "X" indicates a trap.

Exit to High Forest

BANDIT

Alignment:	Chaotic Evil
Creature Type:	Fighter
Fortitude Save:	2
Reflex Save:	0
Will Save:	0
Base AC:	11
Base HP:	12

BANDIT CHIEF

Alignment:	Chaotic Neutral
Creature Type:	Fighter
Fortitude Save:	5
Reflex Save:	2
Will Save:	2
Base AC:	11
Base HP:	42

BANDIT ARCHER

Alignment:	Chaotic Neutral
Creature Type:	Ranger
Fortitude Save:	2
Reflex Save:	0
Will Save:	0
Base AC:	12
Base HP:	12

BANDIT WOMAN

Alignment:	True Neutral
Creature Type:	Bard
Fortitude Save:	0
Reflex Save:	2
Will Save:	2
Base AC:	10
Base HP:	3

There is a small cave in the northwest. A group of bandits has taken over the place as a hideout. It's worth going after this group, whether to steal their loot or to end their evil undertakings. The first few bandits guard the entryway and don't pose much of a threat. To one side of the cave, however, is an archer that stands beyond some decent traps. Try to kill this foe at range before racing over the trigger.

The bandit leader is down the cave's final hallway. A couple of armed men are often found guarding the chief, so an initial burst of missile fire or spells will make it easier to even the odds. Because the tunnel is somewhat narrow, setting traps for the enemy group isn't a bad idea either. Although it's too late to save the prisoner that the bandits have been keeping, their bounty is up for grabs. Two magical rings are in the nearby chests, as is a key. Take this key and stow it for another time.

The chests hold a few modest potions, some gold, and the two rings mentioned above. One of these is a Ring of Scholars (+5 to Lore checks), and the other is often a Ring of Animal Friendship (+12 to Animal Empathy). Neither of these sell poorly, so even characters who won't have a use for the rings will make a tidy profit from such a short undertaking.

Bugbear Cave

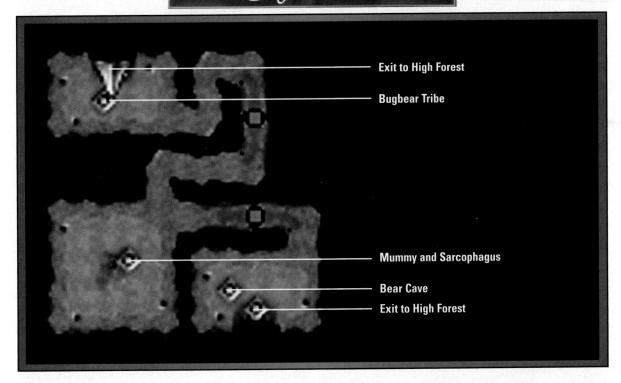

— Exit to High Forest

— Bugbear Tribe

— Mummy and Sarcophagus

— Bear Cave

— Exit to High Forest

BUGBEAR

Alignment:	Chaotic Evil
Creature Type:	Humanoid
Fortitude Save:	3
Reflex Save:	1
Will Save:	1
Base AC:	14
Base HP:	16

BUGBEAR HERO

Alignment:	Chaotic Evil
Creature Type:	Humanoid, Barbarian
Fortitude Save:	6
Reflex Save:	2
Will Save:	2
Base AC:	14
Base HP:	36

BUGBEAR SHAMAN

Alignment:	Neutral Evil
Creature Type:	Humanoid, Sorcerer
Fortitude Save:	4
Reflex Save:	2
Will Save:	4
Base AC:	14
Base HP:	33

CAVE BEAR

Alignment:	True Neutral
Creature Type:	Animal
Fortitude Save:	6
Reflex Save:	6
Will Save:	2
Base AC:	15
Base HP:	68

CRAG CAT

Alignment:	True Neutral
Creature Type:	Animal
Fortitude Save:	3
Reflex Save:	3
Will Save:	1
Base AC:	16
Base HP:	22

DEER

Alignment:	True Neutral
Creature Type:	Animal
Fortitude Save:	2
Reflex Save:	2
Will Save:	0
Base AC:	10
Base HP:	5

MUMMY

Alignment:	Lawful Evil
Creature Type:	Undead
Fortitude Save:	2
Reflex Save:	2
Will Save:	5
Base AC:	17
Base HP:	48

Back in the High Forest, near the southern side, is a cave with two entrances. Once you have the key from the bandit's lair, this dungeon can be entered from either side. Go in through the western entrance first; this opens into a short skirmish against several bugbears with a modest bit of treasure.

The other side of the cavern can be entered directly through the eastern cave opening in the High Forest, or by breaking down the bugbear barricade. A polar bear lives on that side of the cave. You'll find it fighting some wolves that have also stumbled into the area. You can wait until the end of the fight or jump in to hack at everything that moves.

The room within holds a shrine and a sarcophagus. A mummy will summon armed skeletons and attack anyone who comes into the chamber. Area-of-effect magic would be very nice, but many characters may not be advanced enough to bring that to bear quite yet. If that is the case, missile weapons or traps will help to soften the skeletal warriors who come toward you. Even melee types shouldn't come forward to face all of the enemies at once; let the faster skeletons outpace the mummy so that the fight isn't overwhelming. Because the mummy wields a pestilent strike, any resistance to disease will be useful during the battle. The magical belt in the sarcophagus is a Sash of Shimmering, and its magic resistance will aid you before long.

Wyrmling Cave

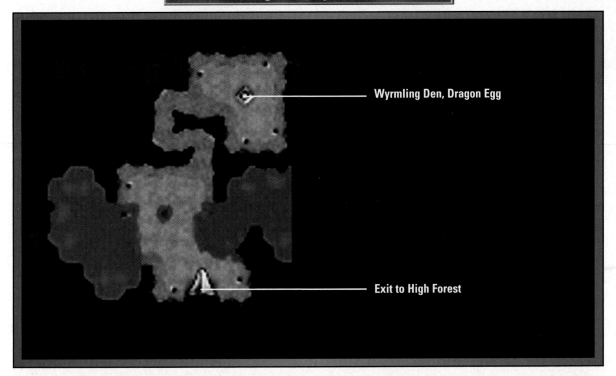

Wyrmling Den, Dragon Egg

Exit to High Forest

WYRMLING RED DRAGON

Alignment:	Chaotic Evil
Creature Type:	Dragon
Fortitude Save:	5
Reflex Save:	5
Will Save:	5
Base AC:	17
Base HP:	59

WYRMLING WHITE DRAGON

Alignment:	Chaotic Evil
Creature Type:	Dragon
Fortitude Save:	3
Reflex Save:	3
Will Save:	3
Base AC:	13
Base HP:	22

A small nest of wyrmlings can be found in one of the two caves in the northeast. This is the first of the two areas and can be reached simply by climbing up a hill. Because the wyrmlings are hardy, it is wise to keep a stash of potions around in case the creatures threaten you. There are magical gauntlets on the opening chamber's floor. In the second cavern, there are more wyrmlings, some Fire Bolts, and a Dragon Egg, which can be sold to the Thayvian wizard Szaren.

Gnoll Caves

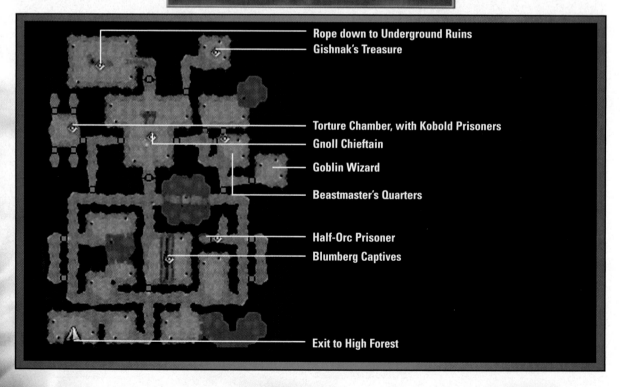

Rope down to Underground Ruins
Gishnak's Treasure

Torture Chamber, with Kobold Prisoners
Gnoll Chieftain

Goblin Wizard

Beastmaster's Quarters

Half-Orc Prisoner
Blumberg Captives

Exit to High Forest

BLACK BEAR

Alignment:	True Neutral
Creature Type:	Animal
Fortitude Save:	3
Reflex Save:	3
Will Save:	1
Base AC:	13
Base HP:	19

BOAR

Alignment:	True Neutral
Creature Type:	Animal
Fortitude Save:	3
Reflex Save:	3
Will Save:	1
Base AC:	16
Base HP:	23

GNOLL ARCHER

Alignment:	Chaotic Evil
Creature Type:	Humanoid
Fortitude Save:	3
Reflex Save:	0
Will Save:	0
Base AC:	11
Base HP:	11

GNOLL LIEUTENANT

Alignment:	Chaotic Evil
Creature Type:	Ranger, Humanoid
Fortitude Save:	5
Reflex Save:	0
Will Save:	0
Base AC:	12
Base HP:	20

GOBLIN WIZARD

Alignment:	Neutral Evil
Creature Type:	Wizard
Fortitude Save:	1
Reflex Save:	1
Will Save:	4
Base AC:	14
Base HP:	19

GNOLL WARRIOR

Alignment:	Chaotic Evil
Creature Type:	Humanoid
Fortitude Save:	3
Reflex Save:	0
Will Save:	0
Base AC:	11
Base HP:	11

KOBOLD

Alignment:	Lawful Evil
Creature Type:	Humanoid
Fortitude Save:	2
Reflex Save:	0
Will Save:	0
Base AC:	13
Base HP:	2

KOBOLD FOOTPAD

Alignment:	Lawful Evil
Creature Type:	Humanoid, Rogue
Fortitude Save:	2
Reflex Save:	2
Will Save:	0
Base AC:	14
Base HP:	12

WORG

Alignment:	Chaotic Neutral
Creature Type:	Magical Beast
Fortitude Save:	4
Reflex Save:	4
Will Save:	1
Base AC:	14
Base HP:	30

The gnoll's lair lies to the north of the wyrmling cave, across a narrow stream. This is the place that you have been searching for. J' Nah and her cohorts are somewhere in the stony tunnels beneath this entrance.

Because the gnolls aren't expecting an enemy to simply walk through their front door, it's possible to get quite a ways into their territory without causing a ruckus. Moving with stealth will aid in this, but it is not required. There are only a few gnolls in each chamber, so killing each group before they can sound one of the many alarms will keep the encounters manageable.

The Downside

Of course, the gnolls won't sit on their hands if one of their warriors manages to strike one of the gongs. If that happens, gnolls from all over the dungeon will converge on you and your party. This isn't a good thing unless you're looking for a real brawl.

If this happens and you don't want to face a legion of gnolls, retreat to the southern part of the dungeon, near the entrance. Not only will this give you a direct route of escape, it will also ensure that the gnolls can advance on you from only one direction!

The first door that you spot as you emerge from the short tunnel that stems from the entry chamber is a large block of solid wood. Even a barbarian won't be able to pound through it in a timely fashion. Ignoring this for the moment, walk down the eastern tunnel and clear the three guard rooms that you pass: two beside the southern part of the hall and the next on the eastern side of the corridor after its bend. The small area across from the final guard room houses a prisoner who can be freed after you deal with the gnolls. The key for the cell is hidden in a box near the cell.

ESCORT THE PRISONER TO FREEDOM

Glendir is a half-orc who has been imprisoned by the gnolls; he is kept away from the general slave population in the caves because he is likely to be more of a threat with others around. You are given the choice to either let Glendir fend for himself or escort the prisoner out to the front of the caves. It doesn't take long to make the extra effort and protect the weaponless half-orc during his escape.

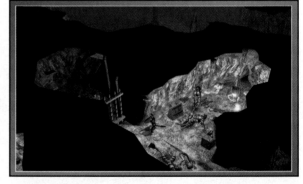

Beyond the next bend in the main corridor is a door that opens into a room and a secondary tunnel. The room holds a gnoll beastmaster; he is quite alert and will sound the alarm unless you use stealth or ranged attacks on him.

The lever in that room opens the gate into the area to the left. The bear pen to the north will stay locked until you pull a second lever—that one is nearby, below a safety fence.

The secondary tunnel to the east connects the complex with another small room. A goblin wizard resides there, and he has a few items that are interesting to steal. Most characters will be quite safe if they rush in and attack the goblin before he can properly respond. Because the wizard will use invisibility for protection, those who cannot detect the invisible may want to use Knockdown and other delaying abilities to keep the goblin pinned before he can cast anything.

Back in the central passage, there is a southern tunnel. A few gnolls in that direction guard the humans from Blumberg. Those people will be more than happy to see a friendly face, at least one that they *think* is friendly. One of the gnoll jailors has a key to the prison doors, although these can be bashed down if there are any problems.

Quest Tip

WHAT TO DO WITH THE PEOPLE OF BLUMBERG

Good characters will be excited by this opportunity to really make a difference. Tell the prisoners that Hilltop is safe and give them 100 gold pieces to help rebuild their lives (total shift of four points toward good).

Demanding payment from the villagers doesn't really do much because the sorry lot has nothing to offer. This can be done multiple times with no effect other than to shift your alignment one point toward evil with each occurrence.

Lying to say that Hilltop is in ruins will also push you one point toward evil.

Killing the prisoners may be an effective way to end their suffering, but it sure isn't a kind or productive way to accomplish this end. This is an extremely evil act and will push you far toward the side of evil.

THE KOBOLD PRISONERS

The western route around the gnoll caves doesn't have much to offer beyond more fighting—there are many guard rooms, a feeding room, and plenty of gnolls. The only room of true consequence is on the northwest edge of the map. The torture chamber that you find has a wicked-looking gnoll in its center. Kill this lone brute and take his key. The door in the upper-right holds what is left of the kobolds that were captured by the gnolls. Nafeeli is their self-spoken leader. You can make a deal with Nafeeli to help fight the gnolls, which won't be much help, really. Or you can agree to let the kobolds go. Nasty sorts may even choose to cut the wretched things down before they can flee, but there is very little to gain from doing so.

SUMMIT WITH THE GNOLL CHIEFTAN

Nothing will stop you from reaching the gnoll chieftain at this point. Chief Gishnak is not a kind or benevolent ruler, but you can reason with him, sort of. Gishnak will order his warriors to attack you until you have displayed considerable skill. Wounding the chief will end the fight and return the gnolls to a more passive state. If you have sided with the kobolds, simply cut down the lesser gnolls at range and whittle down Gishnak when he closes for melee. Otherwise, allow Gishnak to surrender and see what he has to offer.

The gnoll chief will agree to help fight J' Nah if you promise not to harm more gnolls or steal from the tribe. For low-level characters, this is the best chance to defeat J' Nah—she will be a very dangerous adversary. Those with a few extra levels under their belt will need not deal with the gnolls at all; they be can killed, ordered to leave, or given free rein.

The treasure room at the rear of Gishnak's throne area has a Longsword +1, Gloves of the Rogue, and Arrows +1.

After everything is said and done, you can use the rope at the far back of the caves to descend into the ruins.

Underground Ruins

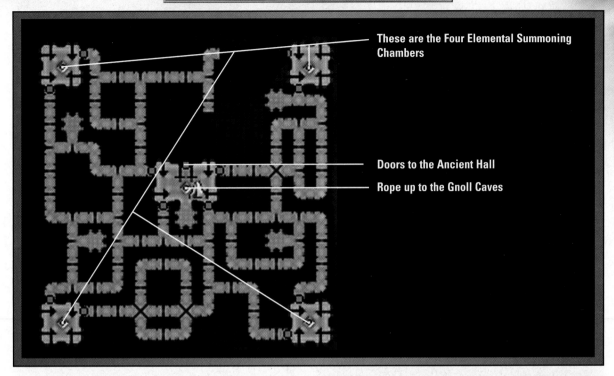

These are the Four Elemental Summoning Chambers

Doors to the Ancient Hall

Rope up to the Gnoll Caves

AIR ELEMENTAL

Alignment:	True Neutral
Creature Type:	Elemental
Fortitude Save:	2
Reflex Save:	2
Will Save:	3
Base AC:	19
Base HP:	72

EARTH ELEMENTAL

Alignment:	True Neutral
Creature Type:	Elemental
Fortitude Save:	2
Reflex Save:	2
Will Save:	6
Base AC:	17
Base HP:	80

AIR MEPHIT

Alignment:	Neutral Evil
Creature Type:	Outsider
Fortitude Save:	3
Reflex Save:	3
Will Save:	3
Base AC:	17
Base HP:	13

EARTH MEPHIT

Alignment:	Neutral Evil
Creature Type:	Outsider
Fortitude Save:	3
Reflex Save:	3
Will Save:	3
Base AC:	16
Base HP:	16

FIRE ELEMENTAL

Alignment:	True Neutral
Creature Type:	Elemental
Fortitude Save:	2
Reflex Save:	2
Will Save:	6
Base AC:	18
Base HP:	60

WATER ELEMENTAL

Alignment:	True Neutral
Creature Type:	Elemental
Fortitude Save:	2
Reflex Save:	2
Will Save:	6
Base AC:	20
Base HP:	76

FIRE MEPHIT

Alignment:	Neutral Evil
Creature Type:	Outsider
Fortitude Save:	3
Reflex Save:	3
Will Save:	3
Base AC:	16
Base HP:	13

WATER MEPHIT

Alignment:	Neutral Evil
Creature Type:	Outsider
Fortitude Save:	3
Reflex Save:	3
Will Save:	3
Base AC:	16
Base HP:	12

HELL HOUND

Alignment:	Lawful Evil
Creature Type:	Outsider
Fortitude Save:	4
Reflex Save:	4
Will Save:	4
Base AC:	16
Base HP:	22

The ruins beneath the gnoll caves have been protected by ancient magic. Luckily, it does not require a mage's skills to survive the traps placed on this level. Instead, the builders put a number of systems in place that can be used to avoid most of the dangers in the region.

A Fountain of Elements

The antechamber across from the main doors of the room houses a pool. This is far more than a scrying pool or something so mundane. Indeed, this is a place of elemental convergence. Silver Tokens can be brought here to summon elementals. It takes a person with substantial Lore to use the pool—many of its original uses have been lost to time and age.

To grab extra tokens, cast cantrips on the four elemental shrines that are out in the maze of hallways. Each can provide an extra token for use on the fountain.

There is a lever at the center of the primary chamber. Before pulling this, take the Potion of Elemental Resistance from the chest at the west side of the room; this will be quite useful later. A blue symbol will appear in the room after the lever is used. This will make your character immune to damage from the level's water traps. The door to the west with a blue hue will lead you toward a room that houses one of the dungeon's four guardians. Follow the trail of blue water spells that ignite through the corridors, being careful not to stray into any of the side hallways; these contain other elements and will still hurt your character. You'll encounter mephits here and there. Although these creatures do not have many hit points, they take some time to kill and will use their ranged attacks to soften your character. Spells of elemental resistance are nice, but do not sacrifice the Potion of Elemental Resistance unless it is necessary for survival.

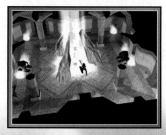

THE FOUR ELEMENTALS

A water elemental will manifest when you enter the chamber at the end of the route. Having a magical weapon will help tremendously in this engagement, but it is not required. Melee characters will likely need to rely on Power Attack to inflict the type of damage they desire.

At low level, some characters simply won't be able to deal with the elementals in this dungeon. Fear not, there are ways to survive even the cruelest challenges. If you are having problems with the elementals, lure the creature out of its room. Kite the elemental back through the tunnels and into an area that has a trap of a different element. These traps will pound on the enemy. You must try to position yourself so that you're standing in a safe corridor while the elemental is just barely inside one of the damaging hallways. This isn't easy, but it is possible with practice. Leading mephits of a different alignment into the room with the elemental will help too; they will often attack both your character and the opposing creature.

Killing the elemental will send you back to the front room. Pull the lever again to switch elements, this time to fire. The entire process must be repeated for fire, air, and earth. The fourth fight is by far the worst. The earth elemental is vicious in melee, having more attacks and a great deal of strength. Use missile weapons and enemy mephits, and lead the being into another element's corridor if possible.

When all four passages have been completed and the elementals are dead, the great doors in the main room will be unlocked. The passage into the ancient hall will be open when you return to the front room.

Ancient Hall

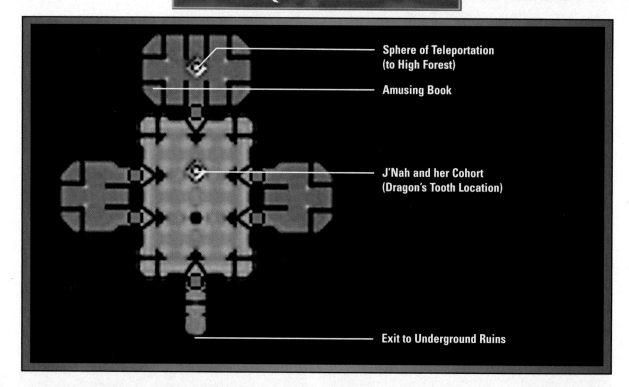

- Sphere of Teleportation (to High Forest)
- Amusing Book
- J'Nah and her Cohort (Dragon's Tooth Location)
- Exit to Underground Ruins

AZITH

Alignment:	Chaotic Evil
Creature Type:	Abberation
Fortitude Save:	3
Reflex Save:	3
Will Save:	6
Base AC:	20
Base HP:	40

J' NAH

Alignment:	Neutral Evil
Creature Type:	Sorcerer
Fortitude Save:	4
Reflex Save:	4
Will Save:	8
Base AC:	13
Base HP:	64

HELL HOUND

Alignment:	Lawful Evil
Creature Type:	Outsider
Fortitude Save:	4
Reflex Save:	4
Will Save:	4
Base AC:	16
Base HP:	22

QUEMOZENG

Alignment:	Chaotic Evil
Creature Type:	Outsider
Fortitude Save:	3
Reflex Save:	3
Will Save:	3
Base AC:	17
Base HP:	21

WARRIOR

Alignment:	Lawful Evil
Creature Type:	Fighter
Fortitude Save:	3
Reflex Save:	1
Will Save:	1
Base AC:	12
Base HP:	21

J' Nah and her cohorts are just a room away. For a short time, you can listen to what the elven sorceress is saying. Although the woman's power is tremendous, it is clear that even she has a superior who is waiting in the shadows. This is an ominous discovery, made more dangerous when you are discovered. If won't be easy to avoid a deadly confrontation now.

The ancient hall isn't very big. There are three side rooms that can be reached from the central chamber. Because J' Nah is patient, you are free to explore these and take the scrolls out of the side rooms. There are some potions tucked away in the eastern library. The northern chamber has a globe of energy that will teleport you out of the entire complex; this essence is activated be feeding it any type of magical energy (lay on hands, arcane or divine spells, etc.). That room also has a book in the corner with a strange tale of gnomes and traps that is inspirational…or something.

CONFRONTING J' NAH

When fully rested, you should use the Potion of Elemental Resistance, then stand behind J' Nah and start a conversation with her. It might be tempting to seek an agreement with the elf, considering the circumstances, but it says a lot that J' Nah is even less trustworthy than Tymofarrar. There is something in the woman's eyes that reads of treachery and ill deeds. This is not someone who can be bargained with easily. Perhaps it is time to use the flask that the dragon gave you.

Without even stopping the dialogue, you should bring up your inventory screen and select the Flask of Powder. Use the item's unique power and select J' Nah. As your character throws the powder over the elf, it will overcome her, distracting her and draining her strength. This is the critical moment of the battle. Hit the sorceress with everything at your disposal. Power Attack

  works well for warriors, the most potent spells for a mage, and anything dire that an archer can summon. Focus everything on J' Nah to bring her down before she recovers. If you made a bargain with the gnolls, Gishnak will show up with his warriors. Be careful not to strike any of them, even with peripheral spells, as this will turn them against you with alarming speed.

The Potion of Elemental Resistance will protect you from the Hell Hound's breath—that creature will start the battle off with a good blast every time. Beyond that, the protection will cushion some of the misery if J' Nah is able to complete her casting of Chain Lightning, which is easily her favorite spell. If the leader falls, the rest of the battle is unimportant. You can even flee, through the main tunnel or by using the sphere of light, to return later. With J' Nah dead, the other creatures will eventually be crushed.

J' Nah has a few light magical items and some gems, but make sure to grab the Dragon's Tooth (one of the four major artifacts) and the Ice Phylactery. The second item will give you a chance to intimidate Tymofarrar and get away without becoming a hero-sickle.

It is time to return to Tymofarrar's cave. Use the hermit to teleport to the kobold caves if you are in a hurry. Otherwise, run all the way up to the Nether Mountains. Use the boulder near the entrance to slip back down to the dragon's lair without delay.

Quest Tip

BARGAINING WITH A DRAGON

There are many ways to deal with the next encounter. When you tell Tymofarrar that J' Nah is dead, the dragon will have little use for keeping you alive. Using a bit of guile, you can get out of the situation without losing a lot of face (literally or figuratively).

Persuade the dragon to honor its pledge.

Intimidate the dragon, using the Phylactery. This option is the best for getting things done safely and easily. Tymofarrar understands that this artifact has incredible powers, so it doesn't want to roll the dice on the matter. With the Phylactery as leverage, you can barter for Deekin's freedom and then ask for the Mask afterward. Using persuasion, the Mask can be acquired for a measly 300 gold pieces. Indeed, this is a trivial expense when compared with how much is gained.

Fighting the dragon is possible, although it's definitely not recommended for anyone below at least sixth or seventh level—even then it's a matter of luck and many reloads. The Ice Phylactery will temporarily transform your character into an ice giant, rendering the dragon's breath useless. Still, Tymofarrar is no slouch in melee combat, and even some heavy buffing ahead of time will not be enough to make things easy. Mostly, it's a matter of hit points; high-level characters will be in good shape, but others will find that Tymofarrar just rips through their defense and takes what is his.

For vengeance, players who are going through the game a second time can try to fight the dragon without using the magic of the Phylactery. Mages can kite the dragon while wielding fireballs, firebrand, and other such magics; archers can use fire arrows with pleasant results; and warriors who are immune to Fear can slug it out at close range (with elemental resistance potions, heavy buffing for damage resistance, and anything else they can get their hands on).

Warriors without immunity to Fear simply shouldn't attempt to fight Tymofarrar.

DEEKIN BLUES

With Deekin's freedom secured, travel to Blumberg. Inform the tiny bard that he is given his life back, whether through Tymofarrar's death or by the gift of Deekin's doll. Deekin is true to his word and will give you what is left of the tower statue. It's time to head home.

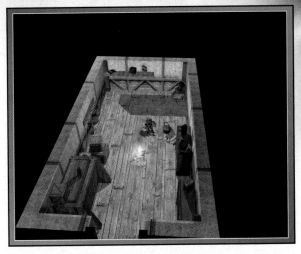

Back in Hilltop, there are several things to do. Fiona is worth talking to. Identify the recent run of magic items and ask the smith about her half-brother. It turns out that Glendir, the half-orc from the gnoll caves, is indeed Fiona's sibling. Although you can pull 100 gold pieces out of Fiona for saving the man, it isn't in her nature to give the money up without a bit of sputtering.

Return all of the artifacts to the recently awakened Drogan, unless they have already been sold. The piece of the tower artifact is all that you need to move into the next chapter. Even with a few artifacts of great power to steal, several incredibly potent creatures were focusing their attention on the item that seemed the least compelling of the group. Now that Drogan has healed, he is quite intent on finding out why this happened. Thus, you are given another duty: to find the archeologist Garrick, a man who can decipher the importance of the tower crystal.

Interlude: Like Sands Through the Hourglass...

Katriana hires a guide and begins her caravan's journey through the Anauroch. The blowing sands and cold nights are the fiercest enemy that you face for some time. With Hilltop and Blacksands behind, there are many questions and a lot of time to ponder them. Katriana mentions that a kobold hired on with the troupe, although he has kept himself out of sight during most of the trip. As luck would have it, Deekin is the wandering mercenary, and he will prove a valuable ally before long.

Anauroch Night Camp

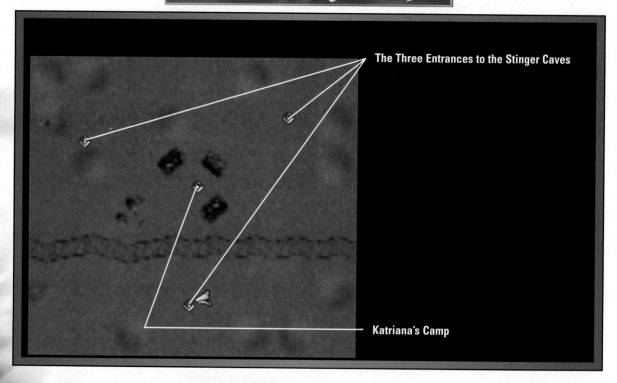

The Three Entrances to the Stinger Caves

Katriana's Camp

STINGER

Alignment:	Neutral Evil
Creature Type:	Humanoid
Fortitude Save:	4
Reflex Save:	1
Will Save:	1
Base AC:	15
Base HP:	26

STINGER OFFICER

Alignment:	Neutral Evil
Creature Type:	Humanoid, Barbarian
Fortitude Save:	8
Reflex Save:	2
Will Save:	2
Base AC:	15
Base HP:	76

STINGER ARCHER

Alignment:	Neutral Evil
Creature Type:	Humanoid
Fortitude Save:	4
Reflex Save:	1
Will Save:	1
Base AC:	16
Base HP:	26

The desert is not a place for the unwary. As the troupe settles down for camp in the evening, there is a sound that hisses above the wind and sands. Before long, Katriana calls the people to arms and stingers begin to scramble over the dunes. Battle is about to commence.

There are several holes in the desert floor that the stingers will climb through. This gives the attackers a chance to come at the camp from a few different angles. Move your character forward to deal with the creatures before they can engage the weaker camp defenders. After the first group is slain, return to the troupe to help slice away the alternate stinger groups.

Nasty characters can fight or choose to sit out and watch the halflings take a beating. Eventually the stingers will fall, but it's fun to see the wretches thrown about.

When all is done, Katriana will approach your character and ask if you saw what befell Zidan, the guide. Of all the people to disappear during the skirmish, he was the worst to lose. Without a guide, the troupe will lose time returning to Blacksands for a replacement. Beyond that, simply turning around to make the return trip will be dangerous. Far better then to search for Zidan and hope that the stingers have not killed him yet.

Ask Deekin to come along for the heroic task. It will help a great deal to have a skilled bard where Zidan has been taken. Not only that, but Deekin is also one of the more versatile and exciting henchman to have in the group. Make sure to have a good supply of missile weapons; even dedicated melee types should grab what they can for ranged battle. If anyone needs a magic bag, be sure to take one from Katriana's store—there won't be many chances to buy these in the future.

Anauroch Underground Tunnel, Stinger Caves

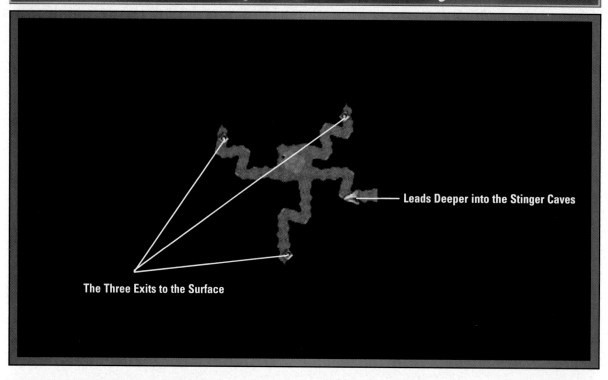

Leads Deeper into the Stinger Caves

The Three Exits to the Surface

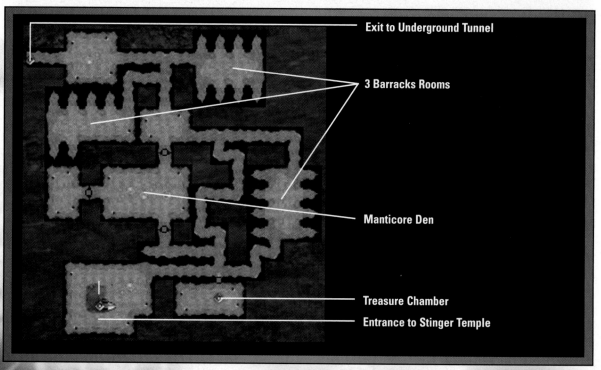

Exit to Underground Tunnel

3 Barracks Rooms

Manticore Den

Treasure Chamber

Entrance to Stinger Temple

MANTICORE

Alignment:	Lawful Evil
Creature Type:	Magical Beast
Fortitude Save:	6
Reflex Save:	6
Will Save:	2
Base AC:	18
Base HP:	80

STINGER OFFICER

Alignment:	Neutral Evil
Creature Type:	Humanoid, Barbarian
Fortitude Save:	8
Reflex Save:	2
Will Save:	2
Base AC:	15
Base HP:	76

STINGER ARCHER

Alignment:	Neutral Evil
Creature Type:	Humanoid
Fortitude Save:	4
Reflex Save:	1
Will Save:	1
Base AC:	16
Base HP:	26

STINGER

Alignment:	Neutral Evil
Creature Type:	Humanoid
Fortitude Save:	4
Reflex Save:	1
Will Save:	1
Base AC:	15
Base HP:	26

There are several large holes that lead into sandstone tunnels within the desert. Following the trail of the camp attackers will take the group directly to one of these entrances. Climb down and prepare to deal with the stingers on their own turf.

There aren't many stingers inside the outer tunnels. All three of the outside entrances connect to a central chamber. A passage to the east will take the group into the proper set of caves where the stingers reside.

The first chamber inside the Stinger Caves has an acid trap at its entrance; try to avoid this, but don't take much time in doing so. There are two archers and four stinger warriors who will try to test the party here. On the whole, the stinger archers are the greater threat; their acid arrows are accurate and hard-hitting. However, the archers are a lot harder to take down unless the group has considerable skill with missile weapons or ranged magic. Melee types must brave the fight with the warriors before turning to missile combat against the archers.

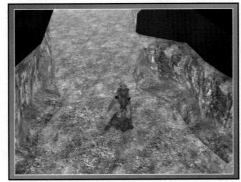

Stinger Archers

It is not a simple matter to deal with stinger archers at close range. The problem is in the stinger ability to burrow through stone at amazing speed. Anyone who attacks a stinger archer directly will find that it burrows to safety. It is almost essential that these obnoxious creatures be brought down with missile fire or magic.

However, rogues can go into stealth mode and creep up on the archers. Sneak attacks have a much better time of cutting down the stingers' evasion than normal melee attacks do.

CLEANING HOUSE

The room in the northeast is a barracks for the stingers. There are a number of stinger warriors in the area, and the chests contain only basic implements that may not be useful to the party—there are healing kits, for those who didn't get any before coming into the dungeon.

The central passage leads south through most of the level; the corridors spill away from the center and open into other barracks rooms. The first of such tunnels leads west. There are a few minor traps you can steal from that room. They're inside chests where they are safe to take, but otherwise this is another trivial chamber.

There are several choices when the party arrives at the next room. The central corridor can be taken to a large room (the only one with doors in this part of the dungeon). There is also an eastern passage that leads toward the same destination in a round-about way. Hmm. Something seems suspicious about the whole area.

A few stingers will attack at this point, one of them wielding a bow. Deal with this group completely before moving out. This might also be a good time to save your game. It isn't a surprise to find that the large chamber is a trap waiting to happen. All of the great doors close, and then a manticore emerges from a side den. This large animal is bestial and has little intelligence, but it can lay down considerable damage up close or at range. Characters with a very high level of animal empathy can try to control the manticore. Even though the result will likely be failure, even a chance at success is worth the risk—having a pet manticore will make the rest of the caves a walk in the park.

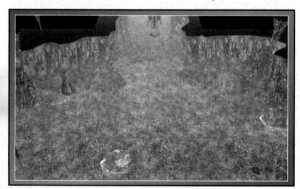 

By clearing out the stingers before entering the chamber, you have ensured that the manticore is isolated. Mages can use the faint cover in the room for hit-and-run magic, archers can do the same, and melee types should get healing potions ready while they close and engage.

When you've defeated the manticore, do not continue south until you've searched its lair. There are some nice items that have been left behind by less worthy champions.

The eastern room, reached from either side, is another barracks for the stingers. This is a place to clear for militant characters that want satisfaction, but few others will find a use for this place.

There are two rooms in the south part of the stinger caves, and both of these are important. The first place of note is a room with a heavy door at its front. Spells, lockpicks, or a number of melee strikes later, the door can be breached. Using power attacks helps for bashing the door, and even then most people won't do a lot of damage between criticals.

On the other side of the door is a room with a statue and many chests. The path to the statue is trapped; this will cease once you destroy the statue. A great deal of the dungeon's treasure is stored in the room, so all can rejoice and loot to their heart's content. Although there aren't any specifically powerful items, characters will find a number of moderate quality magical objects.

The final room has a twisting stone ledge that descends into the shadows. Many stingers guard the path toward the lower area. A harried group may seek shelter by running for the ledge, but it is better to destroy the stingers here before moving forward.

Because the stingers are spread out, using missile weapons to draw the stingers into the side corridor works quite well. This controls the ferocity of the combat and limits the stingers' numeric advantage. A stinger officer in the chamber carries an acid-enchanted halberd; he is best killed at range because of this, but the weapon is a nice find.

Stinger Caves Temple

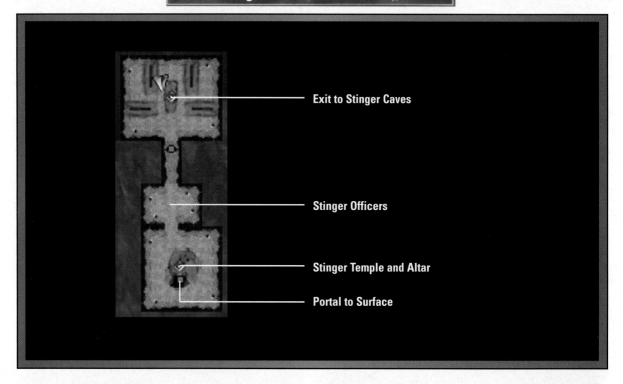

Exit to Stinger Caves

Stinger Officers

Stinger Temple and Altar

Portal to Surface

GHOUL

Alignment:	Chaotic Evil
Creature Type:	Undead
Fortitude Save:	1
Reflex Save:	1
Will Save:	3
Base AC:	14
Base HP:	21

STINGER HIGH PRIEST

Alignment:	Neutral Evil
Creature Type:	Humanoid, Cleric
Fortitude Save:	9
Reflex Save:	3
Will Save:	6
Base AC:	15
Base HP:	62

STINGER

Alignment:	Neutral Evil
Creature Type:	Humanoid
Fortitude Save:	4
Reflex Save:	1
Will Save:	1
Base AC:	15
Base HP:	26

STINGER OFFICER

Alignment:	Neutral Evil
Creature Type:	Humanoid, Barbarian
Fortitude Save:	8
Reflex Save:	2
Will Save:	2
Base AC:	15
Base HP:	76

Only a couple of stinger officers stand between your party and the doors into the stinger temple. There is a tremendous stir of activity on the other side of the temple doors: screams of the angry dead, the skittering of more stingers, and the prayers of an unholy priest. Within is a scene that will cause most people to tarry. There are ghouls *everywhere* in the temple. A couple stingers block a rocky ramp up to an altar, and a high priest is performing some foul ritual at the top of the room.

Before anything starts to move, use all possible haste to get to the high priest and the altar. Both of these must be destroyed before the ghouls can block the way with their wall of rotting flesh.

Warriors must be the most decisive. Charge into the room, get to the other side of the two stingers, and then cut down the high priest. Ignore the guards and the approaching ghouls, and bash apart the altar. If the high priest presents an opportunity, it is sometimes worth moving around him to destroy the altar first anyway. High-hit-point characters are certainly more worried about the priest's spells. Warriors with mediocre hit points but a nice Will Save should risk a run against the altar itself.

Mages and missile wielders can be a bit more creative, but their task is no less difficult. Target the altar first and attack that source of unholy power while moving around the room to avoid the ghouls. Try to stay out of the priest's line of sight when possible, although this won't be more than slight protection. Once the altar is destroyed, the ghouls will die and the high priest becomes the main concern.

Foul Witchery Indeed

The power of the ghouls is linked with the high priest, but it's not what most adventurers would expect. When the priest dies, the ghouls will be driven mad with a surge of energy. This will make the fell creatures even harder to kill without taking damage, and the sheer number of undead creates a fair threat. This is why characters that can risk a preemptive strike on the altar should do so.

Zidan wasn't far from becoming an offering to the stinger's deities, so he is more than happy to get out of the dungeon. Briefly, your choice is whether to be nice or demanding about the whole experience. Refusing any reward from the guide will shift your alignment toward goodness by three points. Forcing the poor soul into giving up 250 gold pieces and his magical Ring of Cyan will slide you three points toward evil. Everything else is doable without substantial consequences. Even if you insult him, the unlucky tracker just has to stand there and take it; otherwise it's back in the hole for old Zidan.

Return to Katriana's camp. The best route out of the dungeon is to use the portal behind the altar, then climb back to the surface through one of the three tunnel holes. There shouldn't be many stingers left in the way, so the party should be quite safe. Up top, everyone will be quite relieved to see Zidan again (for a number of reasons). The halflings are quite willing to reward your character for the trouble.

Quest Tip

A FITTING REWARD

You have several options when Katriana asks what you want in return for such hard work. The troupe is fairly grateful, but a good character needs little else to be warm during those cold desert nights. Tell Katriana to give the reward to Zidan. Your alignment will shift three points toward good.

Politely refusing a reward will keep the halflings in high spirits and improve your reputation. This pushes your alignment toward good by one point. Being a bit gruffer when refusing will negate this alignment change.

When going after the reward, the only big changes are if you try to intimidate Katriana for a couple hundred more gold pieces (+1 shift toward chaos), or if you bargained for a better reward before leaving and refuse the money entirely upon Zidan's return (also a +1 shift toward chaos for being deeply eccentric).

Oasis of the Green Palm

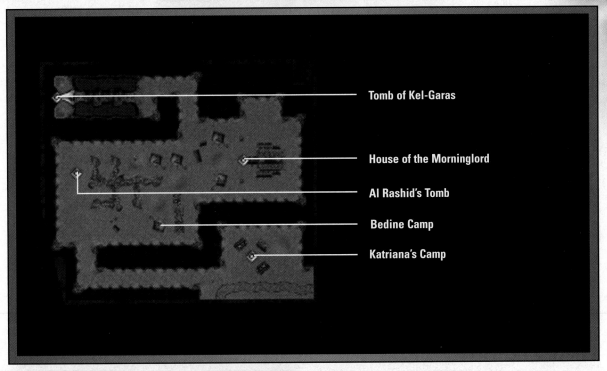

- Tomb of Kel-Garas
- House of the Morninglord
- Al Rashid's Tomb
- Bedine Camp
- Katriana's Camp

ZOMBIE

Alignment:	Neutral Evil
Creature Type:	Undead
Fortitude Save:	0
Reflex Save:	0
Will Save:	3
Base AC:	9
Base HP:	15

If a trip through the Anauroch desert were a simple matter, everyone would be doing it. The next hurdle comes when the caravan starts to run out of water. Fortunately, there is an oasis nearby, but the nomads who control it are not entirely friendly. Katriana wants to get permission to use the oasis without doing anything on her own, and that means your character is tapped for the chore. Katriana has tried to talk with the Bedine nomads before, but her etiquette was found a wee bit lacking.

The Bedine are nomadic, but they don't travel too far from the Oasis of the Green Palm. Travel through the pass at the western side of camp, and your character will come out near the oasis itself. Zombies not far from the pass engage Ali Ibn-Musud and his people. Help the nomads to fight off the undead and speak with their leader after the corpses have been laid to rest in the desert sand.

The Bedine are willing to explain their history in the hope that your group will aid them in removing a vicious curse from the oasis. Because the curse has dried everything up, the entire troupe of halflings will likely die if you don't agree to help the Bedine. Thus, whether you're good or evil, it's necessary to listen and prepare.

The story of the Bedine and Kel-Garas is a very interesting one. Those who wish to learn a bit of history (or anyone who enjoys a splendid bit of background info) should ask Ali about everything he knows. To kill Kel-Garas will take several steps, and the end of the journey will be to face him in the Temple of the Morninglord. Before that, there are several things that you must attend to.

Catacomb of Al-Rashid

Coffin with Desert's Fury

Exit to Oasis

ZOMBIE

Alignment:	Neutral Evil
Creature Type:	Undead
Fortitude Save:	0
Reflex Save:	0
Will Save:	3
Base AC:	9
Base HP:	15

GARGOYLE STATUE

Alignment:	Chaotic Evil
Creature Type:	Magical Beast
Fortitude Save:	4
Reflex Save:	4
Will Save:	1
Base AC:	16
Base HP:	38

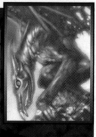

There is a burial chamber to the west, where a legendary weapon of power sleeps. Ali's family has placed the weapon there for a time when it is needed. There are some creatures and enchantments in place to protect the artifact, but these can soon be unraveled.

Inside the tomb, there are several zombies. These are nothing to worry about and can be killed with fair speed. Next, destroy the gargoyle statues that stand as guardians to the tomb. Breaking all four of these will reveal the puzzle that locks Desert's Fury in the tomb. There are marks of an 'X' all around the room, so that is the first clue. Take all seven of the stone blocks around the chamber and place them in an 'X' pattern on the grid of stone plates. The final piece in the 'X' will be left open, but you can move your character to stand on that and complete the pattern. This breaks the seal and leaves Desert's Fury ripe for the taking.

Desert's Fury and Its Forms

The most common form of Desert's Fury is a ball and chain, although mages will often discover a staff instead. In essence, the artifact will take on a form that is usable by its wielder.

In any event, Al Rashid's weapon has a +1 enchantment and is +2 versus undead, and it does a full d8 bonus damage against creatures of the unliving. This is not a bad weapon to keep around even for people who aren't terribly skilled with morningstars.

Tomb of Kel-Garas

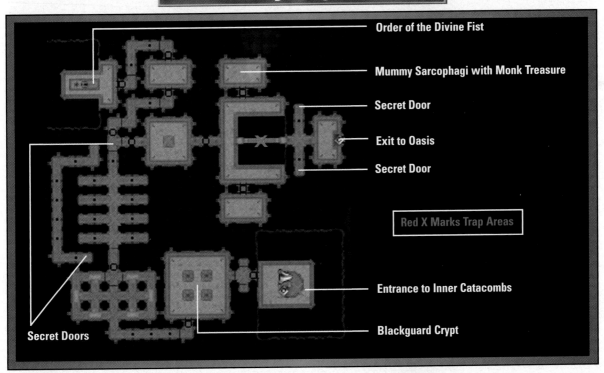

Order of the Divine Fist

Mummy Sarcophagi with Monk Treasure

Secret Door

Exit to Oasis

Secret Door

Red X Marks Trap Areas

Entrance to Inner Catacombs

Secret Doors

Blackguard Crypt

KEL-GARAS

Alignment:	Lawful Evil
Creature Type:	Cleric
Fortitude Save:	8
Reflex Save:	4
Will Save:	8
Base AC:	17
Base HP:	69

ZOMBIE LORD

Alignment:	Neutral Evil
Creature Type:	Undead, Fighter
Fortitude Save:	4
Reflex Save:	1
Will Save:	4
Base AC:	12
Base HP:	49

SKELETON

Alignment:	Neutral Evil
Creature Type:	Undead
Fortitude Save:	0
Reflex Save:	0
Will Save:	2
Base AC:	5
Base HP:	6

SKELETON WARRIOR

Alignment:	Neutral Evil
Creature Type:	Undead
Fortitude Save:	2
Reflex Save:	2
Will Save:	5
Base AC:	15
Base HP:	39

SKELETON BLACKGUARD

Alignment:	Neutral Evil
Creature Type:	Undead, Fighter
Fortitude Save:	5
Reflex Save:	2
Will Save:	4
Base AC:	15
Base HP:	56

MUMMY

Alignment:	Lawful Evil
Creature Type:	Undead
Fortitude Save:	2
Reflex Save:	2
Will Save:	5
Base AC:	17
Base HP:	48

The entrance into Kel-Garas' tomb is in the northwest, beyond a claustrophobic passage between the cliffs. Within are legions of undead and several murderous traps. You enter the area from the east and aren't given many options on how to proceed. The only hall leads west, past a lightning trap with two gargoyle statues. Destroying the statues will cause them to continue attacking for a short time, so it doesn't save time or energy to bother with them, although it is a bit gratifying.

Go behind one of the statues, to the end of the short hallway, and search for a secret door (there is one on each side). Going through these gives you a very good chance to engage the archers in the next room from behind. Your character will be able to slice through the weaker enemies while the tough melee fighters spend time moving into position. It is even possible to duck back out when the archers are done and come in the other side to skunk those skeletal bowmen as well.

The southern chamber off of the bridge room has skeletons and some very light treasure, nothing worthy of mention. To the north, however, is a room with four sarcophagi. Each one of these is trapped and will release a mummy when opened. The good news is that there is a fair bit of magical treasure to be found: often a Monk's Belt, Gloves of the Long Death +3, a Helm of Discharge, and a Small Shield +2.

A Monk's Dream

The mummies in the north part of the dungeon have two perfect monk items. The Monk's Belt grants haste once per day, weapon specialization (unarmed strike), and improved criticals (unarmed strike). This is almost as good as it gets when it comes to ludicrous monk items. The Gloves of the Long Death +3 add extra cold damage, so they are worthy additions too. The same area has a Helm of Discharge that will protect the wearer from the many lightning traps in the dungeon.

THE BURIAL CHAMBERS

The door to the west releases a rank odor when opened. There is a distant buzzing of flies in the air, and when you enter the room, a wave of flies and pestilence will be unleashed. Kel-Garas will manifest and throw a bit of magic around too, but this isn't meant to lay the party low; it's merely a taste of the mage's power. Hurry through the cloud of pestilence and take a moment to breathe in the next hall.

There is a secret door on the west wall if you search around the corridor. The southern stretch has the heat of many fireballs wafting back up the passage; the secret doors allow people to bypass the danger. Before doing that, however, go into the room through the northern doorway. This is the path to a crypt. The order of the Divine Fist waits.

The first resting crypt has four sarcophagi, trapped as usual. Four undead monks will spring from these and attack if even one is opened. The battle isn't very hard, but it helps to stay in the corner and fight the monks two at a time, especially for characters who are weak in melee. Mages are free to flee the room, close the door, and prepare a fireball ambush. It isn't often worth looking through the room for treasure.

The room at the back of the area is where Zaar was laid. This master monk only has some Boots of Hardiness +1, but he fights with the strength of ages. Sending this being on to the next world is a reward unto itself, but the Holy Avenger clutched by a nearby skeleton is even better.

Return to the secret door and use that to avoid the fireball hallway. There are many skeletons inside the hidden area, but these animated dead have little resistance to offer when compared with the conflagration outside. Another secret door will appear at the end of the passage, and you can enter the main tunnels again. Kel-Garas and many of his undead minions will have another run at you then.

Many of the skeletons can be dealt with before confronting Kel-Garas. Destroy the skeletons with divine turning, magic, or brute force. Without their master helping directly, the battle won't be too hard. When enough of the hoard has been cleared, rush Kel-Garas. Again, the mage is not willing or prepared for a full engagement, so he will teleport away after taking a few hits. Because he doesn't work very hard to track down your character, playing hit-and-run games or firing area of effect attacks around corners is a good way to deal with him.

The way forward becomes quite linear again, so there is little doubt as to where to step. Animated warriors guard the next large room, and a blackguard skeleton dominates the cluster of enemies. This is a tough fight for anyone who gets into melee, and most characters should try to use ranged items, missile weapons, and spells to at least soften this dangerous adversary and his troops. The treasure in the area is light, but the blackguard's equipment is very nice and it looks menacing. The helm adds three to saves against mind-affecting spells and to sonic attacks. The armor is Full Plate +1, and the warrior's blade is a Greatsword +1. Although these items may be weak compared with some of the gear that the party has seen, these are great for henchmen, selling, or just for getting that cool, evil look that everyone enjoys.

The last room on the floor has stairs that descend into the inner catacombs.

Inner Catacombs

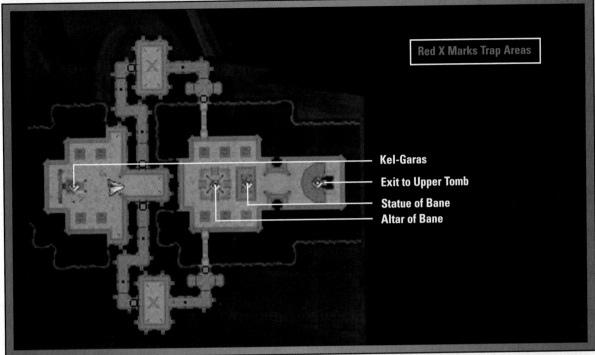

Red X Marks Trap Areas

- Kel-Garas
- Exit to Upper Tomb
- Statue of Bane
- Altar of Bane

KEL-GARAS

Alignment:	Lawful Evil
Creature Type:	Cleric
Fortitude Save:	8
Reflex Save:	4
Will Save:	8
Base AC:	17
Base HP:	69

WRAITH

Alignment:	Chaotic Evil
Creature Type:	Undead
Fortitude Save:	1
Reflex Save:	1
Will Save:	4
Base AC:	13
Base HP:	32

STATUE OF BANE

Alignment:	True Neutral
Creature Type:	Construct
Fortitude Save:	3
Reflex Save:	3
Will Save:	3
Base AC:	23
Base HP:	65

The lower area is large but doesn't take long to sweep through. There are wraiths drifting hither and yon, so it is wise to destroy them as often as possible to keep them from grouping together. Near a Banite altar in the central area is a large statue with ruby eyes. Attacking the statue or trying to steal the eyes will animate this image of Bane, and the being will fight until its death. Magic is the best way to fight the statue, but power attacks are also an option. Most missile weapons won't do much damage to the resistant exterior of the statue.

For any non-evil character, examining the altar of Bane is just a bad idea. Following are the effects of interacting with the altar:

GOOD CHARACTERS

Praying at the altar will shift you five points toward evil.

Pretending to pray will get you cursed.

Spitting on the altar will also get you cursed.

EVIL CHARACTERS

Evil characters that pray faithfully will be fully healed.

Evil characters that pretend to pray will shift three points toward good.

Spitting on the altar will get your main character cursed; your alignment will also shift by three points toward good.

NEUTRAL CHARACTERS

Praying faithfully shifts your alignment five points toward evil.

Pretending to pray shifts your alignment three points toward good.

Spitting on the altar shifts your alignment three points toward good and gets you cursed.

Both of the side tunnels present multiple traps to bypass. Warriors should use speed to get them through, and mages will enjoy elemental resistance spells (lightning and ice will be used), while weaker characters should try to detect and disable the triggers.

Kel-Garas will summon skeletal warriors to defend him before you even reach the last shrine of Bane. Dash around these distractions and take the battle directly to the mage. Fellow casters can rely on Haste to play games with Kel-Garas and his summonings, but anyone with a decent melee game will want to be up close and personal with Kel-Garas during the entire sequence.

Although the shrine above is trapped, there are several magical items in the mix that are worth the effort, including a Cloak of Protection +1. Take the Staff of Blight from the corpse of the fallen mage and leave the area before everything collapses. Without the direct power of the Netherese caster, the tomb has nothing to keep away the desert. Take the staff to the House of the Morninglord, for Kel-Garas is still a threat until all of his power has been undone.

The House of the Morninglord

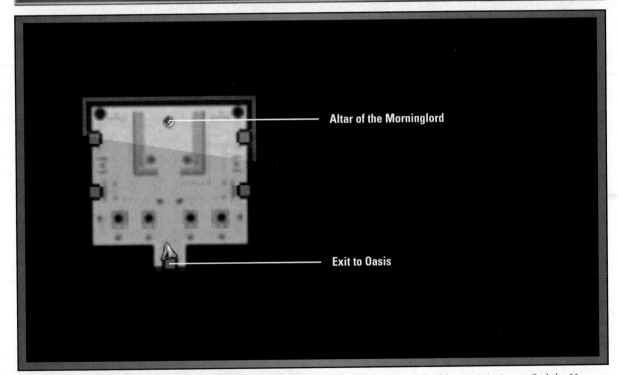

Altar of the Morninglord

Exit to Oasis

ZOMBIE

Alignment:	Neutral Evil
Creature Type:	Undead
Fortitude Save:	0
Reflex Save:	0
Will Save:	3
Base AC:	9
Base HP:	15

After the Bedine speak with you, it is time to find the House of the Morninglord and finish the reign of Kel-Garas. Avoid the zombies who are roaming around and travel to the east (always to the east). The House of the Morninglord was infested with zombies for anyone who approached before dealing with Kel-Garas in his tomb, but the place will be almost clear at this stage. The only reasons for entering the temple earlier would be to kill extra zombies or to take the holy water that is hidden inside the left urn.

169

Kel-Garas will appear again when you approach the altar within the House of the Morninglord. Depending on your character, there are many things that Kel-Garas will be eager to talk about. Knowing how close he is to his final demise, the mage will do what he can to buy time and manipulate the conversation. That is, unless your character is a paladin. Even threatened with death, the Netherese caster will make the first move when he realizes that a paladin has dared to enter his presence.

For the most part, it is fun but unproductive to speak with Kel-Garas. No amount of persuasion will convince this ancient mystic that he should see the error of his ways. Still, it's amusing to watch him try and do the same thing with your character. In the end, the only way to avoid a fight with Kel-Garas is to kill the Bedine leader, Ali.

Agreeing to this foul act will cause the Bedine to rush into the temple. Kel-Garas will give you a knife that can be used on Ali (as a magical item with a unique property). This will instantly kill the hapless nomad, and Kel-Garas will have a newfound measure of freedom and arrogance. For you though, there is only success without remorse. Place the dagger on the altar and it will transform into the Dagger of Bane (+2 to hit, can cause blindness on those struck). The curse will be lifted, and Katriana will have her water.

When it does come down to a fight, expect Kel-Garas to cast a call of blades in front of the bright altar. Two archers will appear to assist Kel-Garas, and he stands in front of the blade wall. For a very short fight, open your inventory, run through the blades, and then use the altar. Put the Staff of Blight onto the altar and the Curse of Kel-Garas will end, as will his life and that of his minions. This is a true victory for the Bedine, and salvation for Katriana's troupe.

Return to the halflings and tell them that the water is free for them. Katriana will move her people onward, and soon the group will arrive at the Ao encampment. Make sure to identify items and get more arrows, scrolls, potions, etc., before moving onward. Katriana presents one of the game's final sources of revenue and trade.

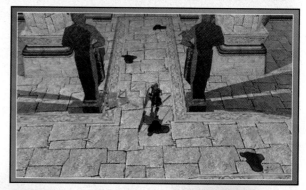

The Winds Whisper of Netheril

Another short journey will place the troupe at the front of a religious encampment. The halflings purchase wine from the people who study the teachings of Ao, but this is also the closest that you can get to the Valley of the Winds using the caravan. Someone in the area should know how to reach Garrick, Drogan's friend.

WHO CARES ABOUT AO?

The Ao encampment has a few things to offer before you travel north. Go in through the main gate. Talking to the guard there will give you a good idea of what the Ao worshippers are like; the guard has no place to go and will try to give a fairly even view of the people in the camp. Ao is an eccentric god, considering that apathy is the central emotion of the faith.

The most interesting things inside the camp are all crammed into the temple, found northwest of the front gate. The archeologist, Garrick Halassar, is there (the man who Drogan asked you to seek). As timing would have it, the mage was nearly killed quite recently. Go to the temple and use a healing item or ability to bring Garrick back from the brink. Once on his feet, the archeologist will talk about the attack on his campsite. This will shift your character's alignment one point toward good.

Then again, it takes time and energy to heal the poor sod, and he hasn't done anything for you. Evil characters can push Garrick for information without aiding him. Others may be happy taking 50 gold pieces from him, supposedly to buy healing equipment, and then leaving for the Valley of the Winds without aiding the coward.

A woman of unknown race led a group of demons in a bitter attack. All of the other archeologists and most of their animals were slain. Garrick was badly wounded, but fate gave him the strength to pull himself away from the area as the woman used a portal to go somewhere else. Garrick doesn't know where the woman has gone, but he is absolutely shaken by her power. Afraid that this foe could use the artifacts of the Netheril, he will beg for you to follow her.

Garrick promises to contact Drogan and let him know that there is a woman after the crystal. Because that artifact carries tremendous potential for destruction, the worst thing that could happen would be for this woman to find it.

After leaving Garrick to his own devices, talk with the Minister of Ao. Asking about the god and then taking the test to become a worshipper is a quick way to get some equipment.

Chaotic Tip

BECOMING AN AVATAR FOR FUN AND PROFIT

Ask to take the Test of Ao, and then answer that thought is the key to the Minister's riddle. Or a river, or snails. In fact, tell the people anything you want. The worshippers will be so impressed that they proclaim your character to be the avatar of Ao. Interesting, and highly exploitable too. Agreeing with these folk will upset the Minister, but it's a nice way to get one or two magical items. Whether you stride around the temple as a deity reincarnate or shirk off the praise with humility, the people will flock before you.

Talking with Rifkin and Talissica afterward will get you a Ring of Protection +3 and an Amulet of Armor +3. Doing this will alienate Telnix. This can be done in a few ways, however, depending on a person's alignment.

Rifkin's moods can push a person toward almost any alignment. Do not let him hurt himself for a shift toward lawful. Use persuasion for a point of chaos; heal him to gain both chaotic and good recognition. In any case, Rifkin will give you his amulet and be quite ecstatic.

Jallisica's ring is very hard to get without gaining a point toward chaos. Only those with access to arcane spells can choose to impress her in a way that isn't chaotic. Otherwise, using divine power, persuasion, or charm will get you the ring but also cause the alignment shift.

Telnix is the hardest nut to crack, for an Ao worshipper at least. He can be persuaded to give up the Cloak of Ao, but Rifkin and Talissica won't believe in your character after that point. Even then, you must not ask Telnix what his gift is or he will become disillusioned and refuse to give it away. Instead, say that you accept his gift because he shows true understanding of your apathy. The cloak grants its wearer a two-point armor deflection bonus, +2 to Constitution, and +1 toward saves versus mind-affecting magic.

The northern path from the Ao encampment leads toward the Valley of Winds. Normally, the camp of mages and archeologists there would be a place to rest and find out about the ruins that they have been exploring. Because of the demon attack that wounded Garrick, everyone in sight is dead or dying. The only thing to do is descend into the ruins and see what vengeance can be wrought.

Excavated Ruins

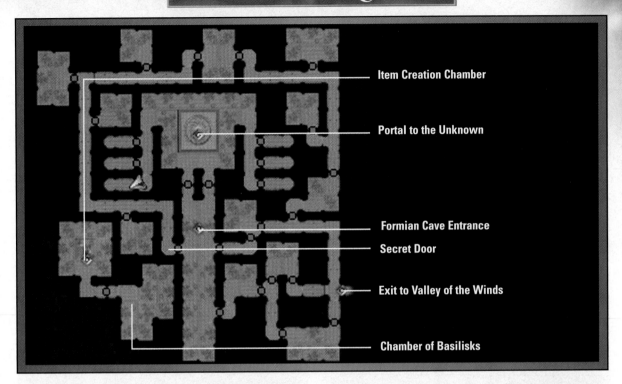

- Item Creation Chamber
- Portal to the Unknown
- Formian Cave Entrance
- Secret Door
- Exit to Valley of the Winds
- Chamber of Basilisks

BLUE SLAAD

Alignment:	Neutral Evil
Creature Type:	Outsider
Fortitude Save:	6
Reflex Save:	6
Will Save:	6
Base AC:	18
Base HP:	60

FORMIAN WARRIOR

Alignment:	Lawful Neutral
Creature Type:	Outsider
Fortitude Save:	4
Reflex Save:	4
Will Save:	4
Base AC:	18
Base HP:	26

BASILISK

Alignment:	True Neutral
Creature Type:	Magical Beast
Fortitude Save:	5
Reflex Save:	5
Will Save:	2
Base AC:	16
Base HP:	45

GREEN SLAAD

Alignment:	Neutral Evil
Creature Type:	Outsider
Fortitude Save:	6
Reflex Save:	6
Will Save:	6
Base AC:	20
Base HP:	67

MINOGON

Alignment:	True Neutral
Creature Type:	Construct
Fortitude Save:	2
Reflex Save:	2
Will Save:	2
Base AC:	18
Base HP:	68

SHIELD GUARDIAN

Alignment:	True Neutral
Creature Type:	Construct
Fortitude Save:	5
Reflex Save:	5
Will Save:	5
Base AC:	24
Base HP:	105

RED SLAAD

Alignment:	Neutral Evil
Creature Type:	Outsider
Fortitude Save:	5
Reflex Save:	5
Will Save:	5
Base AC:	16
Base HP:	52

It's dark under the ground, so everyone should have items with light to make the ruins livable. If you don't have anything appropriate, look around and search the bodies for a light source. No one wants to be eaten by a grue, after all.

The ruins are expansive, and the roving bands of slaads will make everything more difficult. Progress is slow, especially for mages and rogues (both must be more cautious against the numerous foes around each corner), but there is much to gain. Because of the extensive risk from slaads and even some basilisks in the dungeon, we advise saving your game often, even for powerful characters and skilled players.

Kill the Head and the Body Will Die

Slaads are able to summon lesser versions of themselves, although the difference is a subtle one. It is unwise to fight through the summoned slaads because they can be killed immediately by the death of their creator. To improve the chances to doing this, characters should use their strongest attacks on the master (original) slaads during an encounter.

Mages and missile characters can pick and choose their targets, but melee types must run into battle at maximum speed when slaads are spotted. Hurry to engage the original slaads before they can finish summoning the copies; this ensures that the new slaads won't completely block the path to their masters.

In the event you can't get to the real slaads, back away and try to come at the slaads from another angle. Many of the corridors in the ruins have several ways to get around, so backing off is a viable way to reposition for a better strike.

A great deal of the ruins is barren; there isn't much treasure to pick up and the fights are rough. Most people will probably prefer to take the more efficient routes through the rubble, especially after looking through the dungeon a first time.

The southern route from the entrance has little to offer. There are two rooms with a hallway connecting them, and a collapsed ceiling blocks the second chamber by its far doorway. The middle route, going west into the ruins, is also fruitless. There is only one separate room in that choice, and there is a statue trap centered there. A chest in the far wall has some dragon's blood, which will come in handy only for characters that are gathering reagents.

Go north from the entrance to move deeper into the ruins. After the first bend, you can walk north into a series of slaad fights and extra rooms. West is the path for those who want to avoid such things by playing it safe.

Adventurous types will find a blue sphere in the northeast chamber of the ruins. Drawn by the powerful magic there, a green slaad stands mesmerized by the light, although the creature will turn to attack when you arrive. Because the slaad is alone, the fight isn't too tough. Search the body of the fallen slaad to find a Cloak of Arachnida (+2 to poison saves, immunity to Web, can cast Web once per day).

The power of the orb will remain a mystery for a time. Those who have significant Lore skills can read the pillar against the back wall for clues about the item's use. The information there will reveal a great deal, though it is still better to save your game before trying anything.

Orb of the Divine

Three spells can be cast on the globe. These will gather inside the object. When finished, this will transform the artifact into a tool that can be carried with you. Once per day, all of the spells can be drawn back out of the artifact, and they will automatically be cast on the character using the item. Adding the best buffs in the game could make for some lovely combinations. Damage resist spells are certainly high on the list of good choices for the staff. At the other end would be dispel, which would cancel out everything else in the chain. A nice, round mix would include something for elemental resistance, damage resistance, and something to buff a person's armor class or hit points.

Most of the other northern rooms have miscellaneous spell scrolls and reagents. Another trapped statue room, almost dead center at the top of the map, has Acid and Piercing Arrows for archers to take. Other than that, the best choice is to return to the previous western route and go toward the center of the map.

The longer hall leading west will open into a central shaft that covers a great deal of the excavated ruins. Kill the creatures that are fighting in the area; this shows that the slaads are facing some resistance. A group of formians must be living in the hole that dominates part of the main hall. Before going into the hole, look into a couple more of the side rooms in the level.

Across from the main strip are two rooms of interest. The first is beyond the bend in the passage (this would be the last normal room for a person who went all the way around the north route). Several slaads are trying to kill a shield guardian in that chamber. Help the shield guardian by killing the slaads, and then try to convince it that its master is dead. Failure will cause the construct to attack, as will too many questions. Once the shield guardian malfunctions or is destroyed, you can pilfer the skeleton in the corner. This was once the mage who created the shield guardian. There is an Ointment of Stone to Flesh on the body, and you can also take the magical ring and amulet from the "master."

The ring is one of magical defense. These grant +2 to spellcraft, a 14 spell resist, and dispel magic once per day—not a bad find at all. Neither is the Necklace of Fireballs, especially when a character is dealing with hoards of slaads and formians.

The second room is behind a secret door. Look around in the first part of the corridor, just after leaving the main shaft. A door will soon be revealed, but save the game before even stepping through the opening. An entire host of basilisks is on the other side, and their ability to turn creatures into stone is very powerful. Even characters with a 16 Fortitude save are not remotely safe. To keep the strange beasts from using their ability, rush into close combat with the pack; they won't try to stone anything that is engaged with them. Even mages should do this, although having pets, a damage resistance buff, and everything else that can be thrown on would be helpful.

Once the legendary basilisks have been slain, use the ointment on the sphinx in the corner. The wise monster has probably been in its petrified state for many long years. The sphinx introduces itself as Myr and then offers a reward. Because this is a sphinx, it might be best to choose riddles before doing anything else.

The first riddle asked will be an oldie but goodie. It turns out that **Fire** is the answer because it feeds to sustain itself but is weakened and destroyed by "drinking" water. In approval, Myr will explain that four Belladonna roots combined in the defensive urn will add Haste to a mix. This refers to the item creation urns in the next room.

The second riddle is a trick question because the traditional answer would be age (without age, a baby crawls, with it a person stands tall, but too much leads to weakness and frailty). Instead, the answer is **Pride**. Ten organs of extra-planar creatures in the right urn will spawn a rune stone, it turns out.

The third riddle is a match question. Answer by saying that **Ten Males and Six Females** were involved in the skirmish. Instead of learning more about item creation, you will receive experience points for correctly answering this final question.

Truly wacky players with incredibly high animal empathy can go for the most vicious pet ever, should they dare. It takes almost a 40 DC empathy check, but the sphinx can be taken over. Not only is this creature powerful physically, but it also does sonic damage and casts both Fear and Bless. Even better, this pet won't attack you after a period of rest, because the sphinx defaults to being neutral toward your character. With the right items to boost your animal empathy, this could be a very amusing way to clear the dungeon.

The Rune Stone

With all this done, you should have a modest idea of what can be done in the next room. There are two urns that combine reagents and produce an item that will cast offensive and defensive spells simultaneously.

EXAMPLES OF USABLE REAGENTS FOR OFFENSIVE SPELLS

Ruby (1)	Causes fire damage to enemies
Rubies (3)	Causes higher fire damage to enemies
Belladonna (4)	Casts Slow on enemies
Dragon Blood (1)	Creates a gust of wind (knocks down enemies, disperses clouds)
Slaad Tongues (10)	Creates a DC 14 AOE instant kill spell
Fairy Dust (1)	Creates an AOE stun

EXAMPLES OF USABLE REAGENTS FOR DEFENSIVE SPELLS

Ruby (1)	Grants spell immunity to lower level spells and increases spell resistance
Rubies (3)	Grants spell immunity to lower/mid level spells and increases spell resistance
Belladonna (6)	Casts Haste upon activation of rune stone
Dragon Blood (1)	Casts stoneskin
Slaad Tongues (6)	Provides elemental protection
Fairy Dust (1)	Casts improved invisibility upon activation of rune stone

Items that are common to both urns (such as Fairy Dust or Dragon's Blood) need only be placed in one to be counted in each set. Another thing to note is that items that stack inside the urns should not be taken out; they merge into a single item, thus removing them will destroy any of the extras that are inside the urn.

Go back to the main shaft and explore the formian area before proceeding through the doors at the end of the hallway. There is nothing in the formian hive that needs to be seen or acted upon, but it's a fun romp with a lot of fighting.

Formian Hive

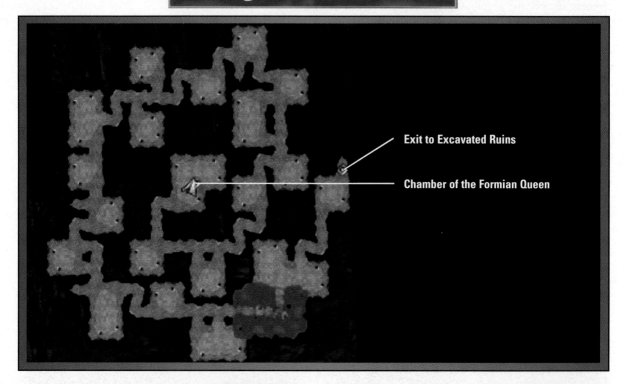

Exit to Excavated Ruins

Chamber of the Formian Queen

FORMIAN MYRMARCH

Alignment:	True Neutral
Creature Type:	Outsider
Fortitude Save:	8
Reflex Save:	8
Will Save:	8
Base AC:	29
Base HP:	102

FORMIAN WARRIOR

Alignment:	Lawful Neutral
Creature Type:	Outsider
Fortitude Save:	4
Reflex Save:	4
Will Save:	4
Base AC:	18
Base HP:	26

FORMIAN QUEEN

Alignment:	True Neutral
Creature Type:	Outsider, Sorcerer
Fortitude Save:	17
Reflex Save:	17
Will Save:	22
Base AC:	24
Base HP:	275

FORMIAN WORKER

Alignment:	Lawful Neutral
Creature Type:	Outsider
Fortitude Save:	2
Reflex Save:	2
Will Save:	2
Base AC:	16
Base HP:	5

There isn't much to the hive. Wander through the linear passage that winds toward the center. There are only a couple of side chambers along the path, and even these have almost nothing to take. There is a bit of gold and you can pick up a number of gems, but mostly this is an opportunity to test out your character's ability to massacre militant ants.

Whether mage or barbarian, halfling or elf, the formians won't pose a serious threat in moderate numbers. Move slowly if your character isn't high enough level, and stay in areas where only a few formians can attack at once. Use ranged weapons and combat control spells (Hold Monster, Tanglefoot Bags, etc.) to slow the rate of advancing enemies. For those with nice equipment or a few extra levels, ignore finesse and plow through the hoard.

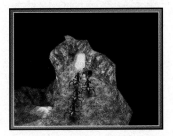  

After half of the level is cleared, the formian queen will contact you and mention that she is ready to speak with you. It's interesting how monsters are more interested in talking after you prove that you can send them up the creek without a paddle. True to form, the queen is all about alliances by the time you get to her. For a somewhat useful magical item, agree to work together in fighting the slaads and their master. Or, if the formians seem like weak and feeble allies, attack the queen and be done with it all.

If civility fails, the queen can actually do a lot more than most of her hive combined. In the throne room, the queen will summon a myrmarch to her aid, and the two of them together have a lot of hit points. Mages will be especially pressed, having foes on two sides. If the rooms behind you are clear, getting breathing room and switching to shoot-and-scoot fighting is a lot safer. Otherwise, it's just a bashing session to see who runs out of hit points and healing first. The queen's treasure is minimal, so fighting the formians is hardly worth the trouble unless you are eager for the battle itself.

For a quick way out of the lair, climb the boulder in the queen's room. This will take you into a secret room in the upper ruins. Two minogons act as sentinels in the chamber, but they aren't too frightening. Even better, there are four chests in the room (one on each side is trapped), and plenty of monetary loot is hidden inside those. The only door in the room will spit you back into the far western hall of the ruins; fight any slaads that remain in that section and return to the central shaft after resting.

Drogan Makes an Appearance

The twin gates at the north end of the shaft conceal the gateway that Garrick was trying to restore. More slaads are inside, unsurprisingly, and a grey one is there to lead them. Strike at the slaads from the gate, and then back away and harass them as they approach. Use area of effect magic and missiles to remove the original slaads, and then close with the grey. A ring is left behind on the leader's body, as are some basic Boots of Striding +2.

Approach the far end of the room once the battle is over. Lo and behold, Drogan arrives to save the day. After the group breathes a collective sigh of relief at the harper's appearance, it is time to unlock the secrets of the portal. All six pillars of the device need to be activated in the correct order for you and Drogan to go through. Garrick was able to restore the device that shows which button to press in the side room at the proper time, but they all look the same. Well, there are two ways to deal with this. Place items in each room to figure out which area is which. Or, consult the following list to know the order of the buttons:

First Button:	Right side, Upper Room (farthest north of the three)
Second Button:	Left Side, Middle Room
Third Button:	Left Side, Lower Room
Fourth Button:	Right Side, Lower Room
Fifth Button:	Left Side, Upper Room
Sixth Button:	Right Side, Middle Room

Touching the buttons in this order will activate the portal; your party will have a chance to pursue the mysterious woman into an ancient city. There are problems, and something happens that will rock Drogan's view of the situation, but there is nothing to be done about it. Undrentide awaits.

THIS CAN'T BE GOOD

You wind up in a dirty cavern, surrounded by statues that seem perfectly lifelike and realistic. Something about the fear-struck eyes in those stones is ominous, but your group must advance toward the city. As with the collapse of the portal, nothing can be changed by what happens next. Life goes on.

After the Darkness Parts

Heurodis was able to get the drop on you, and there wasn't much that you could do about it in the Netherese ruins. As fortune would have it, though, an Asabi slaver-merchant with a bit of foresight has returned you to a more fleshy form. Although the Asabi people are neither kind nor merciful, this slaver sees a great deal of potential in what you can do for him. At least this is better than being a rock for eternity.

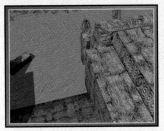

The Lost City of Undrentide

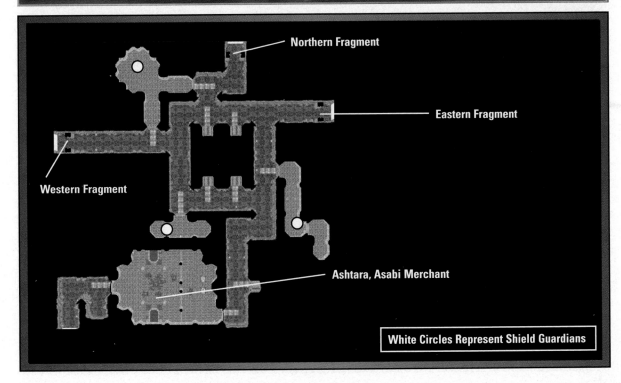

Northern Fragment

Eastern Fragment

Western Fragment

Ashtara, Asabi Merchant

White Circles Represent Shield Guardians

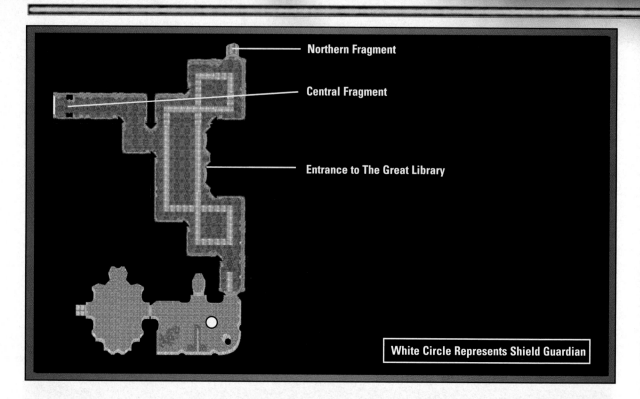

Northern Fragment

Central Fragment

Entrance to The Great Library

White Circle Represents Shield Guardian

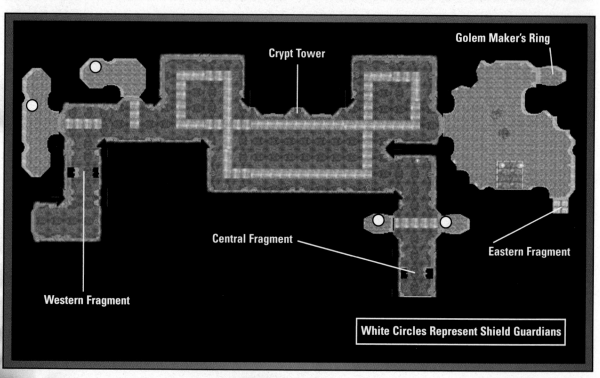

Golem Maker's Ring

Crypt Tower

Central Fragment

Eastern Fragment

Western Fragment

White Circles Represent Shield Guardians

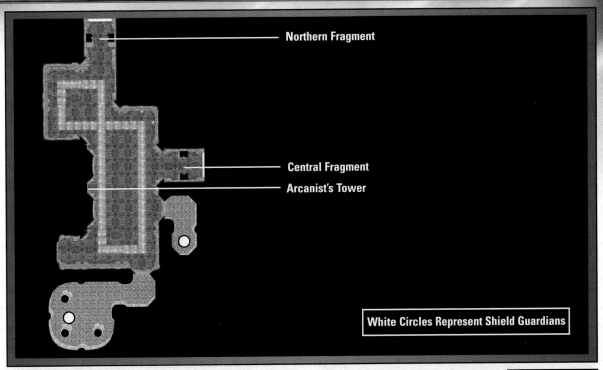

Northern Fragment

Central Fragment

Arcanist's Tower

White Circles Represent Shield Guardians

STONE BUTLER

Alignment:	True Neutral
Creature Type:	Construct
Fortitude Save:	3
Reflex Save:	3
Will Save:	3
Base AC:	26
Base HP:	77

PHASE SPIDER

Alignment:	True Neutral
Creature Type:	Vermin
Fortitude Save:	4
Reflex Save:	1
Will Save:	1
Base AC:	15
Base HP:	37

SHIELD GUARDIAN

Alignment:	True Neutral
Creature Type:	Construct
Fortitude Save:	5
Reflex Save:	5
Will Save:	5
Base AC:	24
Base HP:	105

SWORD SPIDER

Alignment:	True Neutral
Creature Type:	Vermin
Fortitude Save:	4
Reflex Save:	1
Will Save:	1
Base AC:	17
Base HP:	32

GIANT SPIDER

Alignment:	True Neutral
Creature Type:	Vermin
Fortitude Save:	2
Reflex Save:	0
Will Save:	0
Base AC:	14
Base HP:	4

WRAITH SPIDER

Alignment:	True Neutral
Creature Type:	Vermin
Fortitude Save:	3
Reflex Save:	1
Will Save:	1
Base AC:	22
Base HP:	16

DIRE SPIDER

Alignment:	True Neutral
Creature Type:	Vermin
Fortitude Save:	7
Reflex Save:	3
Will Save:	3
Base AC:	17
Base HP:	55

SPITTING FIRE BEETLE

Alignment:	True Neutral
Creature Type:	Vermin
Fortitude Save:	2
Reflex Save:	0
Will Save:	0
Base AC:	10
Base HP:	8

QUEEN SPIDER

Alignment:	True Neutral
Creature Type:	Vermin
Fortitude Save:	7
Reflex Save:	3
Will Save:	3
Base AC:	16
Base HP:	250

STAG BEETLE

Alignment:	True Neutral
Creature Type:	Vermin
Fortitude Save:	5
Reflex Save:	2
Will Save:	2
Base AC:	20
Base HP:	52

BOMBARDIER BEETLE

Alignment:	True Neutral
Creature Type:	Vermin
Fortitude Save:	3
Reflex Save:	0
Will Save:	0
Base AC:	16
Base HP:	13

STINK BEETLE

Alignment:	True Neutral
Creature Type:	Vermin
Fortitude Save:	3
Reflex Save:	1
Will Save:	1
Base AC:	16
Base HP:	19

FIRE BEETLE

Alignment:	True Neutral
Creature Type:	Vermin
Fortitude Save:	2
Reflex Save:	0
Will Save:	0
Base AC:	10
Base HP:	4

HIVE MOTHER

Alignment:	True Neutral
Creature Type:	Vermin
Fortitude Save:	7
Reflex Save:	3
Will Save:	3
Base AC:	16
Base HP:	262

There are thralls banging against a mountain of stone and fallen debris to the west of where you wake. The thralls barely have enough intelligence to get their jobs done, so it isn't worth asking them for information. Instead, walk to the east and meet your temporary master.

Ashtara is a merchant by trade, although the slaver has not been very lucky of late. When Heurodis started to raise Undrentide, many of the ancient tunnels collapsed on themselves. This has trapped Ashtara and some of his surviving thralls in a section of rooms that surround the city's central temple. To earn back your freedom, the Asabi must be given a chance to escape with as much loot as his thralls can carry. Killing the ten golems that reside around the central temple will give Ashtara a bit of breathing room to accomplish this.

Ironically, Ashtara tells you that he learned of Undrentide's location from an Asabi that you killed in the ruins before you were turned to stone. This is, perhaps, one of the things that warms Ashtara to you, because he was planning to kill the rival himself before long.

Travel east, and wander around the Asabi area for a moment. To the north are a couple of the spiders that dominate the ruins. Kill these for a feel of the area's difficulty. Because many of the monsters in the area live inside cracks, holes, and pits, enemies can appear at almost any time within Undrentide, even at close range.

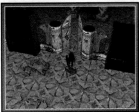

Diamonds in the Rough

Much of the "treasure" in the lost city is rotted, rusted, or otherwise useless to anyone. Yet, there is also a substantial amount of magical loot with potent enchantments. Characters with a decent Lore skill will quickly be able to tell the difference without having to cart around ludicrous amounts of junk. Try to identify everything that you stumble across; some of the random items inside old chests and drawers are incredible.

Buying the Prayer Bag and the Transmogrifying Wand can open the door to many exciting experiments. Throw a couple of items from the table below into the bag and wave the wand over it to produce various planar creatures. Confuse friends, awe your enemies, and keep your hands out of the bag at all times!

	Holy Water	Dragon Blood	Skeleton Knuckle
Meat	Lantern Archon	Steam Mephit	Tyrant Zombies
Bear Hide	Celestial Avenger	Dire Bear	Skeleton Chief
Wolf Hide	Hound Archon	Dire Wolf	Shadow Mastiff

DESTROYING THE GUARDIANS

The first door out in the main hallway opens into the eastern fragment of the city. After a quiet entry, you will soon arrive in a room with a Shield Guardian, a type of golem. These are the constructs that control the barriers into the deeper areas of Undrentide. Although the guardians are priceless relics of another age, they all must be destroyed.

Shield Guardians Don't Have to Be Tough

Anyone who has trouble penetrating the nasty armor and potent magical defenses of the guardians should bypass them until they get the ring in the city's northeast room. The golems' builder had an item that would effectively disable the guardians for a short time, and this will make destroying them a lot easier.

Continue to walk north, fighting beetles and spiders as they appear. Do not try to flee from these, lest you wander straight into a second group—that will not improve matters. Take things slowly to avoid trouble. Any items with freedom of movement will be useful because the spiders use webs so frequently.

The door in the northeast part of the fragment opens into the master builder's room. A stone butler is there, and he is a wealthy source of information. This fantastic golem has intelligence, memory, emotions, and dedication. He will explain

about the builder's ring (which can disable the shield guardians), and he will also reveal a bit about the city's working back in the old days. Asking him about Heurodis and the Mythal will help you to learn what can be done to reach the Temple of the Winds, which is currently barred from passage.

Sadly, this butler will not allow you to take the ring of the master builder. If you wish to destroy the shield guardians the easy way, the stone butler will become your enemy. The best way to keep from killing the butler is to walk inside the door on the eastern side of the room when the golem is on the other side of the chamber. Destroy the chest and take the ring from it quickly, and then flee. The butler will be angry, but he is too slow to follow you for long. Or, if you care not for this majestic creation, pound the block of stone back into obedience. Rocks shouldn't talk back anyway.

Using the golem maker's ring is easy. Put the unique power of the ring on a quickbar slot, and then use it on each shield guardian. This will prevent the creatures from fighting back in the least. The ring need not be equipped to accomplish this.

 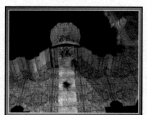  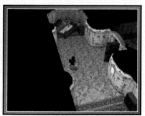

Make sure that the guardian from the eastern fragment is dead, and then kill the other nine shield guardians. Four golems are in the northern fragment; two are in rooms by the western corner. Seek the other two in the eastern hallway, inside two small cubbies.

Three more are in the rooms of the central fragment—all of the rooms show up as light areas on the map.

The final two are in the western fragment, both placed in rooms where powerful nobles once kept their most important possessions. Search these rooms for magical treasure, and return to Ashtara when all of the shield guardians are dead. Sell unneeded equipment and get ready to battle a number of undead (buy or equip any items that will be useful for this).

 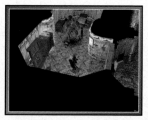  

The next three sections can be done in about any order, but they are arranged for a fairly easy progression through the three towers of Undrentide. Walk back to the northern fragment and enter the crypt tower.

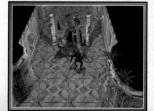 

The Crypt Tower

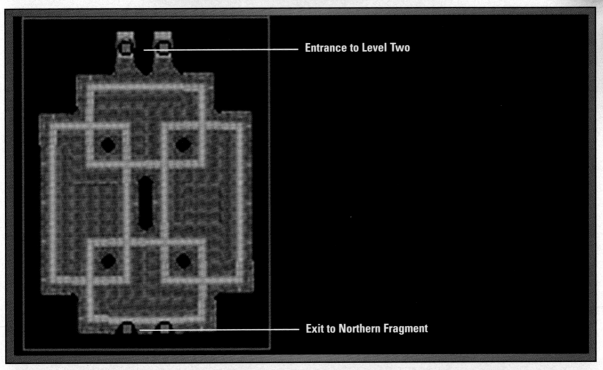

Entrance to Level Two

Exit to Northern Fragment

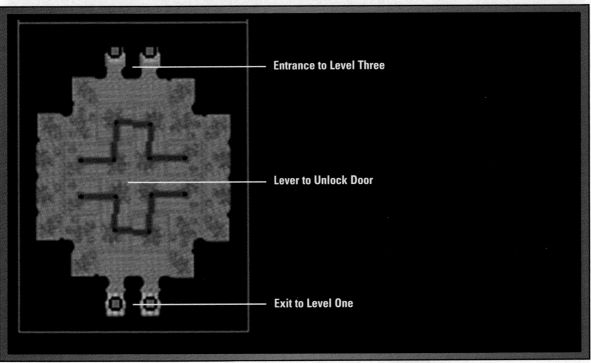

Entrance to Level Three

Lever to Unlock Door

Exit to Level One

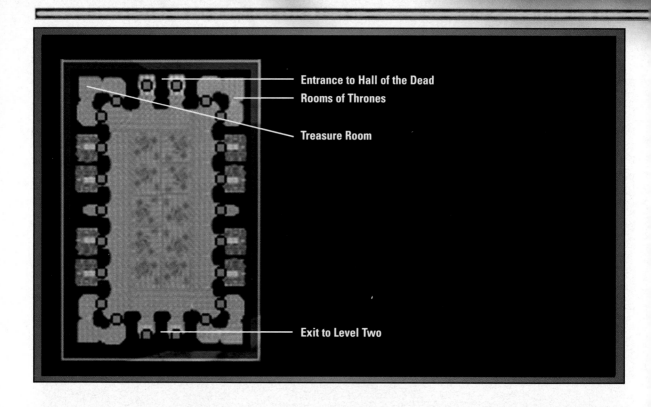

Entrance to Hall of the Dead

Rooms of Thrones

Treasure Room

Exit to Level Two

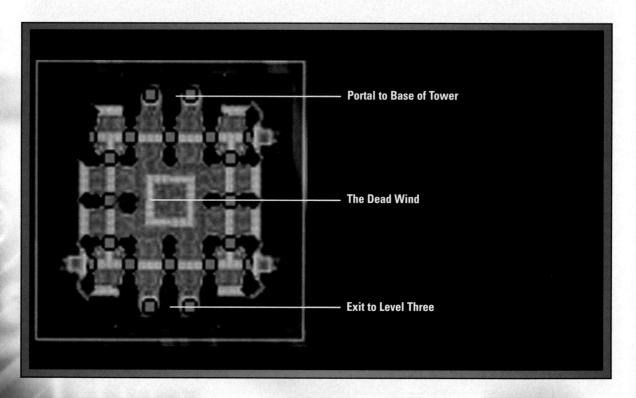

Portal to Base of Tower

The Dead Wind

Exit to Level Three

DISTURBED

Alignment:	Neutral Evil
Creature Type:	Undead, Fighter
Fortitude Save:	3
Reflex Save:	1
Will Save:	4
Base AC:	12
Base HP:	33

BRITTLE BONE GOLEM

Alignment:	True Neutral
Creature Type:	Construct
Fortitude Save:	2
Reflex Save:	2
Will Save:	2
Base AC:	16
Base HP:	60

SKELETAL ARCHER

Alignment:	Neutral Evil
Creature Type:	Undead
Fortitude Save:	2
Reflex Save:	2
Will Save:	5
Base AC:	18
Base HP:	20

SKELETAL CHIEFTAIN

Alignment:	Neutral Evil
Creature Type:	Undead, Fighter
Fortitude Save:	5
Reflex Save:	2
Will Save:	4
Base AC:	15
Base HP:	36

SKELETAL PRIEST

Alignment:	Neutral Evil
Creature Type:	Undead, Cleric
Fortitude Save:	3
Reflex Save:	1
Will Save:	5
Base AC:	13
Base HP:	20

SKELETAL WARRIOR

Alignment:	Neutral Evil
Creature Type:	Undead
Fortitude Save:	2
Reflex Save:	2
Will Save:	4
Base AC:	15
Base HP:	39

SKELETON

Alignment:	Neutral Evil
Creature Type:	Undead
Fortitude Save:	0
Reflex Save:	0
Will Save:	2
Base AC:	12
Base HP:	6

WIND ZOMBIE

Alignment:	Neutral Evil
Creature Type:	Undead, Fighter
Fortitude Save:	2
Reflex Save:	0
Will Save:	3
Base AC:	12
Base HP:	22

THE DEAD WIND

Alignment:	True Neutral
Creature Type:	Elemental
Fortitude Save:	2
Reflex Save:	2
Will Save:	5
Base AC:	9
Base HP:	71

SHRINES OF THE DEAD

The first floor is fairly simple for the observant. There are traps and disturbed undead all over the place, but much of the trouble can be avoided by staying along the light sections of floor—there aren't any traps on these strips. Follow the light patterns and destroy each altar that you reach. This will not only slow the tide of undead entering the area, but it will also eventually reveal a glowing green plume of energy; this is the key to the second floor of the tower. The location of the key is random, so it may be necessary to destroy every altar before you find the key.

Most of the treasure that is lying around will be of little use, but there are a few items that aren't entirely rusted and worthless.

ABSOLUTION THROUGH FLAME

The second floor of the tower is incredibly easy to pass. Burning men wander the area, tormenting themselves with flame and flagellation (mostly internal). It is impossible to learn anything meaningful from these tormented souls because they only cry out the names of their sins. To unlock the far door, pull the lever in the center of the chamber and then move on.

To avoid damage, use elemental resistance or wait for the burning men to move out of your way. This is often unnecessary, but some players don't like their characters to burn their feet.

A MAZE OF BONES

This is the first serious challenge of the tower. Various skeletons cover the entire floor, and the walls move about as they wish. Among the dead are brittle bone golems, dire combinations of magical construction and necromancy. For a safe journey, travel along the sides of the room and avoid the bulk of the fighting. Avoid the doors and cut through any of the walls that take too long to disappear; it doesn't take much effort to break through these magical walls. The doors on the far end are unlocked, so you can run through them and leave the entire floor behind.

Of course, there are other things to do for the more adventurous. The side rooms of this floor are lined with rare undead and interesting treasure. Some of the more exciting are noted here.

To the left of the entrance is a room with a fair bit of magical treasure, including many spell scrolls. This is a good place to spot early on. The next room on that path also has a nice magical item hidden in a pile of bones. A revenant resides in a chest two rooms beyond that. There isn't any nice treasure in the creature's coffin, but it's rare that one sees a revenant at all, so it's worth a trip just to fight one of these odd horrors.

The room in the upper-left has the most treasure in the level. Search through the coffins in the chamber and try to identify the many rusted weapons instead of picking them up. There should be at least three magical items in the mix, as well as some gold and spell scrolls. A specter and a few other undead will come out to fight, but they are hardly a threat for most characters at this point. Mages may want to have creatures summoned to distract the undead, however, to give the caster space and time to wield magic.

The room in the upper-right has a series of thrones. Characters that sit in these will be reduced to near death status or healed to full health. Do not try to experiment when undead are in the room, else you won't have a chance to heal before getting pounded into the floor.

HALL OF THE DEAD WIND

A storm rages at the top of the tower, pulling its fury from the spirits of Netheril. Within the maelstrom is the dead wind, one of the three orbs that you need to reach Heurodis. Even as the smell of rotten flesh fills the area, you must move forward to attack.

The power of the wind will appear at the center of the tower and surround itself with protective energy. While the green sphere is active, the dead wind cannot be damaged. Stay near the wind and protect yourself from the legion of zombies that are summoned to defend the orb. After several rounds of battle, the sphere of protection will briefly fall; switch your focus to attacking the dead wind, and then fight more of the zombies after the protection returns. Most characters will be able to destroy the dead wind after one or two cycles of this pattern.

Take the Dead Wind from the ground when the fighting is over. There aren't many nifty goodies to take, so you should go to the far end of the tower and use the magical doors to teleport out of the crypt tower. Return to Ashtara for more supplies and to identify items, and then travel to the western fragment. Equip anything that protects the wearer from spells and darkness.

The Arcanist's Tower

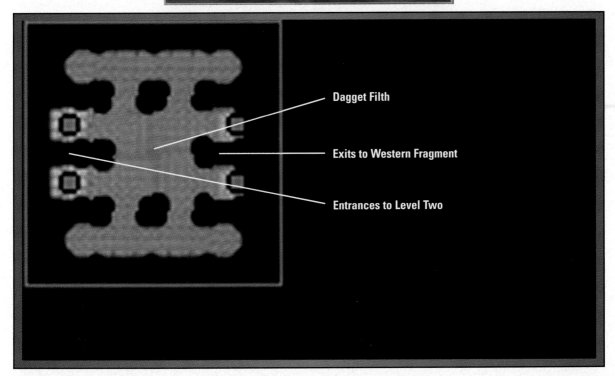

Dagget Filth

Exits to Western Fragment

Entrances to Level Two

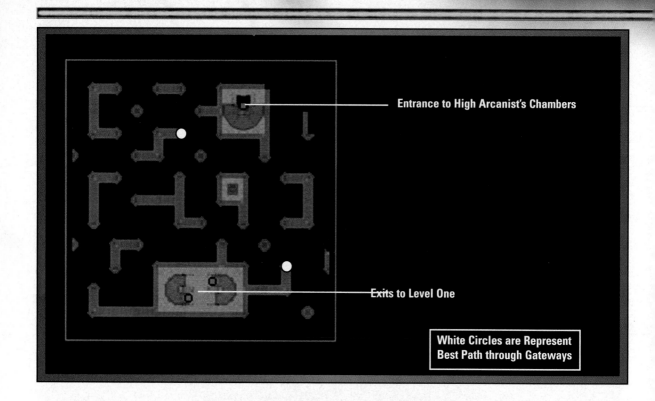

Entrance to High Arcanist's Chambers

Exits to Level One

White Circles are Represent
Best Path through Gateways

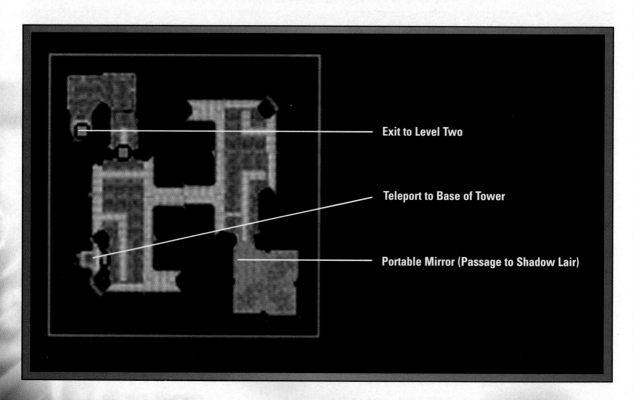

Exit to Level Two

Teleport to Base of Tower

Portable Mirror (Passage to Shadow Lair)

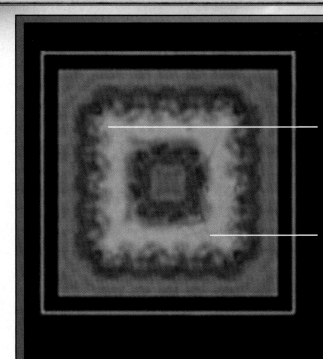

The Dark Wind, Held by the Shadow Lich

Portal back to the High Arcanist's Chambers

SHADOVAR ARCHER

Alignment:	Neutral Evil
Creature Type:	Ranger
Fortitude Save:	5
Reflex Save:	2
Will Save:	2
Base AC:	12
Base HP:	39

SHADOVAR WARRIOR

Alignment:	Neutral Evil
Creature Type:	Fighter
Fortitude Save:	5
Reflex Save:	2
Will Save:	2
Base AC:	10
Base HP:	45

SHADOVAR HEALER

Alignment:	True Neutral
Creature Type:	Cleric
Fortitude Save:	5
Reflex Save:	2
Will Save:	5
Base AC:	9
Base HP:	56

SHADOW LICH

Alignment:	Chaotic Evil
Creature Type:	Undead, Wizard
Fortitude Save:	5
Reflex Save:	5
Will Save:	11
Base AC:	11
Base HP:	82

SHADOVAR MAGE

Alignment:	Neutral Evil
Creature Type:	Wizard
Fortitude Save:	2
Reflex Save:	2
Will Save:	5
Base AC:	12
Base HP:	45

A RAT, AN ELEMENTAL, AND A SHADOW LICH WALK INTO A BAR...

It's quite safe on the first floor of the Arcanist's Tower. It almost seems like things are going to be simple in this place. There isn't any undead, or even the smell of ancient bodies, and a fire elemental and a rat are the only living creatures around. Curiously, the rat is the greater of the two when it comes to importance.

Talk to the rat; the creature's name is Dagget Filth, and he was once the familiar of Undrentide's High Arcanist. Although physically incapable of doing much, this rat has a surprising understanding of what happened to the fallen city and what is going on currently. Ask Dagget about the Shadovar, the collapse of Undrentide, and about the Dark Wind.

The ominous news is that one of the Netherese cities is still around, and the people from that city are trying to steal the Dark Wind before Heurodis does something stupid and gets the city destroyed. Although this isn't a bad idea, you can't let these Shadovar complete their mission. Climb to the second floor and steel yourself for a fight.

A LABYRINTH OF PORTALS

At the top of the steps are a few of the Shadovar that Dagget mentioned. These people have lived in the shadow planes for their entire lives; thus, many of them are mages or other students of obscure lore. The few warriors that accompany the Shadovar are not very impressive, but they do a decent job of distracting people who would otherwise charge down the mages in each group. When possible, accept a few attacks from the warriors if it provides a direct run at the casters who hang back; these are the true threat.

Go to the east from the starting point. The other passages wrap back on themselves and will do nothing to get you to the High Arcanist's chambers. The tricky thing is that the Shadovar have removed most of the material from the tower; simple passage to the other side of the area is no longer possible. Instead, one must use the many portals into the shadow to bridge these gaps. To use a portal, you must kill a Shadovar attacker and take the gem that it carries. Stock up on these, collecting four or so, before proceeding too far.

The way forward from there is quite linear, and the main challenge will be the fights on the plane of shadows. Players that feel threatened by the packs of mages are free to run past the encounters and jump back to the tower's second floor.

Once on the eastern path, the only decision comes in the third shadow area, when the path splits again. Follow the right hall-way and portal, which will teleport you onto the area in front of the stairs. Several Shadovar are waiting there, and their best mages will remain on the stairs to inflict the most damage.

A CONGREGATION OF SHADOVAR

A couple of the ugliest fights await when you arrive on the next floor. Aware of your presence, a full party of Shadovar mages has been sent to stop you. Cast any buffs before leaving the doorway at the top of the stairs.

If you become blinded or otherwise hampered during the ensuing fight, retreat to the previous floor; only some of the Shadovar will follow. This gives wounded characters a better chance of surviving.

When the battle is over, search the far chamber to see what treasure is hidden there. The only major point of interest ends up being a Portable Door. On the bookcase is a tome that explains about the High Arcanist's desire to travel into the plane of shadows and engage the Shadovar leader in a duel. Perhaps that is the Portable Door's purpose. Use the door on the glowing globe nearby to open a portal. The Dark Wind has already been taken to the shadow planes, and you must follow it.

When the battle is over, look in the far chamber to see what treasure is hidden there. The only major point of interest ends up being a **Portable Door**. On the bookcase is a tome that explains the High Arcanist's desire to travel into the plane of shadows and engage the Shadovar leader in a duel. Perhaps that is what the Portable Door is for. Use the magical door to open a portal. The dark wind has already been taken to the shadow planes, and you must follow it. Note that you can even use this Portable Door after you return (this will teleport you to a special merchant's hidden store).

LAIR OF THE SHADOW LICH

Save your game before taking another step, just in case.

As with the rest of the fights against the Shadovar, immunity to darkness is wonderful. Characters without this boon will have an uphill fight on their hands. Either way, the shadow lich and his minions will make tough adversaries.

Try to pick away at the enemy force by creeping around the corners of the room. Because the chamber has a huge pillar in its center, you have a great deal of cover to work with. Pop out, fire missile weapons, and then retreat. Mages can do this with area-of-effect attacks to really have some fun. Even melee characters should be quite wary about taking a direct approach to fighting the Shadovar.

The enemies will try to cast darkness spells and various binding attacks, such as web. If you push too far toward the enemies and are caught in place by a spell, the entire group of casters will unload on you, and that adds up to a lot of damage over a couple of rounds. Keep a few good potions on your quickbar, too.

Once the shadow lich falls, the rest of the process is simple. Clean up the Shadovar and take all of their treasure. The racks along the wall have some interesting pieces of armor and such. For that matter, the lich himself has robes that will interest any mage without scruples. To wear them, you simply have to cut off your old robes and let the new ones graft onto the remaining cloth (long story).

And, of course, take the orb of the Dark Wind before returning to the Arcanist's Tower. The lightning doors outside of the mage's chambers will return you to the western fragment.

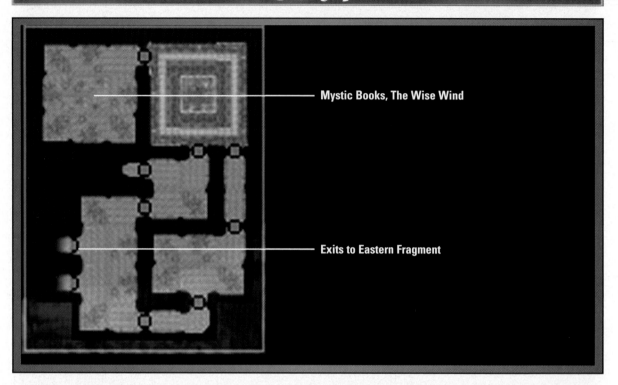

Mystic Books, The Wise Wind

Exits to Eastern Fragment

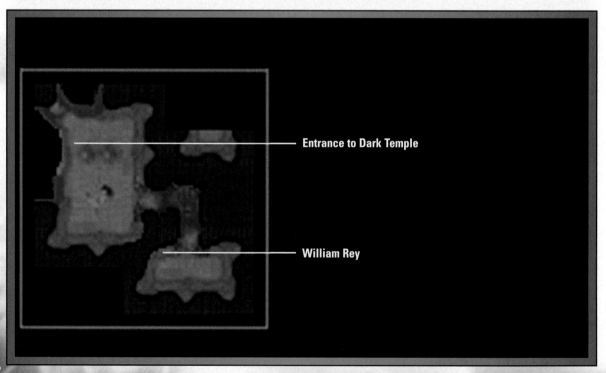

Entrance to Dark Temple

William Rey

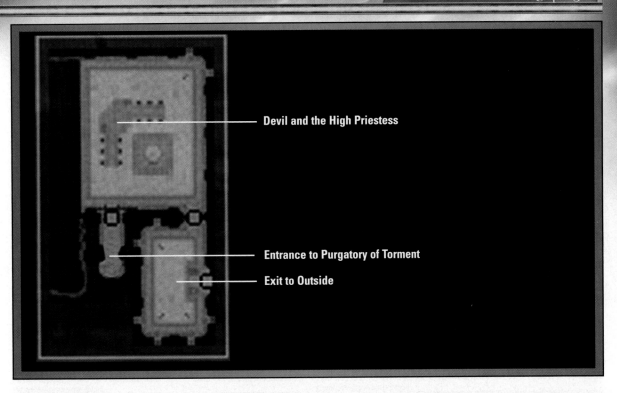

Devil and the High Priestess

Entrance to Purgatory of Torment

Exit to Outside

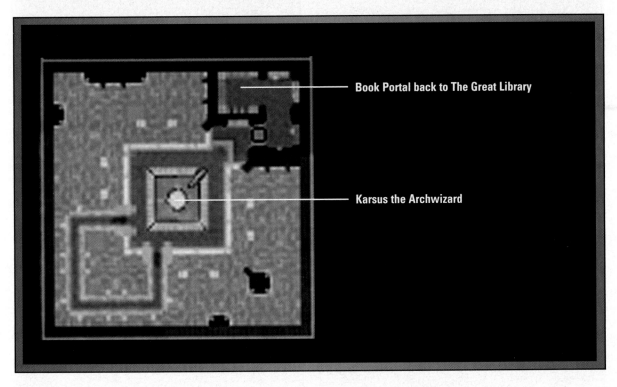

Book Portal back to The Great Library

Karsus the Archwizard

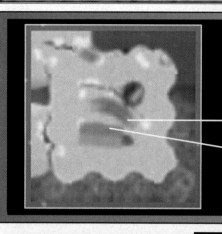

The Wise Wind

Portal to exit of The Great Library

ANCIENT DUST MEPHIT

Alignment:	Neutral Evil
Creature Type:	Outsider
Fortitude Save:	5
Reflex Save:	5
Will Save:	5
Base AC:	17
Base HP:	36

GRAND MATRON

Alignment:	True Neutral
Creature Type:	Cleric
Fortitude Save:	8
Reflex Save:	4
Will Save:	8
Base AC:	9
Base HP:	93

DUST ELEMENTAL

Alignment:	True Neutral
Creature Type:	Elemental
Fortitude Save:	3
Reflex Save:	3
Will Save:	7
Base AC:	19
Base HP:	125

UNHOLY PRIESTESS

Alignment:	True Neutral
Creature Type:	Cleric
Fortitude Save:	5
Reflex Save:	2
Will Save:	5
Base AC:	9
Base HP:	48

DEVIL

Alignment:	Lawful Evil
Creature Type:	Outsider
Fortitude Save:	5
Reflex Save:	5
Will Save:	5
Base AC:	17
Base HP:	33

HELL HOUND

Alignment:	Lawful Evil
Creature Type:	Outsider
Fortitude Save:	4
Reflex Save:	4
Will Save:	4
Base AC:	16
Base HP:	22

SUCCUBUS

Alignment:	Chaotic Evil
Creature Type:	Outsider
Fortitude Save:	5
Reflex Save:	5
Will Save:	5
Base AC:	20
Base HP:	33

WISE WIND

Alignment:	True Neutral
Creature Type:	Elemental
Fortitude Save:	12
Reflex Save:	8
Will Save:	14
Base AC:	10
Base HP:	93

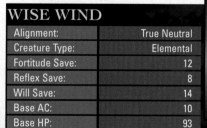

The library of this lost city has fallen into dust and ruin. Unfortunately, the elemental magic of Undrentide has caused this to happen more literally than it otherwise should. Dust mephits and dust elementals coat the rooms of the library, and they fight with abandon. There aren't any tricks to the main areas of the library, either; it's just a matter of slicing away at the elemental beasts until the path is clear.

Elementals are especially easy to lure away from their allies, so hit-and-run tactics are as effective as ever.

The most important room in the library is in the northwest, above the area where you enter. To circumvent most extraneous combat, avoid the southern part of the library and hurry north and then west. There isn't much treasure to be found, but some of the books in the stacks are intact. Even some of the tomes of the Netherese remain. Learn about lichdom, flight, and the Mythal. A very small room in the center of the library has a book on the Temple of the Winds. This describes the process of entering the temple using the three winds. At this point, you already know all of this, but the book is found near several other interesting reads.

There are waves of dust mephits and elementals in the library's final room. Without area-of-effect spells, players are all but forced to rely on limited engagements until the ranks thin out. Boosting your character's Will saves, especially against mind spells, will help with so many mephits casting at once. Look in a bookcase against the wall by the door after the fight; there is a Rod of Resurrection hidden there.

Once quiet descends, save your game and read the book on the other side of the central pillar. The mists of an arcane spell will draw you into the tome, and a story unfolds.

STORY OF A BEGGAR'S LOVE

William Rey stands at the edge of a precipice. This man is crippled, and has not the power to save his lover. She has been taken by evil priestesses and will be sacrificed to their dark patrons. The ending for this tale is quite bleak until you arrive.

William's love, Jendra, is inside the nearby temple. Rush to kill the unholy priestesses there. These women are evil clerics with fair magic but not a lot of melee potential; engaging the priestesses directly is good for all except arcane casters.

In the adjoining chamber of the temple is a devil, guiding the hands of his fell worshippers. Sad is the sight, for Jendra has already been given to increase this creature's strength. Kill the devil and the priestesses to stop their terror, and then seize a Quill that the high priestess of the group was carrying. A strange artifact, indeed, and one worthy of keeping. Take the treasure from the temple's chests and move into the final room. There is a book within, and another story. This one shares little joy as well.

UNREDEEMED

Karsus, the Archwizard of Undrentide, is the focus of this tale. Trapped in a dimension of torment, the mage still pays for his acts of hubris. Succubi tear at his body and mock his spirit, and nothing will ever stop the pain for him. Yet, you can offer brief respite by going to his aid. Kill the demons and speak to Karsus. The archwizard will not accept kind words, and ultimately he must be slain for any chance at redemption. Take the dead mage's staff and a Vial of Ink before leaving. Walk to the back of the area and use the book there to escape this realm.

REWRITING THE PAST

Players who believe in goodness and virtue may want to change the brooding nature of the stories with the artifacts that were recently taken out of the books. Even selfish characters might consider this for gaining allies in the upcoming battle against the wise wind. Either way, the following sections are entirely optional.

To make the stories end on a better note, use the ink and pen to rewrite the book and enter the story a second time. This time, Sir William Rey has arrived ahead of you. His love for Jendra was strong and his body was able to match that devotion. The priestesses lie dead, and the ritual was never completed. In thanks, the knight promises to come to your side when you strike at the wise wind.

Change Karsus' text also, and then read onward. An angel stands in the place where the archwizard was once tortured, and she tells you that Karsus has been taken away by the spirits of goodness. He has left the message that he too will return to aid you against the wise wind, in tribute for all that you have done.

A TRAP, AN ENDING

Whether you have secured the aid of William and Karsus or not, the quill and ink will offer a chance to strike at the wise wind. Walk around the library to the other large tome, and begin to write a story. This tale will explain how the wise wind has been defeated and captured by a great adventurer in a time of need. The city of Undrentide stirs from its centuries of slumber.

The wise wind will appear in a quiet location, and even alone you will be able to defeat the orb without too much trouble. Have buffs set to prevent various Will and mind effects from landing, and summon any available creatures to help engage the wind in melee combat. The other orbs had much better tactical positions to protect themselves, so this becomes a matter of making the rush and finishing the task quickly. Take the fallen orb when the battle ends and return to Undrentide.

Now that all three of the winds are under your control, Heurodis won't be able to keep you out of the city's greatest temple. Make one final run back to Ashtara for trading items, and then go to the city's central fragment.

Having a great deal of insight will reward wise characters with a chance to battle the final wind in a better location, where there is treasure underfoot! This won't make the actual attack against the artifact easier, but it does provide one of the few chances to reap some benefits from this strange realm.

Standing Before the Temple of the Winds

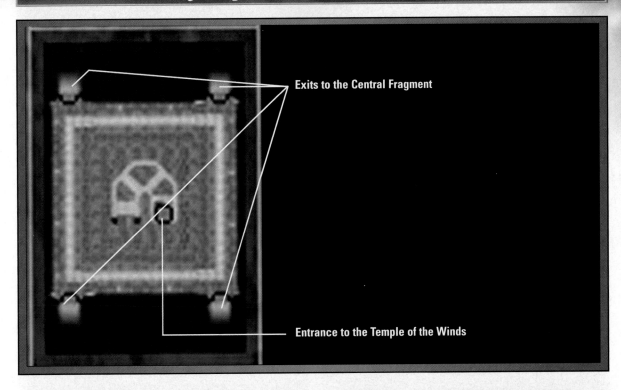

Exits to the Central Fragment

Entrance to the Temple of the Winds

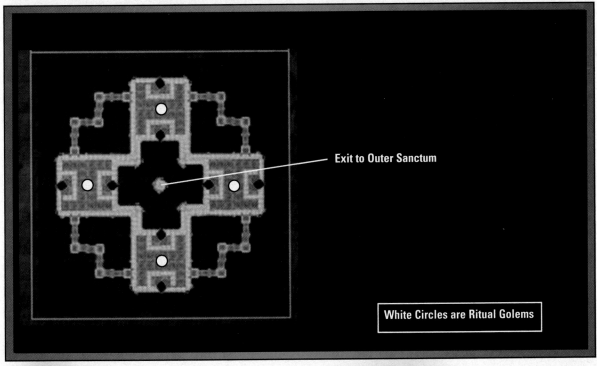

Exit to Outer Sanctum

White Circles are Ritual Golems

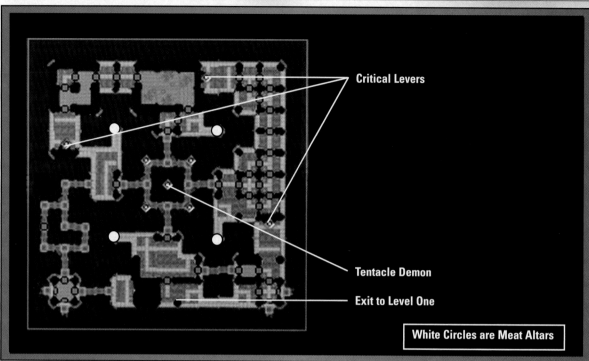

Critical Levers

Tentacle Demon

Exit to Level One

White Circles are Meat Altars

BATTLE HORROR

Alignment:	True Neutral
Creature Type:	Construct
Fortitude Save:	4
Reflex Save:	4
Will Save:	4
Base AC:	11
Base HP:	71

MEDUSA HANDMAIDEN

Alignment:	Lawful Evil
Creature Type:	Humanoid
Fortitude Save:	5
Reflex Save:	2
Will Save:	2
Base AC:	15
Base HP:	33

CLAY GOLEM

Alignment:	True Neutral
Creature Type:	Construct
Fortitude Save:	3
Reflex Save:	3
Will Save:	3
Base AC:	22
Base HP:	60

ALLIP

Alignment:	Chaotic Evil
Creature Type:	Undead
Fortitude Save:	1
Reflex Save:	1
Will Save:	4
Base AC:	11
Base HP:	26

HELMED HORROR

Alignment:	True Neutral
Creature Type:	Construct
Fortitude Save:	4
Reflex Save:	4
Will Save:	4
Base AC:	11
Base HP:	71

WRAITH

Alignment:	Chaotic Evil
Creature Type:	Undead
Fortitude Save:	1
Reflex Save:	1
Will Save:	4
Base AC:	13
Base HP:	32

IRON GOLEM

Alignment:	True Neutral
Creature Type:	Construct
Fortitude Save:	6
Reflex Save:	6
Will Save:	6
Base AC:	30
Base HP:	99

SPECTRE

Alignment:	Lawful Evil
Creature Type:	Undead
Fortitude Save:	2
Reflex Save:	2
Will Save:	5
Base AC:	13
Base HP:	45

STONE GOLEM

Alignment:	True Neutral
Creature Type:	Construct
Fortitude Save:	4
Reflex Save:	4
Will Save:	4
Base AC:	26
Base HP:	77

WISP

Alignment:	Chaotic Evil
Creature Type:	Aberration
Fortitude Save:	3
Reflex Save:	3
Will Save:	6
Base AC:	20
Base HP:	40

SKELETAL DEVOURER

Alignment:	Chaotic Evil
Creature Type:	Aberration
Fortitude Save:	3
Reflex Save:	3
Will Save:	7
Base AC:	25
Base HP:	85

MYTHALLAR

Hardiness:	5
Fortitude Save:	16
Reflex Save:	0
Will Save:	0
Base HP:	15

HEURODIS

Alignment:	Lawful Evil
Creature Type:	Humanoid, Wizard
Fortitude Save:	11
Reflex Save:	8
Will Save:	13
Base AC:	20
Base HP:	135

All doors in the middle of the central fragment lead into the outer sanctum of The Temple of the Winds. The magical barriers that surround the temple's only entrance are infallible to tools of war, magic, or spirit. Only the union of all three orbs will bring down the temple's barrier, now that Heurodis has begun to bring the city back to its place in the heavens. By placing those three orbs into the container in front of the stairs, you will take the next step toward ending this violation of Undrentide's rest. Climb the stairs after the shield falls and prepare for the worst—a properly timed save game wouldn't be a bad idea.

RITUAL OF THE HANDMAIDENS

The temple's first floor is not normally guarded. A glance will show that it requires a fair amount of magic for Heurodis to block the stairway to the next floor. To maintain the power of this artificial blockade, all of Heurodis' handmaidens have remained here to continue a strange ritual. Although it's hard to determine the exact nature of the spell they are powering, these hand-maidens will keep you from going any further unless they are killed. The focus of the lesser medusas' spells is a series of golems (i.e., a Clay Golem, Stone Golem, Battle Horror, and Helmed Horror). This presents a formidable combination, since the golems will activate once the rituals are disrupted.

Mages will have the best chance to sow chaos into the enemy ranks without a lot of resistance; the handmaidens are centered around their golems, thus creating ideal targets for fireballs and other blast-radius spells. Archers too have a fair chance to deal damage before enduring a

heavy response. Note that the outer passages around the room are heavily trapped, so it is perilous to flee down those just to gain a few extra shots against the medusas.

Buffs that improve saving throws are nice here—anything to prevent petrification is doubly desirable. And a bit of damage resistance against the golems wouldn't hurt either, although they are often fought one at a time because of their dispersion. As with basilisks, it is easier to engage handmaidens directly once they get into medium range and are able to use their various magic powers! In short, fight at long range or at point-blank.

Once all four of the golems are dead, the ritual of locking will dissipate and the doors to the upper level will become active again. Make time to rest, both physically and mentally, before going through that portal.

AN UNMATCHED EVIL

Although the Mythallar that control the floating city are only a single floor away, the distance is far greater than it appears. Between you and the stairs in the southwest is a convoluted level filled with undead abominations. At the center of the twisted ledges is a horror of tentacles, flesh, and teeth. Nothing short of dragons or the gods themselves could take on the creature that now resides in the temple. No matter how much time you spent looking around for nifty pieces of treasure, the tentacle demon is not safe to play with.

The idea behind this area is simple; you must pull the four levels at the pseudo-spokes around the center so that the path will open before you. Travel to one side, kill the monsters there, collect meat to distract the tentacle beast, use the meat, and then rush to repeat the process in the next section. Once understood, this isn't too hard to complete, but the sheer number of monsters makes this an extremely trying victory to achieve.

If your character has any Rings of Regeneration, put them on while moving around the level. There won't be a lot of time to rest, and attrition becomes a dire threat after enough waves of floating undead or skeletal devourers have had their time to swarm. Although mages have a chance to unleash wave after wave of area-of-effect spells, the cruel number of encounters will test the greatest sorcerers. It's time to break out healing potions, wands, and other expendable items. Because the enemies are undead, weapons like Desert's Fury will be useful, as will buffs against evil. Fighters should equip their most defensive items (magical shields over two-handed weapons, armor class over strength, and so forth).

The first piece of meat and the lever for the southern door is to the east. Fight through those rooms and look in the corner first. After securing a hunk of meat, turn to the north and walk toward the chamber with four levers. Three of these can-

not be used; they can only be pulled from areas near the other corners. Use all your strength to crank the lever that is not glowing with mystic energy. This unlocks the portcullis south of the central ledge.

Walk to the center, but do not pass through the portcullis yet. Leave the meat on the altar that is west of the gate. This will attract the mighty behemoth that lurks below, drawing it away from its post in the center. Hurry to reach the east-

ern quadrant of the room, and then continue northeast for a second piece of meat. The lever is nearby, just to the west, and this completes the second leg of the process. Use the meat again, complete the northern route in the same manner, and then go to the west. After killing the undead and pulling the fourth lever there, the door to the upper level will open.

HEURODIS WAS BLIND TO HER DESTINY

Save your game again before moving forward to engage Heurodis. The medusa has lost her ability to turn enemies into stone, in the name of the Mythallar, but she is not frightened in the least. Surrounded by the power of the Netherese stones, she is immune to almost all manner of mundane and mystical attack. This feeds the creature's already monstrous arrogance, and she taunts you for a time. Whether good or evil, charismatic or thick as a block of wood, your character has no choice but to fight.

Defeating Heurodis would be pretty tough if the Mythal stones weren't fairly easy to destroy. The heart of the medusa's power will travel around the circle of stones. Exposing the matriarch requires that her power be trapped in a single stone and then purged. Archers have the easiest time; fire to destroy a stone in front of the energy, and then block the path behind it as well. It only takes two or three rounds to do this and destroy the final piece of Mythal. Mages should note that the stones have a very high Fortitude save (it is a 16), so spells that pound against the Mythallar have a somewhat lower chance of having their full effect. Warriors can use Power Attack to rip the pieces in half. Destroy a piece well ahead of the moving energy, and then get behind the wave of light before it bounces back. Blasting a second stone will trap the energy completely, leaving it defenseless.

However this is done, a quick player will prevent Heurodis from getting more than a spell or two cast before her defenses crumble. Mages should send all manner of creatures or henchmen to combat the medusa at this point; throw spells out to protect and strengthen your allies, and then flip over to direct attack spells when the battle seems to reach a controlled level.

Warriors have a very simple rush on their hands once the Mythallar fall. Heurodis has a full spread of arcane spells, so getting her into melee is the best possible solution. Use buffs or extra equipment to defend against the medusa's aura of Fear if needed—paladins are devastating against her, having both immunity to Fear and splendid saves versus her spells. The matriarch's mediocre armor class is such that Power Attacks might be warranted for some characters, especially paired weapon wielders or finesse fighters.

Although archers face Heurodis at range, when she is at her best, the medusa's advantages are minimized by having an NPC to distract the caster. This type of climax becomes a slugfest of missile accuracy against Heurodis' nasty spellcraft.

When the epic battle is over, Heurodis and her resurrected city will begin to crumble together. Although it looks like all may be lost, the portable mirror of the High Arcanist offers salvation. Leaping through the shadowy doors leads into the unknown, but it's still preferable to being buried under a million tons of brick, stone, and skeletons. For the second time in its bitter history, Undrentide breaks against the sands of the desert. The legacy of the Netheril once again flutters and is swept aside.

What follows for your hero and the companions of Hilltop is another story…

NEVERWINTER NIGHTS
SHADOWS of UNDRENTIDE
Official Strategy Guide

by Michael Lummis

©2003 Pearson Education

BradyGAMES® is a registered trademark of Pearson Education, Inc.

All rights reserved, including the right of reproduction in whole or in part in any form.

BradyGAMES® Publishing

An Imprint of Pearson Education
201 West 103rd Street
Indianapolis, Indiana 46290

ISBN: 0-7440-0268-0

Library of Congress Catalog No.: 2003107500

Printing Code: The rightmost double-digit number is the year of the book's printing; the rightmost single-digit number is the number of the book's printing. For example, 03-1 shows that the first printing of the book occurred in 2003.

06 05 04 03   4 3 2 1

Manufactured in the United States of America.

BradyGames Staff

PUBLISHER
David Waybright

EDITOR-IN-CHIEF
H. Leigh Davis

MARKETING MANAGER
Janet Eshenour

CREATIVE DIRECTOR
Robin Lasek

LICENSING MANAGER
Mike Degler

ASSISTANT MARKETING MANAGER
Susie Nieman

Credits

TITLE MANAGER
Tim Fitzpatrick

SCREENSHOT EDITOR
Michael Owen

BOOK DESIGNER
Chris Luckenbill

PRODUCTION DESIGNER
Bob Klunder

RULE YOUR GAME

Rule Neverwinter Nights™
with labeled game hotkeys

Neverwinter Nights™

Zboard™

THE ULTIMATE KEYBOARD BUILT BY GAMERS FOR GAMERS

Get the most out of *your game* with the customized Zboard™ for *Neverwinter Nights™*. The Zboard™ is a revolutionary interchangeable keyboard system with labeled commands and full color graphics to fully immerse you in the game.

A total of 69 labeled game commands divided into easy-to-use groups: *Chatting, Inventories, Dungeon Master* and more.

Visit
WWW.IDEAZON.COM/NWN
for details and special promotions

Compatible with:

SHADOWS of UNDRENTIDE™

Access the radial menu
with one touch

ideazon

The interchangeable keyboard simply snaps into the Zboard™ Base. Zboard™ Base sold separately.